Voters Begin to Choose

Also by Ian McAllister
The Northern Ireland Social Democratic & Labour Party

Also by Richard Rose & Ian McAllister
United Kingdom Facts
The Nationwide Competition for Votes

Also by Richard Rose
Public Employment in Western Nations
Understanding Big Government
Understanding the United Kingdom
Do Parties Make a Difference?
Can Government Go Bankrupt? with Guy Peters
What Is Governing? Purpose and Policy in Washington
Managing Presidential Objectives
Northern Ireland: A Time of Choice
The Problem of Party Government
International Almanac of Electoral History, with T.T. Mackie
Governing without Consensus: An Irish Perspective
People in Politics
Influencing Voters
Politics in England
Must Labour Lose? with Mark Abrams
The British General Election of 1959, with D.E. Butler

Edited by Richard Rose
The Welfare State East and West, with Rei Shiratori
Fiscal Stress in Cities, with Edward Page
The Territorial Dimension in United Kingdom Politics, with P.J. Madgwick
Presidents and Prime Ministers, with Ezra Suleiman
Electoral Participation
Britain: Progress and Decline, with William B. Gwyn
Challenge to Governance
Elections without Choice, with Guy Hermet and Alain Rouquie
New Trends in British Politics, with Dennis Kavanagh
The Dynamics of Public Policy
Comparing Public Policies, with Jerzy Wiatr
The Management of Urban Change in Britain and Germany
Electoral Behavior: A Comparative Handbook
Lessons from America
European Politics, with Mattei Dogan
Policy-Making in Britain
Studies in British Politics

Voters Begin to Choose

From Closed-Class to Open Elections in Britain

Richard Rose and Ian McAllister

The great tragedy of science —
the slaying of a beautiful hypothesis by an ugly fact.

T.H. Huxley

SAGE Publications · London · Beverly Hills · New Delhi

SAGE Publications Ltd
28 Banner Street
London EC1Y 8QE

SAGE Publications Inc
275 South Beverly Drive
Beverly Hills, California 90212

SAGE Publications India Pvt Ltd
C-236 Defence Colony
New Delhi 110 024

British Library Cataloguing in Publication Data

Rose, Richard, 1933-
Voters begin to choose: from closed-class to open elections in Britain.
1. Voting — Great Britain — History — 20th century
I. Title II. McAllister, Ian
324.941′085 JN956

ISBN 0-80399-743-4
ISBN 0-80399-744-2 Pbk

Printed by J.W. Arrowsmith Ltd, Bristol, UK

Contents

Tables and figures

Appendix tables

Figure

Introduction: facing the future

The competition for votes in Britain today is open not closed. The old class-equals-party model of politics is no more — if it ever was. In its place we need a model which recognizes that more than two parties compete for votes; that voting behaviour reflects more (and more changeable) influences than static identification with class and party; and that party government as we have known it since 1945 is now vulnerable.

The most familiar model of electoral competition, class equals party, is a closed model. It is simple in the extreme, admitting the minimum of classes and the minimum of parties. It also implies the minimum of change: little or no short-term movement of voters between two parties, and long-term changes following the gradual alteration in the relative size of the two classes. But simplicity is purchased at a very high cost. The gap between the model and reality was apparent in Britain a decade ago (Rose, 1974; 1980). Today, the fact of three-party competition makes evident the need to return to first principles.

The electorate today is wide open to change; three-quarters of voters are no longer anchored by a stable party loyalty determined by family and class. More voters float between parties — or are wobbling in their commitment to one party — than show a lifetime loyalty to a particular party. At different points in the 1979-83 Parliament, the Labour, Alliance and Conservative parties could each claim the support of nearly half the electorate in the Gallup Poll; at another point each had the support of less than one-quarter of voters. On 9 June 1983 the electorate divided in such a way that the Conservatives gained an overwhelming majority in Parliament. But the Conservatives won 61 per cent of the seats in the Commons with only 42 per cent of the vote. Since then opinion polls and by-election results have often shown that no party has the support of as much as two-fifths of the electorate, thus emphasizing the prospect that no party may have a majority in the next House of Commons (Bogdanor, 1983; Butler, 1983).

The question facing many voters today is not whether to maintain an established party loyalty. It is: Which of the parties supported in the past should I vote for next time? The openness of the electorate cannot be explained as the result of social change. Changes in class structure require decades or generations to accomplish, because of the slow rate at which society alters. Yet electoral change has occurred with rapidity in Britain. In 1974 the Conservative vote fell to its lowest point since 1859; in 1983 the Labour vote dropped to its lowest share since 1918, and the Alliance vote rose to the highest point for the Liberal tendency since 1923. In default of similarly great changes in class structure, specific political events such as changes within the Labour Party, the departure of dozens of Labour MPs to form a Social Democratic Party and an Alliance with the Liberal Party, and the 1982 Falklands War must also be taken into account.

So open is electoral competition today that it is not even clear how many parties seek popular support. In the 1983 election more than half a dozen parties won seats in the House of Commons. The strongest parties (the Conservatives and Labour) and the weakest (the Scottish Nationalists and Plaid Cymru) are easily identified. But it is not clear whether one-quarter of voters supported two separate parties — (the Liberals and the Social Democrats) — or a third grouping, the Alliance that they form for electoral purposes. Northern Ireland adds four more parties, inflating to double digits the total number of parties with seats in the House of Commons.

At least ten different parties will be defending seats in the House of Commons at the next general election. Whatever the outcome of that election, it will mark a discontinuity with the past. If the result is similar to 1983, it will re-inforce a party system very different from that previously prevailing. If the result is a substantial departure from 1983 — whether a hung Parliament without any majority, or an overall Labour majority — this will introduce a fresh discontinuity. There is no convincing reason to expect a return to the status quo ante: competition between two parties and the decline of one mechanically causing the other to rise.

Confronted with evidence of substantial shifts in electoral behaviour and in the names and fortunes of parties, students of elections have four alternatives. The first is reliance upon tradition, repeating shibboleths of the past as if elections since February 1974 had never happened. These elections may be ignored because they were not discussed in books that a journalist or teacher read when a student. The results may be dismissed by politicians to whom they are politically uncongenial or because they are uncongenial to intellectual theories about how the electorate ought to behave.

A second alternative is to reformulate existing theories of electoral competition in an attempt to rescue them. Those who believe that class *ought* to determine voting may alter the conventional definition of occupational class in hopes of discovering a good fit between social classes and Conservative, Labour and Alliance voters. Those who expect parental party preferences to determine voting may search for a missing link in the chain of political socialization that can explain why family loyalties no longer determine voting today. Those who have learned the intricacies of calculating the swing of votes between the Labour and Conservative parties may do this in more and more refined ways, even though the great movement of votes in 1983 was not a swing between the major parties but a shift from both the Labour and Conservative parties to the Alliance. However, theories should not be accepted because of their ingeniousness, rhetoric, or logic. Theories must be tested by confrontation with electoral evidence.

Thirdly, the disparity between present and past electoral behaviour can be described as a dealignment of voters. Yet if dealignment was a novelty in the early 1970s (Sarlvik and Crewe, 1983), by the second half of the 1980s it must be considered the status quo. At best, such a characterization is negative knowledge. It is a statement that electoral competition today differs from the past; it is not a description of the present. A positive characterization of electoral competition requires more (Wald, 1982; Williams, 1985).

This book adopts a fourth approach, an analysis of electoral competition that starts from first principles, and takes the 1983 British election result as the basis for testing theories and generalizations adduced in the past. Since that election contradicts much that was once believed to be true, voting surveys from the past are also re-examined. Not only is it possible that things ain't what they used to be; perhaps they never were! Instead of examining particular theories as if they must be wholly right or wholly wrong, we ask: Under what circumstances and to what extent is each of significance today? Voting is explained by a model of lifetime learning. The model is open in the sense that voters are always potentially able to think afresh. But it is in no sense empty, explaining four-fifths of the variance in the Conservative-Labour vote (Table 7.3).

In facing the future, we start from the present. To a substantial extent, future choices reflect present judgements of past achievements (Fiorina, 1981). The Parliament elected in 1983 is the point from which parties will compete at the next general election. One-quarter of MPs elected in 1983 will be Members of Parliament after the year 2000 — unless changes in party competition increase instability in the careers of MPs.

To concentrate solely upon the outlooks of voters is to commit what Scheuch (1966) terms the individualist fallacy, drawing inferences about the actions of complex political organizations from data about individuals. This is often misleading, for the pressures within party organizations are different from those within the minds of ordinary voters (Rose and Mackie, 1984). Moreover, for any given distribution of the popular vote, the distribution of seats in the House of Commons can vary widely.

To understand electoral competition, we must examine parties as well as voters. The most important political events of the 1979-83 Parliament were not initiated by changes in electoral opinion but by party politicians: the moves that altered the structure of power within the Labour Party; the creation of the Social Democratic Party and the Alliance; and Mrs. Thatcher's maintenance of a distinctive economic policy notwithstanding unprecedented levels of mid-term unpopularity in opinion polls.

Voters can only choose in response to the alternatives put before them by parties. The alternatives now before an elector are not the same as in the House of Commons. At Westminster the Labour Party is the official Opposition, with eight times as many MPs as the Alliance. But in most parliamentary constituencies, voters are not offered a choice between a Conservative MP and a Labour challenger. The Alliance is more likely to be the challenger to the Conservative incumbent, and Labour a more or less poor third (McAllister and Rose, 1984: Table 9.4). The translation of voters' preferences into representation in the House of Commons depends not only upon how individuals vote, but also upon where they vote and the ranking of parties in their constituency.

The first two chapters set out four models of electoral competition, defined by whether class determines voting and whether there is minimal or multi-party competition. The alternatives range from the familiar closed-class model to open electoral competition. Election results since 1945 show that even before the emergence of the Alliance, Britain had become a multi-party system. Chapters III and IV marshal voting surveys since 1964 to test theories of the class determination of the vote. However class is defined, its impact is limited.

A new perspective on the social structure of the electorate is set out in chapter V, identifying four major blocs, defined by socio-economic interests as home-owners or tenants and as trade union members or non-members. The freedom of the electorate from class determinism is further demonstrated by the weakness of the intergenerational transfer of party loyalties from parents to children, analysed in chapter VI. The extent to which voters' political principles influence voting is examined in Chapter VII, which concludes with a lifetime learning model that takes into account the cumulative effect of all the factors influencing voting, and shows which are most important. The hypothesis — *We are all Alliance nowadays* — emphasizes the extent to which voters' views are common across party lines; it is examined in chapter VIII. When the electorate is sufficiently in agreement so that the distance is limited between Conservative, Labour and Alliance voters, any party can benefit from an electorate in flux.

In this book the authors have drawn upon a substantial body of studies by themselves and other scholars about voting behaviour and party competition. As the senior author commenced writing about British general elections in 1959, re-examining elections since has been a reminder of the contingency of knowledge, and of the need to test old generalizations against fresh evidence in order to understand the process by which elections are won and lost.

In order that the reader can see evidence clearly for himself or herself, the book is full of tables showing the relationship between voting and many potential influences. It is particularly important to describe the precise degree to which influences are strong or weak, since a number of our conclusions challenge accepted ideas about the determinants of voting. Particular care has been given to the way in which voter surveys are percentaged. Many tables are a matrix giving the percentage of total voters having a combination of social and political characteristics. These are the figures that add up to produce election results. Students of electoral competition should always pay heed to what is politically as well as statistically significant.

The sample surveys intensively analysed here have been generously provided by several sources. The Gallup Poll has made available their unique massive samples of voters during election campaigns. The Data Archive of the Economic and Social Research Council at Colchester has made available surveys of British elections since 1964, conducted under the direction of David Butler and Donald Stokes, 1963-70; Bo Sarlvik and Ivor Crewe, 1974-79; and Anthony Heath, Roger Jowell and John Curtice in 1983. The earlier studies were funded principally by the Economic and Social (formerly Social Science) Research Council; the 1983 study was funded jointly by Pergamon Press, Jesus College Oxford, and the ESRC.

In examining election results historically, F.W.S. Craig's invaluable books, particularly *British Electoral Facts, 1832-1980*, have been used. Only those who remember the problems of searching for accurate and consistent data about British general elections before Fred Craig's work was published can appreciate the value and magnitude of his efforts.

In the course of writing, and especially in rewriting this book, helpful comments were received from Vernon Bogdanor, Richard Holme, Anthony Mughan, Edward Page, Jorgen S. Rasmussen, Rosemary J. Rose, Donley T. Studlar, Peter Taylor-Gooby, and

Kenneth Wald. The translation of this book via word-processor, computer and typesetter from a rough typescript into a finished typeset book was greatly facilitated by the efforts of Mrs. J.M. Roberts and Dr. Phillip L. Davies of the Centre for the Study of Public Policy at the University of Strathclyde, and Rupert Harding and his colleagues at Sage Publications Ltd.

1
Opening up electoral competition

Electoral competition involves two very different but complementary groups, individual voters and political parties. An election result is not just the product of organized party efforts, nor is it produced solely by the choices of individuals. It is produced by the interaction between parties and voters. Obvious though the point is, it is often overlooked. One school of election commentators concentrates upon the activities of party politicians; this is the distinguishing characteristic of the Nuffield studies of British elections since 1945 (Butler and Kavanagh, 1984). Another group concentrates upon the social and political characteristics of individual voters, as recorded in sample surveys. A generation of computer-trained academics finds this approach congenial (Butler and Stokes, 1969; Sarlvik and Crewe, 1983), and public opinion polls generate interest among party leaders too (Rose, 1985).

Electoral competition is interactive because both parties and voters are necessary to produce an election outcome. Without parties, voters would have no nationally relevant means of discriminating between competing candidates; candidates in one constituency would be isolated from candidates in the other 649 constituencies. The bond of party gives voters in every constituency the choice between a Conservative, Labour or Alliance government. Without parties, voters would have no means of holding the government of the day responsible. Without voters, a party has no chance to influence events in Parliament or government. Whatever their merits, voteless parties exert no influence on government and receive little attention in the media. Recent decades have shown how a Liberal or Nationalist party is ignored politically unless and until it wins votes and seats in Parliament. While parties structure the choice of electors, voters influence a party's seats in the House of Commons.

Because an individual can only favour a single candidate on the ballot paper, elections in Britain make it appear as if each individual gives unqualified support to one party. In the Republic of Ireland and in Northern Ireland, by contrast, a voter can show a liking for more than one party through the single transferable vote, ranking candidates in order of preference. In the United States, candidates for different offices — President, Senator, Representative and so forth — usually appear on the same ballot. An American can thus split his or her vote between Republican and Democratic candidates for different offices. In primaries, Americans choose between different candidates within a party.

Very few voters follow a party line on every major issue of the day. A vote is not a 100 per cent endorsement of everything that a party says or stands for. It is a rough indication of a preference, favouring one party as either a greater good or a lesser evil. Voters whose choice is only on balance cannot be called closed-minded partisans; if not already floating voters, they are wobbling in commitment to their current party.

Before nationwide opinion surveys were regularly undertaken, there was widespread ignorance among party leaders and political commentators about what ordinary voters thought. Views of voters were usually projections of what elite commentators thought (Rose, 1967). Today there is widespread dissemination of major generalizations purportedly proven by voting studies and opinion polls. There is arguably now more need for attention to be given to the role of parties in electoral competition.

The purpose of this chapter is to set out four alternative models of the relationship between parties and voters. The closed-class model, in which two parties compete for support and votes are determined by class, is often used to characterize electoral competition in Britain, or treated as the norm for competition everywhere. But it is not the only form of competition, and it has been losing strength. Therefore, this chapter will also consider the dynamics of transition from closed to open electoral competition.

Four models of parties and voters

To characterize electoral competition, we need to consider differences between voters who are determined and indeterminate, and differences between minimal and multi-party competition. The two sets of attributes can then be combined to make a fourfold typology of electoral competition.

When the electorate is *determined*, voting reflects the persisting structure of society. Individual votes are not cast according to the voluntaristic choice of individuals, or transitory influences of a particular election, such as the personality of a party leader. Class is the most familiar social structure determinant of voting, although it is not the only possible influence upon party preferences. Religion, language, national identity and race can also structure party loyalties (cf. Rose and Urwin, 1969). The established pattern of party competition can itself influence voting, insofar as individuals are socialized by their parents to identify with a particular party. In a determined electorate, individuals do not make choices; an election registers the social and political influences that determine votes.

In an *indeterminate* electorate, short-term influences upon voters are much more important than social structure or enduring party identifications. Instead of voting according to one's class or as one's parents did, an elector may cast a ballot in response to a topical but transitory issue; because of temporary problems at work; or because of the personality of a local candidate or national party leader. Short-term influences are inherently more volatile than long-term influences. In default of the stability induced by social structure or durable party identification, voters have a weak commitment to their current party, and some will float between parties from election to election.

The electorate in Britain has historically been viewed as determined. According to Gilbert and Sullivan, late Victorian voters were born either a little Liberal or Conservative (Butler and Stokes, 1969:45), a proposition not without some factual foundation when religion influenced voting, and religious loyalties were transmitted within the family from generation to generation (Wald, 1983). The rise of the Labour Party in the twentieth century also supports the idea of voting being determined by social structure. Labour is perceived as a party mobilizing working-class voters, with a middle-class counter-mobilization by the Conservatives.

Indeterminate electorates tend to characterize competition at the earliest stages of the introduction of the suffrage, when nationwide political parties have yet to be established. When individuals had little experience of elections, long-standing party commitments had no time to mature. Both voters and politicians could easily move between political groups that later crystallized into parties. Today, indeterminate voting can be regarded as a sign of post-modern elections; the United States is the prototype of such a system. In America the decline of political parties has resulted in a substantial fraction of the electorate voting for candidates from different parties at the same election, since Congressional and gubernatorial office as well as the Presidency are on the same long ballot. In a post-modern electorate, social structure and political structure are of limited consequence compared to transitory influences (cf. Wattenberg, 1984).

Competition at elections can be either minimal or multi-party. The *minimum* required for competition is two parties. In a one-party election a voter has no choice but to approve the candidate nominated or to refrain from giving positive support; there is no alternative. This absolute minimum is very rarely found, even within authoritarian single-party regimes (Hermet, Rouquie and Rose, 1978). In a one-party system, the party may give voters a choice between more than one candidate of the ruling party. In democratic elections, the minimum choice is between two parties.

Multi-party competition occurs when three or more parties contest elections. The existence of three candidates means that the voter's choice is not reduced to a simple judgement between Ins and Outs. A third party may be perceived as a clear alternative, for example, yellow as against red and blue, or combining elements of its competitors as grey or tartan plaid. If four or more parties contest elections, the choice of the electorate is even more open. When opposition parties are multiple, they can differ in their grounds for opposing the government, and in the frequency with which they vote against or support the government of the day. A third party may normally be part of a governing coalition, as in Germany, or consigned to the ranks of opposition, as at Westminster.

Students of British politics have long considered minimal competition as normal. The first-past-the-post electoral system has been assumed to relegate a third party to minor party status; the great majority of votes cast for it are wasted, being ineffective in electing MPs. The structure of the House of Commons focuses attention upon the choice between the party in office and the party second in seats in the House of Commons, which has the official title of Her Majesty's Loyal Opposition.

Neither in principle nor in practice is minimal party competition certain. Generalizations about the weakness of third parties can also be applied to second parties. Equally noteworthy, first-past-the-post electoral systems often award some seats to third parties, and Britain is no exception. Coalition government rather than single-party government is the norm in most parliamentary systems, and in Britain minority or coalition government has been a recurring feature of modern British politics (Butler, 1978).

Combining characteristics of the electorate and of parties produces a fourfold typology of electoral competition (Figure 1.1). The closed-class model — a minimal number of parties and a determined electorate — is but one of four logical possibilities. The other alternatives are fixed-track, structured or open competition.

FIGURE 1.1
Four models of electoral competition

	Parties	
Electorate	Minimal: 2	Multiple: 3 plus
Determined	CLOSED-CLASS	STRUCTURED
Indeterminate	FIXED TRACK	OPEN

Closed-class competition

(A minimum number of parties, and a class-determined electorate.) When two social groups determine voting, electoral competition is a duopoly. To say that parties compete is an exaggeration, for each party is not so much seeking to win votes from those committed to its opponent as it is seeking to mobilize the maximum vote from electors already predisposed in its favour by their social position. Northern Ireland has been an extreme example of closed (albeit not class) competition. In the days of the Stormont Parliament, Protestant Unionists and Catholic Nationalists often did not even bother to contest seats, for the dominance of one religion in a constituency made the other's cause hopeless with a first-past-the-post ballot (Elliott, 1973:98). In seats where the two religions were evenly balanced, each side made great efforts to mobilize the maximum number of electors committed to it by social loyalties. Class, a central feature of modern societies, could be expected to be at least as strong an influence in Britain as is the pre-modern force of religion in Northern Ireland.

A duopolistic system of electoral competition is stable as well as closed. In a closed system, people do not choose how to vote but whether to vote; in a voting booth social loyalties dictate party preference. Social loyalties can reflect a lifetime of political socialization, starting with children learning loyalties from parents and being maintained by contemporary influences. For example, a manual worker's son who is a manual worker would *be* Labour rather than choosing Labour, and a middle-class businessman's daughter who became a headmistress would *be* a Conservative. Analyses of the social bases of party support go so far as to speak of the 'freezing' of party commitments (Lipset and Rokkan, 1967; but cf. Rose and Mackie, 1984).

In Britain the class-equals-party model gives concrete expression to the idea of closed competition. The electorate is divided into two classes, manual and non-manual workers, and competition is considered to occur between two parties, Conservative and Labour, each with a class basis of support. Whilst historians and sociologists might argue about which came first — class pressures leading to the creation of class parties, or opportunistic efforts of politicians to mobilize class support for their party — there is agreement about the assumed result. In the frequently quoted statement by Peter Pulzer (1967: 96): 'Class is the basis of British party politics; all else is embellishment and detail.'

Structured competition

(A determined electorate and a multiplicity of parties.) Electoral competition is structured when the electorate is closed, giving each party a firm base of electoral support, and also divided into a multiplicity of groups; thus, the parties do not constitute a duopoly. The Netherlands has been a classic example of a structured system of multi-party competition, because the electorate has been determined along two dimensions, religion and class, each sustaining separate political parties (Lijphart, 1974). In Scandinavia, there are separate agrarian, middle-class, and religious parties dividing the anti-socialist vote, as well as a Socialist party with a working class base (Berglund and Lindstrom, 1978).

Proportional representation facilitates structured competition, enabling a party with a relatively limited but socially structured appeal (for example, a party for Swedish-speakers in Finland) to win seats in proportion to its votes. Under proportional representation, seats in Parliament are not subject to big shifts in response to small swings in popular preferences, as is the case in Britain.

Structured competition has not been normal in England, because of the absence of a third class to sustain a third party, as well as the bias of the first-past-the-post electoral system. But in the United Kingdom as a whole, the presence of nationalist parties makes it possible to argue that electoral competition in Scotland and Wales is structured by national identity or language in addition to class politics (Madgwick and Rose, 1982). In Northern Ireland, the existence of the bi-confessional Alliance Party, appealing to the small fraction of Protestants and Catholics who are consciously bi-confessional (for example, partners in a mixed marriage), introduces a small third party in a highly determined party system (McAllister and Wilson, 1978).

Fixed-track competition

(An indeterminate electorate and minimal parties.) Even when the electorate is indeterminate, the number of parties need only be two. Anthony Downs' (1957) model of party competition describes movement back and forth between parties along a single dimension. In America, the Republican and Democratic parties are the alternatives between which indeterminate voters move.

The fixed-track model implies mobility by parties as well as voters. In a proportional representation system, parties would need to change their positions in order to prevent the emergence of new parties. In the first-past-the-post electoral system, parties can respond more slowly, because of the inbuilt advantages of parties with many MPs. But move the parties must, if they wish to remain competitive in the long run. In theory perfectly competitive parties might adapt their position whenever public opinion changed. In practice, parties are not infinitely adaptable, and may maintain unpopular positions in the face of electoral pressures for change, as the Labour Party demonstrated before the 1983 election.

The familiar British notion of elections reflecting a swing of the pendulum (Jennings, 1961: 32) is an example of the fixed-track model of electoral competition. The metaphor of the pendulum emphasizes the movement of voters, yet the pendulum maintains its course on a fixed track between two points. Even voters on a random-walk search for a party would find only two parties to choose between. Insofar as the fixed dimension of competition reflects economic issues, then the electorate could shift to the right when economic conditions made this appear reasonable, and to the left in response to changes in the economy (cf. Alt, 1979).

Open competition

(An indeterminate electorate and a multiplicity of parties.) Voters can make a fresh choice at each general election; their votes need not be pre-determined by social structure. In this model, the parties between which voters choose are multiple rather than minimal. Uncertainty is much higher, for a larger portion of the electorate has a weak partisan commitment, or floats between parties. A decline in one party's vote does not assume a rise in the other's as in a fixed-track party system. For example, in the present Parliament a decline in Conservative support could benefit either Labour, the Alliance or both.

An indeterminate electorate is inherently mobile, because the preferences of voters are not anchored in social structure or in a long-standing identification with a particular political party. Whereas the fixed-track model implies a constant left-right dimension along which voters shift, voters in open competition can go in any number of different directions. There is no fixed single dimension to which issues can be related, such as economic conditions. Voters float because they are 'weightless', lacking strong commitments to parties or to socio-economic interests.

In open competition parties add to the disorientation of the electorate, because they too are mobile rather than anchored by persisting loyalties to groups and interests. Instead of representing classes that aggregate interests on a stable basis, parties can be 'catchall' organizations seeking to represent everybody (Kirchheimer, 1966). In such a competitive environment, parties cannot be confident that any substantial bloc of voters is their own. A successful attack by Conservatives upon Labour or vice versa may not benefit the other party but could work to the benefit of the Alliance.

In open electoral competition, parties are not fixed to a particular location in political space; they are under great pressure to move in pursuit of whatever appears to be the dominant electoral trend of the moment. For example, the Conservatives under Margaret Thatcher have had to continue support for social programmes to protect their chances of re-election, and Labour has had to take into account the interests of home-owners and a growing middle-class in order to compete for a majority in Parliament.

Once voters are no longer determined by fixed points in social structure and political space, parties are under pressures to be indeterminate too. For example, a decay in class loyalties can lead an anti-Socialist party to become a catchall party, adding working-class to middle-class support. The result is unipolar competition (Rose and Urwin, 1969: 33), with one party appealing to fixed trade union and working-class interests, while other parties are free of any fixed commitments. The outcome can be completely open competition, as the working-class party begins to seek middle-class support as well.

In a closed-class system of electoral competition, the alternatives are clearcut and predictable; in an open system, uncertainty is predominant. The mobility of voters is paralleled by the mobility of parties. A voter trying to turn one party out of government must think not only about his or her individual vote but also about how others will vote — and how party leaders will react. The number of uncertainties increases, and with it the risk that elections will not produce results that most voters desire.

The dynamics of competition

Whatever the particular type of electoral competition at the moment, the most interesting political questions concern the dynamics of change from one type of competition to another. This is particularly true in the state of British electoral competition today.

Logically, the electorate could change from being determined to indeterminate, indeterminate to determined, or exchange one social dimension of determination for another. For example, instead of landed aristocrats versus urban bourgeoisie, the electorate could divide as middle-class versus working-class. The number of parties could change from two to many, because of a disintegration of established parties, or from many to two as parties coalesced. The history of presidential elections in America offers a very good example of the recurring splintering *and* re-integration of short-lived breakaway parties. Another possibility is flux in parties. France not only has a multiplicity of parties at each election, but also frequent changes in the names of parties between elections.

Historically, the creation of a party system has been viewed as a process of mobilizing voters into determinate groups giving stable support for parties, whether multiple or two (Lipset and Rokkan, 1967; Rokkan, 1970). After 1884, Labour representation groups sought to replace older divisions within the middleclass along religious lines by dividing an electorate enlarged by franchise reforms into a middle-class Conservative Party and a working-class Labour Party.

After generations of universal suffrage, the prospect of contemporary parties finding new groups to mobilize is virtually nil. The lowering of the voting age to 18 and the addition of immigrant groups to the electoral register have been noteworthy, but involve numbers too small to support a new political party nationwide. An alternative possibility is that a new party mobilize existing social groups along a new dimension of competition (Schattschneider, 1960); the efforts of Nationalist parties in Scotland and Wales exemplify this. Yet the limited vote for the Nationalists has shown that national identity is of secondary importance in structuring votes within Scotland and Wales, and is even less important in a British context (McAllister, 1982; McAllister and Rose, 1984: chapters 5-9).

The basic logic of social structure determining parties is easy to state in the form of a general sociological theory of how groups ought to behave. But actually turning social loyalties into party loyalties is much more difficult to achieve in practice. Most social groups are *not* capable of determining votes; for example, feminist groups have not mobilized a majority of women as a party on their own. Nor does the American moral majority (*sic*) test its claim to be a majority by organizing as a political party. Pressure groups fear that an electoral test would demonstrate their inability to determine the votes of their members.

In contemporary Western societies, the demobilization of the electorate (that is, a shift from determined to indeterminate voting) is seen as a correlate of changes from a traditional industrial structure to a post-industrial society. Parties can no longer count on voters being delivered by childhood indoctrination in a fixed social structure. Parties must compete by offering distinctive policies to electors who, like consumers, are fickle, valuing novelty rather than tradition in voting.

In post-war Britain the analysis of electoral competition normally starts from the assumption of a closed-class system. But this need not imply closed-class competition in perpetuity. For this to happen several conditions would have to be met. First of all, society must continue to be divided into two and only two principal groups. Secondly, the relationship between social structure and party voting must remain strong or increase. Third, two and only two parties must offer themselves to the electorate.

Society does not stand still. Prototypical groups of party loyalists, such as elderly coalminers, and retired Home Counties colonels or their widows, are a small and declining proportion of the electorate today. Electoral competition will remain closed only if social changes do no more than alter the size of the classes supporting the established class parties, for example, increasing the number of Conservative-voting home-owners or of Labour-voting trade unionists. Closed competition may also be sustained if the parties can assimilate new social groups to established institutions. As Eric Hobsbawm (1981) has emphasized in *The Forward March of Labour Halted?*, this can no longer be taken for granted. Equally the ups and downs of the Conservative Party in the past two decades have demonstrated that it is not the automatic beneficiary of any Labour loss of support.

In consequence of a decline in class voting, a closed system can gradually evolve into a fixed-track system, if the two established parties are sufficiently flexible to adapt their appeals to the electorate. A decline in the class determination of voting need not mean a decline in economic issues salient to the electorate. It may simply reduce the certainty of working-class voters supporting Labour, and middle-class voters supporting the Conservatives. Instead of voting lifelong social loyalties, electors could vote their perception of current economic interests. The competition between the Conservative and Labour parties in the 1960s was not so much about alternative visions of society as it was about which party would be better at producing the economic growth that the whole country needed.

In contemporary Britain the Conservative and Labour parties can continue to be perceived as standing for distinctive economic or class interests, for example, the Conservatives as opposed to inflation, and Labour to unemployment. Even if a party claimed to oppose both unemployment and inflation, voters could reckon that one was better than the other at dealing with each problem. In such a situation, individual voters could float back and forth, depending upon whether they thought government should give priority to reducing inflation, or reducing unemployment. To the casual eye, the prevalence of economic issues would make it appear as if class issues were still pre-eminent. But careful analysis could reveal that salient economic issues cut across rather than paralleled traditional class alignments.

A third possible trend — a shift from deterministic to structured electoral competition — is not plausible in Britain. Such a shift would require the emergence of a third political party that drew its vote from a distinctive social group different from the middle class and the working class. The absence of social groups not already mobilized within the electorate makes this difficult to conceive, and the electoral system restricts seats in the House of Commons to parties capable of concentrating their support in some constituencies. If race structured voting, then a Black Britain party could win a few constituencies populated predominantly by immigrants and their descendants. But since immigrants are usually an electoral minority in the constituency in which they live, such a party could not be effective nationwide.

The Alliance demonstrates that a third party can come forward, but its electoral support is not determined. The Alliance does not claim to be the party of the educated (less than one-quarter of the electorate) or of the *Guardian* readership (less than one-twentieth). Instead, it seeks to be a party representing everyone; its appeals consciously reject the language of class interests.

Finally, a closed system can evolve into open electoral competition through the reduction of the electoral influence of all social loyalties. Instead of the grounds for voting being fixed, voters would be ready to move, being influenced at different times by the personalities of party leaders, general party images for competence, or social and economic issues. Open party competition produces persisting uncertainties about the outcome of an election, because many different influences are at play, and can work in different partisan directions.

Open electoral competition is visibly present when more than two parties can demonstrate that they are effective competitors in national elections. This was the case in Britain in the 1920s, but the collapse, though not disappearance, of the Liberal Party led most political commentators to treat the British party system as having minimal competition. Since support for Liberals was more often manifest at by-elections than general elections, the Liberal Party role could be considered minor compared to the Conservative and Labour parties. But this assertion has been difficult to sustain since the 1974 "Who governs?" elections, when confrontation between the Conservative and Labour parties led a quarter of voters to reject both alternatives. The creation of the Alliance, which came within 2.2 per cent of matching Labour's vote in 1983, makes the status quo a three-party system.

Just as the evolution of electoral competition in the early days of universal suffrage can be described as a move toward a closed system, in post-industrial societies social changes imply a movement from closed to open competition. The transition can involve a mixing of models. A portion of the electorate can still vote according to class loyalties, while another is completely open. Two established closed parties may continue to win the majority of the vote, while a third appeals to indeterminate electors. Fixed-track and deterministic alternatives could be transitional stages in a world in which political alternatives are no longer reduced to two.

An open system of electoral competition is also vulnerable to change. For example, a party with indeterminate support can collapse, leaving two parties with firm social bases of electoral support. If Mrs. Thatcher has actually created social divisions 'on a scale hardly seen since the English Civil War', as general secretary Norman Willis told the 1985 Trades Union Congress, this process of polarization should create closed-class competition.

The four models of electoral competition make us aware that whatever pattern prevails at the moment need not persist. The models identify alternatives for a Britain that is currently in flux. Deciding which model most accurately describes Britain in the 1980s is a matter for empirical analysis, and the best evidence is given by the British electorate when parties seek their votes.

2
The multiplicity of parties in Britain

Why have parties at all? This question is prior to considering the number of parties in a political system. The justification for party politics is both normative and practical. At the normative level, competing parties are essential in the definition of democracy as we know it. Politics is about articulating and reconciling different views of how a country should be governed. Parties put forward different views about government. Democratically elected governments have the authority to take actions binding everyone, including those who voted for their opponents.

The practical justification for parties is recognized in almost every system of government, Communist or Fascist as well as democratic. Parties mobilize support from the mass electorate, having a directive role in non-competitive systems, and a representative role in democratic systems. Furthermore, parties produce values and policies independent of the civil service of the permanent state. Without the external influence of party upon government, election results would change very little, since civil servants endure and are not accountable to the electorate (Rose, 1974a: chapters 15-16).

In democratic systems parties normally have two main activities: nominating candidates to contest elections, and aggregating interests in support of policies for government. At a general election candidates cannot be expected to materialize from nowhere, and voters want an indication of the political views of candidates; parties provide this. Prior to the formation of mass parties in late nineteenth century Britain, many voters were deprived of a chance to cast a ballot because hundreds of constituencies were uncontested, and many MPs were returned unopposed. When parties seek votes from a mass electorate, party leaders must aggregate the political demands of groups of limited size, such as owners of company shares or coalminers, into broad-based appeals.

Two parties is the minimum for democratic electoral competition. A variety of reasons are conventionally offered to explain why there should be only two parties. The first-past-the-post electoral system is one reason; it awards no seats to parties that finish third. A second party wins seats if and only if it can concentrate sufficient support in some constituencies to finish first. Labour concentrated its vote in the 1983 general election, and the Alliance failed to do so. In English-speaking countries using the first-past-the-post system, three (or more) parties are normal (Rose, 1983: 34). America is no exception, for Democrats and Republicans compete within as well as between parties.

The need to focus responsibility upon the government of the day is a second major reason offered for the existence of two and only two parties. The party in government is the first party, and the party second in Parliament is deemed the only alternative. But reducing the choice to two parties presumes what is not necessarily true, that each of the two parties will alternatively be acceptable to a majority of the electorate. This is spectacularly not the case in the Orange-and-Green party choice in Northern Ireland. Electoral competition can lead to polarization between two antithetical parties.

A third reason for assuming that party choice should be minimal is the reduction of problems of government to two points on a single left-right dimension. Class and economic interests can be deemed so pervasive that every kind of issue is related to class. Moreover, preferences about issues are assumed to be internally consistent; voters on the left will support left positions on all issues and voters on the right act similarly.

Insofar as theories of duopolistic competition are correct, then only closed-class or fixed-track competition could be valid. But are such theories true? Each of the foregoing arguments could be reversed to show why a multiplicity of parties should contest an election. The introduction of a third party may not seem like a large quantitative increase, but politically it is very significant. It increases the choice of the electorate by 50 per cent. The votes a third party wins are usually taken from the support of one or both of the other two parties; each party is thus faced with competition on two fronts.

The argument that policy alternatives can be reduced to only two positions is very questionable. Along a left-right dimension there is a centre position. The Alliance often projects itself as a group that is middle-of-the-road, as against the alleged extremes of the Conservative *and* Labour parties. A party can also differ in its mix of policies. The Alliance could offer a third alternative by agreeing with the Labour Party on some issues, for example, government should act to lower unemployment, and with the Conservatives on other issues, such as trade unions having too much power.

The argument that government unpopularity leads to opposition popularity is theoretically flawed, for it presupposes that voters must always endorse one of the two established parties. The 1979-83 Parliament saw both Conservative and Labour leaders fall in popularity simultaneously. Together they claimed the endorsement of only 44 per cent of the electorate in the Gallup Polls in autumn, 1981. In the 1983 general election, the vote for both the Conservative *and* the Labour parties went down. The 1983 Parliament has seen the rejection of both parties' leaders continue; Margaret Thatcher and Neil Kinnock are each below David Steel and David Owen in Gallup Poll monthly ratings, and voting preferences continue to divide three ways.

While the British electoral system favours duopoly in the House of Commons, this can be breached. A third party can win seats by concentrating its votes in a limited number of constituencies (e.g. Northern Ireland), or a party's nationwide vote can rise to such a point that the party is over the threshold at which substantial numbers of seats can be won for each additional per cent of votes. In a Parliament with no majority party, even parties with only a few seats can be relevant to control of government (Sartori, 1976: 300ff). In the 1974-79 Parliament, a Liberal Party with 13 MPs formed a pact with a Labour government lacking an overall majority. In the Parliament elected in 1983, the weakness of the official opposition, Labour, also renders Alliance MPs irrelevant in division lobbies.

The problem of counting parties can be resolved by considering a variety of aspects of party competition. Is it seats in the House of Commons, or votes nationwide? If it is votes nationwide, then is the nation the United Kingdom, Great Britain or England? Because there are many different ways in which parties can be deemed to count, this chapter will first review different kinds of evidence of multi-party competition, and then consider changes across time and space in the dimensions of multi-party competition.

Multi-party not minimal party competition

The nomination of candidates to contest elections is the activity that distinguishes political parties from pressure groups and a host of other political organizations. Therefore, the fundamental test of the number of parties in the British party system is: How many parties consistently nominate candidates to fight elections nationwide? The rise or fall in the number of candidates fighting an election indicates the extent to which party competition is becoming more open or closed.

In the nineteenth century, hundreds of seats were normally not contested at general elections. In Hanham's (1959: 191) words, 'general elections were not general'. Instead of two organized teams of candidates fighting every constituency under a common programme, there were hundreds of more or less isolated constituencies in which particular local circumstances determined whether or not there would be an electoral contest, and who the candidates would be. In some seats returning two MPs, each party would nominate only one candidate, thus dividing between them the representation for the constituency, and depriving its voters of a choice.

Between 1832 and 1865 an average of 45 per cent of all seats in the House of Commons were uncontested, and from the first election after the 1867 Reform Act through 1880, 26 per cent. The 1885 election, immediately following the major franchise expansion of 1884, was the first in which less than 100 constituencies were uncontested. In 1900, 243 seats were uncontested, more than one-third of the total. By 1931, 67 were uncontested. Only since 1945 has virtually every seat been contested by at least two parties at each general election (Craig, 1981: Table 14.09).

The era since 1945 has seen a change in the number of candidates contesting seats. From 1945 through the 1970 general election, the average number of candidates was normally less than three a constituency, and in elections from 1951 to 1959 a majority of constituencies were contested by only two candidates, thus meeting the definition of minimal party competition. The Liberal nomination of 475 candidates in 1950 actually confirmed the minimalist model, for 319 Liberals lost their deposits. The Liberals did not contest so many seats again for another 24 years (Table 2.1).

TABLE 2.1
Candidates at general elections, 1945–83

Election	Number	Av. per seat	Seats with only two candidates
1945	1,683	2.6	174
1950	1,868	3.0	113
1951	1,376	2.2	495
1955	1,409	2.2	489
1959	1,536	2.4	373
1964	1,757	2.8	194
1966	1,707	2.7	234
1970	1,837	2.9	185
1974 Feb.	2,135	3.4	38
1974 Oct.	2,252	3.5	0
1979	2,576	4.1	3
1983	2,578	4.0	0

Source: Craig, 1981: Table 1.39.

Since 1974 three or more candidates have been the rule in a constituency. In 1979 and 1983 an average of four candidates fought a constituency. This reflected the nationwide effort by Liberals and Alliance, reinforced by Nationalists in Scotland and Wales; it also reflected the presence of many candidates standing as independents or as "one-man" parties in England. In October, 1974 and in 1983 every Westminster constituency had at least three candidates.

A party that nominates more candidates ought to win a larger share of the popular vote, but this is not always the case. The first seat that a newly formed party fights is one of its strongest; yet a one-man party that fights a single seat and wins 50 per cent of the constituency vote there has gained only 0.08 per cent of the total national vote. Nor can a party expect to keep its share of the vote constant when expanding the number of constituencies fought. For example, if a party fought 25 seats, it might win an average of 25 per cent of the vote in each constituency; this would be 1.0 per cent of the total national vote.

The number of seats fought and a party's level of popular support are interdependent. When popular support is rising, a party is encouraged to fight more seats. In February, 1974 the Liberal Party organization was overwhelmed by candidates coming forward unprompted by the organization, because of a groundswell of Liberal support. Nominating candidates is no guarantee of creating a surge in support. In 1950 the Liberals made a great effort to fight nationwide, but the polarization of popular support between the Conservative and Labour parties caused the additional Liberal candidates to fare badly. In 1979 the National Front thought that popular disillusion with successive Conservative and Labour governments would aid its cause, trebling its candidates. But every one of the 303 National Front candidates lost his deposit, and the average candidate polled a derisory one per cent of the vote. The nomination of candidates to seek votes nationwide is a necessary but not sufficient condition of a party winning a significant share of the national vote.

The post-war fortunes of the Liberal Party illustrate the interdependence of the number of candidates and popular support (Table 2.2). In 1945 the Liberals fought about half the seats, winning an average of 18.6 per cent of the vote cast in constituencies contested. In 1950 an effort to win more votes by nominating more candidates caused the average Liberal constituency vote to fall by 6.8 per cent. By cutting back severely on the number of candidates, the Liberal share of the vote per contested seat rose by more than a quarter by 1955. As Liberal support rose in the late 1950s and early 1960s, its share of the vote per contested constituency rose, and more candidates were nominated. Yet because the Liberals were only able to fight half or less seats, the party's national vote was limited.

The tide of Liberal support in 1974 was evidenced by the very substantial increase in the number of candidates nominated, combined with an increase in the average Liberal vote per seat. It rose to 23.6 per cent in February 1974. By consistently contesting constituencies nationwide since, the Liberals have found that they are vulnerable to losing as well as gaining support. The Liberal share of the vote fell in October, 1974 and again in 1979. In 1983 the Alliance vote was up, but only 2.4 per cent of the increase in Alliance support from February, 1974 was due to increased support in contested constituencies. Most of the increase came from increasing by one-fifth the number of seats the party fought.

TABLE 2.2
Liberal candidates and votes won, 1945–83

Election	Candidates No.	Total vote %	Av. vote per contested seat %
1945	306	9.0	18.6
1950	475	9.1	11.8
1951	109	2.6	14.7
1955	110	2.7	15.1
1959	216	5.9	16.9
1964	365	11.2	18.5
1966	311	8.5	16.1
1970	322	7.5	13.5
1974 Feb.	517	19.3	23.6
1974 Oct.	619	18.3	18.9
1979	577	13.8	14.9
1983 (Alliance)	633	25.4	26.0

Source: Calculated from Butler and Sloman, 1980: 208–10.

Post-war party competition has seen an ebb and flow in popular support for the Liberal Party, and also for the Scottish National Party and Welsh Nationalists (see Rose and McAllister, 1982: Table 4.5). But these fluctuations have occurred within a pattern of increased organizational capability to contest elections. By maintaining a nationwide electoral presence in election after election, Scottish and Welsh Nationalist parties have raised their minimum vote when popularity is waning, and raised their maximum when support is waxing.

The credibility of multi-party competition is rising too, for parties are winning fewer and fewer seats with at least half the vote. In pure two-party competition, one candidate must win at least half the vote. When votes are divided three ways, this may occur if the party is very strong in a constituency or one of its opponents is very weak, but it is not a necessity. When opponents collectively win a majority of votes, then the incumbent party is vulnerable in three ways: the loss of votes to the second-place party; the transfer of votes from the third place to the second-place party; or a combination of both movements.

From 1945 through 1970 the great majority of MPs, whether

fighting one or two opponents, won more than half the votes cast in their constituency. In the elections of 1951 and 1955, 94 per cent of all MPs were returned with absolute majorities. In the eight elections of the period, an average of 79 per cent of seats were won with an absolute majority, and one in five with a minority vote (Table 2.3).

However, since February, 1974, 52 per cent of all MPs have been elected by less than half the vote in their constituency. The proportion of candidates elected with less than half the vote rose to 64 per cent in February, 1974. It was slightly less in 1983, 52 per cent, because of the Labour Party's disastrous showing in opposition. Most MPs sit in Parliament thanks to divisions in the vote for their opponents, and the majority party in the Commons consistently gains a minority of votes nationwide.

TABLE 2.3
The credibility of multi-party competition, 1945–83

Election	Seats won on minority vote		Lost deposits		
			Con.	Lab.	Lib./All'ce
	No.	%	(as % of seats contested)		
1945	174	29.0	1.0	0.3	24.8
1950	187	29.9	0.8	0.0	67.1
1951	39	6.2	0.5	0.1	60.5
1955	37	5.9	0.5	0.1	54.5
1959	80	12.7	0.3	0.1	25.4
1964	232	36.8	0.8	1.3	14.2
1966	185	29.4	1.4	0.5	33.4
1970	124	19.7	1.6	1.0	55.4
1974 Feb.	408	64.3	1.3	4.0	4.4
1974 Oct.	380	59.8	4.5	2.1	20.2
1979	206	32.4	0.5	3.5	52.5
1983	336	51.7	0.8	18.8	1.7

Sources: Craig, 1981: Tables 5.01, 14.11, 14.12; Craig, 1984: 98.

The law defines a serious candidate as one who wins at least one-eighth of the vote in a constituency, thus securing the return of a cash deposit required as a means of discouraging frivolous candidates. A party that does not command enough support to save its deposit is far removed from the prospect of winning a seat. It has so low a share of a constituency's vote that a further decline in support would have only a limited impact upon the result.

From 1945 through 1970 Conservative and Labour candidates on average lost fewer than one per cent of their deposits. The Liberal capacity to save deposits fluctuated; the party lost 67 per cent of its deposits when fighting nationwide in 1950; the proportion fell in 1951 and 1955 but only because of a drastic cutback in candidates. From

1959 through 1966 the Liberals saved deposits in most of the seats they fought, but in the 1970 election they again lost more than half their deposits (Table 2.3). Consistently, a majority of other candidates lose their deposits.

Since 1974 the pattern of lost deposits has altered greatly. In February, 1974, the Liberals lost fewer deposits than Labour, and in October, 1974, saved four-fifths of their deposits. In 1979 the Liberals lost most of their deposits, but the number of lost Labour deposits also increased. In 1983 Labour candidates lost more than ten times as many deposits as the Alliance. In the last four British general elections, the Liberals and the Alliance have shown that they have credible candidates. Labour now faces a problem of credibility in the 119 seats in which it is meant to represent the official opposition, but lost its deposit in 1983.

The actions of party politicians have now institutionalized multi-party competition. The Liberal Party and Scottish and Welsh Nationalists have organized the nomination of candidates to benefit from popular protest against the established duopoly parties (Van Mechelen, 1982). The changes in the Labour Party that led to the creation of the Social Democratic Party and the Alliance between the SDP and Liberal leaders have also been important. The leaders of successive Labour and Conservative governments have made an important, albeit negative contribution, dissipating support through their actions in office. Each change has had implications for the electorate. None has been initiated by popular demand; they have reflected initiatives by party politicians.

TABLE 2.4
From minimal to multi-party competition, 1945–83

Election	Con.	Lab.	Duopoly (% all votes)	All other
1945	39.6	48.0	87.4	12.6
1950	43.4	46.1	89.5	10.5
1951	48.0	48.8	96.7	3.3
1955	49.7	46.4	96.1	3.9
1959	49.4	43.8	93.2	6.8
1964	43.4	44.1	87.5	12.5
1966	41.9	48.0	89.9	10.1
1970	46.4	43.1	89.4	10.6
1974 Feb.	37.9	37.2	75.0	25.0
1974 Oct.	35.8	39.2	75.1	24.9
1979	43.9	36.9	80.8	19.2
1983	42.4	27.6	70.0	30.0

The importance of initiatives by party leaders is demonstrated by examining changes in the support of the established duopoly parties, (Table 2.4). Minimal competition between parties increased from 1945 until the mid-1950s. The two duopolistic parties took 87.4 per cent of the vote in 1945, and 96.7 per cent in 1951. In the 1960s the Conservative and Labour shares fluctuated and tended to fall. But at the three elections between 1964 and 1970 the two duopolistic parties took between seven-eighths and nine-tenths of the total vote. While the electorate was less fixed in the 1960s, the decline in one party's share was matched for the most part by an increase in the vote for the other. Between 1945 and 1970 the Labour share of the vote fell by 4.9 per cent, and the Conservative share rose by 6.8 per cent.

Since 1970 both the Conservative and Labour parties have had their share of the vote decline. Labour won two elections in 1974 with much the same share of the vote that the Conservatives had gained in suffering an enormous defeat in 1945. In 1983 Mrs. Thatcher's victory was won with a lower share of the vote than Sir Winston Churchill and Sir Alec Douglas-Home had secured in losing the 1950 and 1964 elections. Labour's share of the vote since February 1974 has consistently been lower than at any general election since 1931.

The impact of the creation of the Alliance can be measured by contrasting the position of the established parties just before the Gang of Four broke with the Labour Party to found the Social Democratic Party, and a year later. In December, 1980 the Conservative support in the Gallup Poll was well down, and the Labour vote was ten per cent ahead of the government. Yet the combined support for the two established parties remained virtually the same as in the 1979 general election, 80.5 per cent. While the strength of the duopolistic parties was less than in 1970 or 1951, movement between the two established parties was consistent with the model of minimal party competition.

The capacity of a new party coalition to alter voting was demonstrated by the creation of the Alliance. By December 1981 the Alliance had the support of 49.5 per cent in the Gallup Poll; less than one-quarter favoured each of the traditional duopolistic parties. Third-force strength was more than three times what the Liberals had a year earlier and more than six times the Liberal vote in 1970. Alliance support did not hold at this mid-Parliament peak, but it remained high enough in 1983 to advance the third-force vote beyond its previous height. In 1983 Labour's average vote per candidate was lower than at any general election since 1900. In the four elections since February, 1974, the established duopolistic parties have together won an average of 75 per cent of the vote, as against 25 per cent taken by third-force parties. Minimum party competition belongs to an era now past.

The several faces of multi-party competition

Multi-party competition can take many forms, from highly stable competition between half a dozen parties in Switzerland to the shifting of the names as well as the number of parties in France, the Netherlands and Israel. In Britain the extent of multi-party competition varies with the measures employed; it differs between nations within the United Kingdom, and between measures of MPs and of popular votes. Yet by any relevant indicator, Britain now has multi-party competition.

The shift from minimal to multi-party competition has occurred throughout the United Kingdom. Even though the Conservative and Labour shares of the vote differed between nations, in 1951 duopoly was everywhere strong, accounting for 97.6 per cent of the vote in England, 96.4 per cent in Scotland, 91.3 per cent in Wales, and 72.8 per cent in Northern Ireland (Table 2.5). Other parties drew votes chiefly from a fringe of a fringe, that is, remote rural seats in Scotland, Wales and Northern Ireland (Rose, 1968, Table 7; Rose and McAllister, 1982: Table 9.21).

TABLE 2.5
Division of votes within the United Kingdom, 1951–83

Election	Con.	Lab.	Total	Lib./All'ce	Nat.	
		(% vote within nation)				
England						
1951	48.8	48.8	97.6	2.3	n.a.	
1974 Oct.	38.9	40.1	79.0	20.2	n.a.	
1983	46.0	26.9	72.9	26.4	n.a.	
Wales						
1951	30.8	60.5	91.3	7.7	0.7	
1974 Oct.	23.9	49.5	73.4	15.5	10.8	
1983	31.1	37.5	68.6	23.2	7.8	
Scotland						
1951	48.6	47.9	96.4	2.7	0.3	
1974 Oct.	24.7	36.3	61.0	8.3	30.4	
1983	28.4	35.1	63.5	24.5	11.8	
Northern Ireland[a]						
1951	59.3	13.5	72.8	0	27.2	Irish
1974 Oct.	0	1.6	1.6	0	62.1	Un'st
					29.8	Irish
1983	0	0	0	0	57.1	Un'st
					33.2	Irish

[a] 1951: Ulster Unionist Party, which broke links with the British Conservative Party in 1972. 1974 and 1983: Un'st = all Unionist and Loyalist candidates; Irish = all favouring Irish unity.

The October, 1974 election produced a noteworthy nationalist vote and depressed the strength of the duopolistic parties in Scotland and Wales. There was also a major fall in their vote in England, where the combined Conservative and Labour share dropped to 79 per cent. In the exceptional circumstances of Northern Ireland the duopoly had virtually nil vote because the Ulster Unionists broke their electoral alliance with British Conservatives and the Labour Party effectively withdrew from contesting seats. The duopoly's share of votes rose throughout Great Britain in 1979, but only by five per cent.

The 1983 election demonstrated that each nation of the United Kingdom now has multi-party competition; the only difference is the number and names of the multiplicity of parties. The Alliance is not a Celtic fringe party: it is strongest in England. The duopolistic parties have difficulty in taking two-thirds of the vote in Scotland and Wales because competition from the Alliance is augmented by Nationalist candidates. In Ulster even the simple Orange-Green duopoly of votes has become more complex, because of divisions between Official Unionists and Democratic Unionists, and between the Social Democratic & Labour Party and Provisional Sinn Fein (McAllister and Rose, 1984: chapter 8; Elliott and Wilford, 1983).

The first-past-the-post electoral system tends to create a duopoly of seats in Parliament. Since 1945 one party has almost always had a minority of the popular vote converted into a majority of seats. The two largest parties win more than nine-tenths of the seats in the Commons, but the relationship between seats and votes has not been constant. As long as the Conservative and Labour parties enjoyed a duopoly of the popular vote, the disproportional element in the electoral system was limited. The two parties' combined share of seats differed from their combined vote by as little as 1.9 per cent in 1951, and by an average of 6.6 per cent between 1945 and 1970.

The disproportionality of the electoral system has increased since 1974, because the Liberal and Alliance vote nationally has not been concentrated in ways necessary to win seats in proportion to votes. Since February, 1974, the two established parties have on average taken 19 per cent more seats in the House of Commons than their combined share of the popular vote. In 1983 the gap was the widest in more than half a century; together, the Conservative and Labour parties won 70 per cent of the vote and 93 per cent of the seats.

The British electoral system exaggerates the consequences of shifts in votes between a multiplicity of parties. In a proportional representation system, a shift of a few per cent in votes will produce a shift of only a few per cent of seats in Parliament. But in the first-past-the-post system, a shift of a few per cent in votes usually has a disproportionate effect. As Alliance support reaches or exceeds one-third of the vote, the Alliance share of seats would become less disproportional. A large increase in the Alliance vote could even lead one of the other parties to become a victim of disproportional under-representation (Butler, 1983). The greater the potential shift in parliamentary seats because of small shifts in votes, the more open and intense the competition.

A century of party competition since 1885, the first election in which a majority of males had the right to vote, emphasizes two points. The first is the *variability* of electoral competition across time. Secondly, minimal party competition has usually *not* been the norm. Competition between two and only two parties has characterized only one-quarter of the past century (Table 2.6).

From 1885 through 1910 multi-party competition existed in two or three dimensions. In Ireland, Nationalism versus Unionism divided Catholic and Protestant voters. Since Ireland returned 101 of the 670 seats in the House of Commons, Irish MPs, whether Nationalists or Unionists, were important at Westminster. Within Britain the Conservatives and Liberals also reflected attitudes toward Unionism, but the principal dimension of differentiation was the religious divide between supporters of the established church and non-conformists (Wald, 1983: 90). The two major parties averaged more than 90 per cent of the vote, but this was only because of the large number of uncontested seats in Ireland, and the absence of Labour candidates emphasizing class differences.

From 1918 through 1935 multi-party competition was the rule. The Conservative and Labour parties, which ended the period as the two largest parties in the Commons, together averaged only 76 per cent of the vote in seven elections. The Liberal, Labour and Conservative parties each were involved in splits or coalitions, introducing competition within as well as between parties. The Liberals were split at the 1918 general election by Lloyd George, and Labour was split at the 1931 election by Ramsay MacDonald. The Conservatives fought as part of a coalition in 1918 and 1931. The period saw the emergence of class-based voting for the Labour and Conservative parties (Miller, 1977), but the pervasive characteristic was variability in the names and numbers of parties in constituency competition.

The 1945 general election introduced an era of minimal party competition between Conservatives and Labour, which persisted through the 1970 election. The two-party share of the vote averaged 91 per cent, and at the constituency level Conservative and Labour candidates were almost invariably the only credible candidates for seats. The two parties were very evenly matched; the difference in their average share of the vote in eight elections was less than one per cent. Moreover, the two parties were deemed class parties, competing for support from a more or less closed electorate.

Multi-party competition has again been the rule since 1974. In the past four elections the combined Conservative and Labour share of the vote has averaged less than in the confused period of multi-party competition between 1918 and 1935. The weakness of the two established parties is particularly striking, since neither has yet been characterized by a great split like that which rent the Liberals during the First World War. While the number of leaders breaking away from Labour in 1981 was no greater than in 1931, the vote for the breakaway Social Democrats was much greater than for the followers of Ramsay MacDonald then. Moreover, the direction of change is not, as in the interwar era, toward consolidation into two class-based parties, but away from a closed-class model of party competition.

TABLE 2.6
Party systems of the United Kingdom since 1885

Votes	(mean %)	
1885–1910: Two-dimensional		
Conservatives and Liberal Unionists	47.3	93.0
Liberals	45.7	
Irish Nationalists	3.6	
Labour	2.6	
1918–1935: Multi-party		
Conservatives	44.8	76.3
Labour	31.5	
Liberals	19.9	
Others	3.8	
1945–1970: Two-party		
Labour	46.1	91.3
Conservatives	45.2	
Liberals	7.1	
Others	1.6	
1974–1983: Multi-party		
Conservatives	40.0	75.2
Labour	35.2	
Liberals	19.2	
Others	5.6	

A distinctive feature of British general elections since 1974 has been the relatively low share of the vote of the winning party. In February, 1974 the Labour government's share of the vote was lower than that won by any governing party since 1832 with one exception. The vote of the Conservative victors in 1983 was, with one exception, lower than that of any government with a working majority since 1832.

In modern British elections, multi-party competition is normal. Minimal party competition is not an iron law of the electoral system or of British political culture; it is specific to one period, and that period is now part of the past.

3
Testing the closed-class model of voting

Familiarity breeds belief, but belief in class as the chief determinant of voting behaviour is not proof of its actual importance. Before the introduction of sample surveys, Conservatives could dismiss the idea of class divisions as inconsistent with their belief in the organic unity of society, and Socialists could argue that class *had* to be (or ought to be or eventually would be) the sole determinant of voting. In the absence of evidence, a clash of beliefs could continue indefinitely and inconclusively.

In its simplest form the class-equals-party model of voting is a closed-class model of electoral competition. Class is said not only to determine voting, but also to result in the minimum of competing parties; the middle class votes Conservative, and manual workers vote Labour.

Two obstacles to the acceptance of a closed-class model immediately come to mind. Firstly, because three-fifths of the electorate is working class, then the Labour Party should win every election. Only an eccentric belief, such as party preference defining class, is consistent with election results that give substantially less than half the vote to Labour, in theory the party of manual workers. There is also a need to explain deviations: why does so much of the working class vote Conservative (Nordlinger, 1967; McKenzie and Silver, 1968; Kavanagh, 1971) or Alliance? And why do some middle-class electors vote Labour? (cf. Rallings, 1975; Garrard et al.,1978; Alt and Turner, 1982).

Given the flaws in the link between class and party in Britain today, one response is to proclaim the need for more or better theory. A sociologist normally interprets this as requiring a refinement of definitions of class. Anyone who has ever worked with the British census definitions of class is well aware of their atheoretical nature. While it is reasonable to refine a core concept in sociology, the study of voting behaviour requires attention to politics as well. We cannot assume that because a theory postulates that class ought to determine voting that this in fact occurs. To do this is to be guilty of a particularly naive or arrogant form of sociological reductionism (Sartori, 1969). We must consider how class differences may be translated into competition between parties, and whether or not such theories are strongly supported or rejected by empirical evidence.

The rise of multi-party competition in Britain raises a second problem. A three-party system can be a closed-class system only if the number of classes is increased to three. For example, the Alliance vote could come from an intermediate lower middle class. If three classes each favour a different party, party competition is structured with deterministic voting and multiple parties. Alternatively, the Alliance could draw its votes from a cross-section of all classes; it would thus be an open party competing with two closed-class parties.

In testing the relation between class and voting either of two extreme criteria are sometimes applied. The first extreme argues that any departure from a purely random relationship between class and party — for example, one per cent more manual workers favouring Labour, and one per cent more middle-class voters favouring the Conservatives — is proof of the influence of class. But a relationship that is only one per cent better than random is almost completely open. The complementary error is to assert that any departure from a perfect fit between class and party rejects class determination. But if nine out of ten electors vote for their class party, the relationship is virtually closed. Because social relationships are probabilistic not mechanistic, the association between class and party is best expressed in degrees on a scale from 0 to 100. The proper question is not whether there is a random or completely deterministic relation between class and party, but how much or how little relationship is there?

The first requirement is to set out the basic ideas and methods for testing ideas about class and voting. Secondly, the relationship between class and voting at the 1983 British general election is tested with a variety of conceptions of class; the cash value of their influence is measured, and all are found to be weak today. The relationship between class and party since 1964 is examined; it was limited then, and has declined since.

The idea of class voting

Although everyone discusses class when writing about British society, the word is not used in the same way by different authors. Nor is evidence from election surveys analysed in the same way. Since so much of what follows emphasizes relatively fine distinctions between different definitions and measures of class, it is well to begin by emphasizing what is common in nearly every discussion of class.

First of all, class is defined as the dominant division of the electorate. Other social characteristics that cut across class differences, such as religion, language, or national identity, are considered of no political consequence. Insofar as these characteristics appear significant in Wales, Northern Ireland or Scotland, they are dismissed as trivial in size, or simply as indicating the "un-Britishness" of these parts of the United Kingdom (Rose, 1982). European evidence of the importance of such non-class influences as religion is ignored, because it is drawn from alien nations. So too is evidence about the high degree of class voting in Scandinavia (Rose, 1974b: 15).

Secondly, classes are defined by material economic conditions. Class is not meant to be just an idea put about by social scientists or interested politicians; classes and class relations are inherent in the economy and society. The specific way in which classes are defined varies from theory to theory. Usually, class is defined by a single occupational attribute. This precludes the possibility of an individual being in a mixed class, that is, middle class in one characteristic such as income, but working class in another, such as doing manual work. The American practice of combining education and income as well as occupation in a composite measure of socio-economic status is not normally followed in Britain.

Thirdly, classes are defined as having a hierarchical relationship; some classes are above others. This is explicit in old-fashioned phrases distinguishing upper, middle and lower classes. Such language is no longer in general use today, and the old aristocratic upper class is numerically trivial, and unimportant electorally. Classes are usually described as middle and working, or as manual and non-manual. Whatever the labels, classes are not arrayed along a horizontal dimension, such as a left-right scale. Nor are they set out nominally without any transitive order, as are the colours blue, yellow and red. Classes are defined in "over" and "under" terms, implying the subordination of one to another. In Marxist models relations between classes are assumed to create conflict; functionalist models tend to emphasize the complementary roles of different classes.

Theories of class differ substantially in the rationale for distinguishing strata within society, and in the particular attributes used to assign electors to different classes. For example, the historic Marxist definition of classes distinguished between capitalists, the owners of the means of production, and all others, whether manual workers or middle-class employees. The 1918 Constitution of the Labour Party similarly states that the party appeals to 'the workers by hand or by brain'. A party that successfully did this would not be engaged in electoral competition but in political hegemony, for together these groups constitute more than 90 per cent of the electorate in every Western country.

The conventional practice is to define class according to the social status or prestige of different occupations. Very considerable efforts have been invested in classifying hundreds of occupations into social strata that are then ranked from top to bottom (cf. Glass, 1954; Bott,

1957; Butler and Stokes, 1969; Goldthorpe and Hope, 1974; Treiman, 1977). Rankings normally differentiate more than two strata, for example, identifying divisions between skilled and unskilled manual workers, and an upper middle and a lower middle class. Analysing voting by a multiplicity of strata is not meant to eliminate the distinction between middle class and manual workers, the point on the social continuum at which a shift occurs from predominantly Conservative to predominantly Labour support.

Social scientists differ about the rationale for grouping occupations into classes, and distinguishing between the middle and the working class. A sevenfold definition of classes will necessarily produce distinctions absent in a three or fourfold classification. But the elaboration of more distinctions does not necessarily produce a better understanding of voting. The more classes created, the greater the need to collapse many strata into a few in order to test whether the votes cast for Britain's three parties are class-determined. In practice, different theories normally produce only marginal percentage differences in the assignment of people to social strata. Whatever the definition, a semi-skilled factory worker is invariably labelled as working class, and a teacher as middle class.

Subjecting general theories to empirical testing with survey data forces an author to clarify what is sometimes left obscure in writings. A computer will do whatever a researcher instructs — but it must be given explicit instructions, and it will follow these literally and uncritically. Even the definition of a voter is contingent not mechanical; standard conventions have had to be developed to deal with non-voters and supporters of minor parties. Survey analysis also forces a researcher to specify what criterion or criteria are to be used for assigning people to classes, and what names (or less meaningfully, what numbers) are to be given the classes thus created.

Two large sets of survey data are available for the analysis of voting in Britain. The Gallup Poll has surveyed every British general election since 1945 (Gallup Poll, 1976). The unique advantage of the Gallup Poll is the large number of persons interviewed; in 1983 a total of 8,948 persons were asked about their party preferences during election campaign surveys, and 4,146 in a special election-day survey undertaken by Gallup under BBC sponsorship. Since 1963, when David Butler and Donald Stokes launched the first, nationwide academic study, post-election surveys have been conducted under the title of the British Election Studies (see Appendix A).

The large number of interviews makes Gallup Poll data particularly useful for analyses requiring the subdivision of the electorate into many groups. The British Election Studies are conventionally used in academic analyses, and will be employed here, sample size permitting.

Fortunately, an unusually large sample of 3,955 was interviewed in 1983. Like the Gallup Poll, the British Election Studies have considerable continuity in questions from election to election, thus facilitating trend analysis. Upon occasion, the choice of survey is dictated by the presence of a question on one but not the other study. In addition to the tables in this book, thousands more were generated by computer, and the authors frequently made comparisons between results given by the two surveys. No substantive political differences were found, and the minor arithmetic differences were usually within the expected range of sampling fluctuations.

The starting point in survey analysis is the distribution of the sample between the parties (see Appendix B). The analysis of Liberal voters has presented a particular problem to students of elections. When the Liberals contested half the seats or less, then election results could not fully measure Liberal support, because much of the electorate did not have a chance to vote Liberal. Moreover, the relatively low level of Liberal support meant that in a conventional sample survey the number of Liberals was few. For the same reason, Liberals could have little influence on overall patterns of voting; hence, a case could be made for setting them aside. The pioneering Butler-Stokes (1969) study of British voting often did just that. The emblem that introduced each section was a symbol of closed electoral competition, a fourfold table of dichotomies between Conservative and Labour, and middle class and working class voters. The second edition, published in 1974, omitted this device. The inclusion of Liberal and Alliance votes is even more important in trend analysis, since the rise of this third party is one of the biggest changes in voting in a generation. In consequence of the growth in multi-party competition, the Liberals were more fully covered in analyses of the 1974-79 elections (Sarlvik and Crewe, 1983). However, Franklin (1984: 488) has continued to omit the Liberal/Alliance vote. In 1983 the Alliance must be given full attention, since its share of the popular vote was almost equal to that of Labour.

Statistics about the relation between class and voting can be produced in very different ways. Conventionally, a relationship is expressed as the proportion within a given class favouring each party. The figures add up to 100 per cent across each row of a table (for an example, see Table 3.10). The assumption is that if the national vote is divided between three parties in the proportions 45 per cent, 35 per cent, and 20 per cent, any departure within a row reflects the influence of class. If a party gets 45 per cent of the vote nationally but 60 per cent of the vote within the upper middle class, that class is said to favour that party. This conclusion is valid as far as it goes — but it tells us little about the outcome of electoral competition.

The proportion of votes that a party wins within each class cannot be summed, for classes differ substantially in their size. For example, the upper middle class is smaller than the lower middle class, and the skilled working class is larger than the lower middle class. Thus, if different parties each had the same advantage in different classes, they would end up with very unequal shares of the national vote. For example, in 1983 Labour won a majority of the votes among blacks (but not whites), among Glaswegians (but not non-Glaswegians) and among voters in mid-Glamorgan (but not elsewhere in Wales or England). As Harrop and Rudd note (1983: 384), to say that 'among black Glaswegians now living in the Rhondda, Labour's campaign worked like a dream' is technically correct. But it obscures the electoral disaster that the party suffered among the remaining 95 per cent of the electorate.

To understand electoral competition, the votes cast within a class for each party must be described as a percentage of all the votes cast in an election. For example, if a party won two-thirds of the vote of a class constituting one-third of the electorate, it would thereby obtain 22 per cent of the total vote (for example, see Tables 3.1-8). If another party won half the vote of a group constituting two-thirds of the electorate, it would thereby gain 33 per cent of the total. Such statistics provide an awareness of the distribution of the vote as it actually is. Expressing the distribution of the vote as a percentage of the matrix (that is, all the cells in a table) makes evident the competitive advantage of being favoured by a larger rather than a smaller class. Calculating the percentage of the vote for each cell means that the support given a party can be summed across classes, thus showing the extent to which class determines voting in the electorate as a whole.

The relationship between class and voting

Because of the great attention given to the nuances of class in Britain, it is best to test class voting with a variety of differing definitions of class. Using the same method to test each alternative definition of class (see Appendix B) makes it possible to compare results to see which approach best determines voting, or whether all are equally strong or weak. Because of a substantial amount of operational agreement between different definitions of class, the resulting tables should have much in common.

The logic of analysis can be illustrated by examining a situation in which there is undoubtedly a very high level of determination of voting by social structure, namely, religion and party in Northern Ireland.[1] Expressing the relation between religion and party in terms of the percentage of Protestants and Catholics voting for their respective parties would underline the obvious but obscure the important. It would show that 93 per cent of Protestants vote Unionist, and 86 per cent of Catholics vote for Irish unity parties. Such a calculation can be interpreted as showing that religion is equally important in determining the vote for Unionist and Irish unity parties. There is a difference of only 7 per cent between Protestants voting Unionist and Catholics voting for Irish unity parties.

However, the politically important point is that Protestant voters outnumber Catholics by a ratio of three to two. Unionist parties always win a majority of votes in Northern Ireland elections, because Protestants are an absolute majority of the electorate. These two points are clearly shown by setting out the evidence as a percentage of the matrix; 56 per cent of the electorate are Protestants voting Unionist, and 33 per cent Catholics voting for Irish unity parties (Table 3.1).

TABLE 3.1
Structural determination of the vote: religion and party in Northern Ireland[a]

Total %		Unionist[b]	APNI[c] (% of all votes)	Irish unity[d]
60	Protestants	**56** *	4	–
1.5	Other	1	**0.5** *	–
39	Catholic	1	4	**33** *
	Total share of vote	(57.5)	(8.5)	(33)

Index of Determination, calculated from cells with an asterisk, 89.5 percent; Standardized, 80 percent.

Source: Calculated from Market Research Bureau of Ireland election survey for the *Irish News*, Belfast.
[a] All tables refer to the 1983 election unless otherwise noted.
[b] Includes Official Unionists and Democratic Unionists.
[c] Bi-confessional Alliance Party of Northern Ireland.
[d] Includes Social Democratic and Labour Party and Sinn Fein.

An Index of Determination can be calculated by adding the percentage of voters who actually support the parties that deterministic theories predict will receive their votes. The Index of Determination of Northern Ireland voting by religion is 89.5 per cent, that is, 56 per cent Unionist-voting Protestants plus 0.5 per cent persons without a religion voting for the Alliance Party of Northern Ireland (APNI) plus 33 per cent Irish-unity Catholics. Ulster voting is highly determined, for the Index is much closer to the absolute maximum, 100 per cent, than to the absolute minimum, 0.

If the relationship between religion and voting in Northern Ireland were random, then the arithmetic Index of Determination would be lower but not zero. If each party's vote reflected a cross-section of the electorate, then the Unionists, Irish unity parties and APNI would each draw 60 per cent of their vote from Protestants, 39 per cent from Catholics, and about 1 per cent from others. Such a random relationship would produce an Index of Determination of 48 per cent. To control for random association, a Standardized Index of Determination can be calculated. It is the difference between the observed index and what would be randomly expected, divided by the proportion of vote not attributable to random association. In the case of Northern Ireland, the Standardized Index of Determination is also very high, 80 per cent.[2]

The Index of Determination has the advantage of being easily calculated and showing the proportion of all votes cast along group-determined lines. For comparison, the Standardized Index is necessary because it discounts the support that a party could expect to receive randomly, whatever the size of its core group of supporters. Both measures record the strength of association between group characteristics and voting on a scale from 0 to 100.

ABC1/C2DE Class

Of the different operational definitions of class, the most widely used is the occupational stratification devised by the British Market Research Society (1963; Monk, 1968), often known as the ABC1/C2DE scale, after the labels given middle class and working class strata respectively. Each person is assigned a class according to the occupation of the head of household. *Upper Middle Class* (A): e.g. company directors, doctors, high-ranking Army officers; *Middle Class* (B): e.g. junior executives; managers of medium size shops, medium-rank Army officers; *Lower Middle Class* (C1): e.g. nurses, bank clerks, junior civil servants, typists, police sergeants; *Skilled Working Class* (C2): e.g. carpenters, electricians, bricklayers, police constables; *Unskilled Working Class* (D): e.g. semi-skilled labourers, unskilled factory workers, bus conductors, Army privates, etc; *The Poor* (E): e.g. casual workers and those lacking regular occupation; elderly persons dependent solely on pensions. On this basis, 39 per cent of the electorate is assigned to the middle class (ABC1) and 61 per cent to the working class (C2DE). This stratification system is well known, and virtually all survey interviewers are trained to apply it.

When the ABC1 definition of occupational class is applied to voters in the 1983 election, the theory of class determination is rejected (Table 3.2). The proportion voting Conservative or Labour in each class tends to resemble partisan differences in the electorate as a whole. In 1983, 22 per cent of voters were middle-class Conservatives,

5 per cent more than would be expected randomly, and 22 per cent of manual workers Labour, 5 per cent more than randomly expected. The Index of Determination is 44 per cent, the sum of random and non-random voting for class-typical parties. The Standardized Index discounts the effect of random voting; it is 15 per cent.[3]

TABLE 3.2
Vote by class: ABC1/C2DE

Total %		Con.	All'ce (% all votes)	Lab.
(39)	Middle class			
2	Upper middle (A)	**1** *	0.4	0.1
13	Middle (B)	**8** *	3	2
24	Lower middle (C1)	**13** *	7	4
(61)	Working class			
31	Skilled workers (C2)	13	8	**10** *
18	Semi-skilled and unskilled (D)	6	5	**7** *
12	Poor (E)	4	3	**5** *

Index of Determination, 44 percent; Standardized, 15 percent.

Source: Gallup Campaign Study, 1983.

The largest number of deviant voters, that is, those casting ballots in ways inconsistent with class voting theories, is in the working class. In 1983 the 22 per cent of the electorate consisting of working-class Labour voters was outnumbered by the 23 per cent that were working-class Conservative voters, and 16 per cent working-class Alliance voters. Of the total electorate, 39 per cent consisted of manual workers who did not vote for their class party, and 22 per cent of those who did. In the middle class, there was more of a tendency for voters to support the party said to represent the class; 22 per cent of the electorate voted Conservative, as against 10 per cent favouring the Alliance, and 6 per cent Labour. While a majority of the middle class favoured the Conservatives, more than four out of ten middle class voters did not vote for the party said to represent that class.

One response to such evidence of the openness of the electorate is to regard theories of class voting as misleading, and abandon them. An alternative is to develop a sociological theory that stratifies the electorate into classes that show a stronger fit between class and party and thus yield a substantially higher Index of Determination. Six alternative stratification schema will be tested in turn. However, the use of different labels does not imply that the theories are completely unrelated. All are based upon characteristics of occupation, and with one exception emphasize a distinction between manual and non-manual workers. Nor do changes in nomenclature and in the rationale for dividing the electorate alter underlying social and political characteristics of voters.

Butler-Stokes

The original Butler-Stokes study (1969: 70ff; see also, Kahan, Butler and Stokes, 1966) made an effort to modify the Market Research Society approach to intermediate occupational groups. The C1 group was differentiated into two strata, described as skilled or supervisory non-manual (C1A) and lower non-manual (C1B). The former tended to identify subjectively with the middle-class, and the latter with the working class. The modification was limited in its overall impact on the Market Research Society categories. Of the 24 per cent assigned in 1964 to the C1A class, 15 per cent were still in the middle class after the Butler-Stokes revision. Only 9 per cent, those in class C1B, were placed differently from those in the ABC1/C2DE schema.

In analysing voting behaviour, the crucial test of a method of stratifying voters is how well it apportions voters to class-typical parties. By this standard, the Butler-Stokes method fails. As the authors themselves showed, a majority of Class C1B (54 per cent) as well as of Class C1A (58 per cent) voters favoured the Conservatives, in 1964; in Class C2, 62 per cent favoured Labour (Butler-Stokes, 1969: 77). Assigning Class C1B to the working class actually lowered the overall Index of Determination by three per cent. Not surprisingly, Butler and Stokes (1974:75) abandoned the use of this modification in their second edition.

TABLE 3.3
Vote by class: Butler-Stokes

Total %		Con.	All'ce (% all votes)	Lab.
12	Higher manager, professional (A)	**7** *	4	1
16	Lower manager, administrative (B)	**8** *	5	3
6	Skilled, supervisory, non-manual (C1A)	**4** *	2	1
11	Lower non-manual (C1B)	**6** *	2	2
25	Skilled manual (C2)	9	6	**10** *
20	Semi-skilled and unskilled manual (D)	6	4	**10** *
10	Residual, poor (E)	5	2	**3** *

Index of Determination, 48 percent; Standardized 18 percent.

Source: British Election Study, 1983; Cf. Butler and Stokes, 1969: 70ff.

Applying the Butler-Stokes stratification schema to voting at the 1983 British general election confirms that class does not determine party preference (Table 3.3). The Standardized Index of Determination is 18 per cent, slightly higher than in the Gallup Poll ABC1 analysis, reflecting marginal difference between the surveys (see Appendix B). Class C1B, initially regarded by Butler and Stokes as working class, continues to be predominantly Conservative. Only one-fifth of this border-line stratum votes Labour, whereas two-fifths of the lower C2 stratum does. Whatever the original rationale, the Butler-Stokes attempt to modify the definition of class structure does not produce a good fit between class and party.

Oxford Social Mobility Survey

A very ambitious attempt to develop a new stratification system for British society was undertaken as part of the 1972 Oxford Social Mobility Survey (see Goldthorpe and Hope, 1974; Goldthorpe, 1980; chapter 2). The Oxford Social Mobility Survey added two attributes of occupation not normally explicit in conventional prestige models of stratification: autonomy at work, differentiating self-employed persons from employees of organizations, and the exercise of authority, differentiating directors, managers and foremen in factories from those under orders from others. Combining these distinctions with more conventional class indicators generated 35 strata, which were then collapsed into seven. The schema was not strictly hierarchical, although it included an unambiguous top class, as well as intermediate and lower groups (cf. Goldthorpe, 1980: 39ff). As in any stratification schema, the strata overlap substantially with pre-existing categories of the Market Research Society and Butler-Stokes.

While the primary object was to analyse social mobility, the directors of the Social Mobility Survey did consider the electoral implications of their research, hypothesizing a very different trend from what has subsequently occurred. Labour was expected to maintain its position as the natural party of the working class. The weakening of class determinism was viewed as largely a middle-class phenomenon.

> Mobility patterns and trends may also be reckoned as a major factor, on the one hand, in maintaining the tie between the Labour Party and the working class, and indeed in increasing the solidarity of working class partisanship; and, on the other, in bringing about the observed growth in Labour support within the middle class. (Goldthorpe, 1980: 270).

Empirical testing of the fit between this approach to class and voting was left to others.

Class Trichotomy: Robertson

A member of the Essex group conducting the British Election Studies of the 1970s, David Robertson (1984: 108ff), re-examined voting in 1979, proposing a stratification system with three classes, labelled upper, intermediate, and lower. The so-called upper class is not an exclusive grouping; it contains one-third of the electorate, and is virtually identical with the original Butler-Stokes definition of the middle class.

The novelty of Robertson's approach is the explicit recognition of an intermediate class, composed of those whom Butler and Stokes classified as group C1B, lower non-manual, plus manual foremen and self-employed manual workers from the skilled working class. The rationale for the amendment is drawn from the Oxford Social Mobility emphasis on autonomy and authority at work. This is reckoned to justify removing from the working class foremen holding authority, and self-employed persons. This distinction is not consistently employed, however, for the intermediate class also includes lower non-manual workers lacking in authority and autonomy. What Robertson calls the upper class is subdivided into those with autonomy (for example, self-employed professionals), those with authority (for example, managers and directors), and non-manual supervisors who have little autonomy and are subject to authority as well as exercising it.

TABLE 3.4
Vote by trichotomized class: Robertson

Total %	Classes	Con.	All'ce (% all votes)	Lab.
(33)	Upper			
12	Higher manager, professional (A)	**7** *	4	1
16	Lower manager, administrative (B)	**8** *	5	3
6	Skilled supervisory, non-manual (C1A)	**4** *	1	1
(19)	Intermediate			
8	Lower non-manual (C1B)	5	**2** *	2
7	Foremen and technicians	3	**2** *	2
4	Self-employed without employees	2	**0.6** *	1
(48)	Lower			
18	Skilled (C2[a])	6	4	**8** *
20	Semi-skilled, unskilled (D)	6	4	**10** *
10	Residual, poor (E)	5	2	**3** *

Index of Determination, 43 percent; Standardized, 15 percent.

Source: Derived from British Election Study, 1983, applying guidelines in Robertson, 1984: 112, to class schema as reported in Tables 3.3 and 3.5.
[a]As in Market Research Society and Butler-Stokes, fewer foremen and self-employed assigned to intermediate class.

The three-class approach is relevant in current British political circumstances, because of its potential for explaining multi-party competition, with the Alliance the party of the intermediate class. Morever, creating an intermediate class reduces the size of the working class. The likelihood of Labour maintaining dominance in the working class is thus increased notwithstanding its fall in vote. Robertson also attempts to show that the three classes constitute groups with distinctive political attitudes. However, the relationship between attitude factors, class, and party is not clearly documented, and appears limited (Robertson, 1984: 228, 113ff).

The creation of three classes does not improve the determination of voting by class (Table 3.4). The upper class is consistently Conservative, but the intermediate class is not predominantly Alliance, for the Conservatives secure a majority of votes in this group, and the Labour vote is almost at the same level as Alliance support. In the lower class, the Labour Party is the leading party, but with less than half the votes. The Standardized Index of Determination is low, 15 per cent. None of the nine categories identified is predominantly Alliance. This three-class theory does not explain voting in a three-party system.

Class Trichotomy: Heath, Jowell and Curtice

An elaborate and extensive classification of the electorate, derived from the Oxford Social Mobility Study, has been undertaken by the organizers of the 1983 British Election Study, Anthony Heath, Roger Jowell and John Curtice (1985). Their novel treatment of the working class emphasizes the extent to which different definitions of class reflect contrasting choices by social scientists.

The division of the electorate by Heath, Jowell and Curtice follows that developed by John Goldthorpe and Catriona Llewellyn in the analysis of the 1970 census (Goldthorpe and Hope, 1974), which modifies conventional occupational stratification to take into account authority at work, manual foremen being distinguished from skilled manual workers because they exercise authority; and self-employed persons being placed in a separate stratum since they have autonomy.

A novel result of the approach is that the working class is reduced in size by almost half. Skilled, semi-skilled, and unskilled manual workers constitute only 36 per cent of the voters in the Heath, Jowell and Curtice study, compared to 61 per cent when the Market Research Society schema is employed (cf. Tables 3.2 and 3.5). In this stratification model, the equivalent of the middle-class — professionals, managers, and self-employed persons with some authority or autonomy — becomes the largest single class, constituting 41 per cent of the electorate, virtually the same in size as the middle-class defined by the ABC1 schema. The intermediate class, consisting of routine non-manual workers and manual foremen and technicians, is slightly larger than in Robertson's three-fold schema.

TABLE 3.5
Vote by head of household class: Heath, Jowell and Curtice

Total %		Con.	All'ce (% all votes)	Lab.
(41)	Authority and Autonomy			
14	High professional, managerial (1)	**8** *	5	1
17	Lower professional (2)	**9** *	5	3
10	Self-employed petty bourgeois (4)	**7** *	2	1
(23)	Intermediate class			
14	Routine non-manual (3)	7	**4** *	4
9	Manual foremen, technicians (5)	4	**2** *	3
(36)	Working class			
17	Skilled manual (6)	5	4	**8** *
19	Semi-skilled, unskilled manual (7)	5	4	**9** *

Index of Determination, 49 percent; Standardized, 18 percent.

Sources: British Election Study, 1983: Goldthorpe-Llewellyn schema.

The Heath, Jowell and Curtice schema "minoritizes" the working-class. The fact that routine non-manual workers such as secretaries and clerks do not get their hands dirty is regarded as making them superior to the working-class, even though they lack authority or autonomy; this is a status judgement. Manual workers who exercise authority as foremen or enjoy autonomy as skilled technicians are also regarded as apart from the working class. In effect, the working-class is made into a residual minority, a virtual lumpenproletariat of manual workers lacking authority, autonomy, job security, and social esteem. Class determinism makes Labour's 1983 defeat appear as part of an inexorable social process more than as a setback produced by political mistakes that could be set right by the departure of Michael Foot, ending internal wrangling within the party, and abandoning or playing down unpopular policies.

In political terms, the Heath, Jowell and Curtice stratification schema could be interpreted as proof of the "democratization" of social relations in Britain, since 64 per cent of the electorate is now middle-class, or at least "not working class". The non-working class groups are not socially homogeneous but each has at least one positive attribute regarded as middle-class in the Oxford schema, whether autonomy, authority or status.

The tripartite division of classes, and particularly the minorization of the working class, is fortuitously suited for analysis of the 1983 election, since Labour was very much a minority party in its share of the vote. The differentiation of the middle class is also appropriate in an election in which the Alliance was almost as successful as Labour in competing for votes, and more successful within the conventionally defined middle class. In practice, the minoritization of the working class does not produce a stronger link between class and party. The Standardized Index of Determination is 18 per cent, the same as that produced by applying the ABC1 schema to the same data (cf. Tables 3.3 and 3.5). As in all the other models examined, the Conservatives are most favoured in the top class. But Labour does not have the support of a majority in the much reduced working class. Moreover, the intermediate class is *not* disproportionately Alliance; the Conservatives draw nearly half the vote in this group, and Labour does slightly better than the Alliance.

By looking only at individual strata and the percentage of the vote within a stratum, it is possible to argue that a degree of political distinctiveness is found among each of these classes (Heath, Jowell, and Curtice, 1985: chapter 2). For example, the so-called petty bourgeois class of self-employed is 71 per cent Conservative. But this stratum cannot characterize the British electorate as a whole, for it consists of less than 10 per cent of it. To characterize the whole electorate thus it would be necessary to demonstrate that large as well as small strata show an equally strong link between class and party. In fact, Heath, Jowell and Curtice's own analysis (1985: Table 2.3) shows that only 36 per cent of the electorate is in a stratum where as many as half vote for one party. No party secures as much as half the vote among the working class, foremen and technicians, or routine non-manual electors. Most of their strata are split three ways, rather than being predominantly for one party.

The relationship between class and voting can be further tested by another innovation recommended by Heath, Jowell and Curtice (1985: 22ff; see also Dunleavy and Husbands, 1985: 124-29), classifying voters on the basis of their own occupation, rather than the occupation of the head of household, the conventional practice in social research. This recognizes the autonomy of each individual, regardless of gender. Since votes are cast by individuals and not just by male heads of households, it can be argued that occupational class should be assigned to each person individually. However, this neo-liberal emphasis upon the autonomy of the individual ignores the significance of the family as a social and economic unit (Rose, 1985a). Furthermore, it presupposes that class differences are so important that they will create political divisions within families whose members work in different strata.

Adopting an individualist classification of respondents increases the minoritization of the working class; it falls to 31 per cent of the electorate. A substantial fraction of households consists of a husband in a manual occupation, and a wife who has a non-manual job as a salesperson, a secretary or a clerk or had such a job before becoming a housewife. The intermediate class becomes the largest stratum in the electorate, and the working class the smallest (Table 3.6).

TABLE 3.6
Vote by respondent's class: Heath, Jowell and Curtice

Total %		Con.	All'ce (% all votes)	Lab.
(33)	Authority and Autonomy			
8	High professional, managerial (1)	**5** *	3	1
17	Lower professional (2)	**8** *	5	3
7	Self-employed petty bourgeoisie (4)	**5** *	1	1
(36)	Intermediate class			
30	Routine non-manual (3)	15	**8** *	7
6	Manual foremen, technicians (5)	3	**1** *	2
(31)	Working class			
11	Skilled manual (6)	3	2	**5** *
20	Semi-skilled, unskilled manual (7)	6	4	**10** *

Index of Determination, 43 percent; Standardized, 15 percent.

Sources: British Election Study, 1983: Goldthorpe-Llewellyn schema.

In theory, classifying voters by their own occupation rather than by that of the head of household should produce a better fit with voting, by reassigning persons who would otherwise be "subordinated" in the class of a parent or spouse. But this does not happen. Instead, the Standardized Index of Determination for respondent's class falls to 15 per cent, a drop of three per cent from that for the same people classified by the occupation of the head of household.[4] The top class, those with authority or autonomy at work, become less Conservative; there is very little change in the link between class and party in the intermediate and working classes. Ironically, the result of reclassification according to neo-liberal individualism emphasizes the importance of cross-class ties within the family (see also pp. 70ff).

Public/private production classes

In an era of big government, a pure interest-group division of the labour force can contrast public employees with those working in the private sector. Public employees depend upon government organizations to determine wage rates, and tax revenues pay employees in health and education, and often subsidize employees in nationalized industries. Public employees are thus an extreme example of creatures of the state, because they are dependent on the state for work (Dunleavy and Husbands, 1985: 18ff). Public sector workers in Britain are very disproportionately unionized (Parry, 1985: Table 2.7), and the link between unions and the Labour Party has been seen as a guarantee of continued public employment. The Thatcher government has emphasized cutting back the number of public employees by the privatization or contraction of nationalized industries, and by reducing the numbers employed in the civil service and local government. A lengthy argument about production classes being more important than conventional occupational class has been advanced by Dunleavy (1980: 382), who asserts that conventional Marxist thinking supports this view, and rejects what he labels as 'empiricist and Weberian' analyses.

TABLE 3.7
Vote by public/private production classes

Total %		Con.	All'ce (% all votes)	Lab.
66	Private sector	**30** *	17	18
34	Public sector	14	9	**10** *

Index of Determination, 40 percent; Standardized, 3 percent.

Source: Gallup Campaign Study, 1983.

Testing public employment's impact upon voting shows the unimportance of this distinction. In 1983 Conservatives were the most favoured party in both the private and the public sectors (Table 3.7). Labour drew only one per cent more of the vote from public sector workers than did the Alliance, and the two parties also took virtually the same share of the vote in the private sector. The Standardized Index of Determination is thus extremely low, 3 per cent.

In the mixed economy welfare state, working for government is not the only way in which government can make individuals depend upon it for an income. Government pays more people for not working than for working; pensioners, recipients of unemployment benefits and other income-maintenance grants outnumber public employees (Parry, 1985: Table 2.12). Those in receipt of a primary income from government, whether in employment or not, would be expected to be more Labour, and those not receiving a cash benefit from government to favour the party of Margaret Thatcher.

In 1983 the British Election Study classified 47 per cent of voters as either working in the public sector or receiving an income-maintenance grant as their primary source of income.[5] This group was

40 per cent Conservative, Labour was favoured by 34 per cent, and 26 per cent voted Alliance. Among voters in the private sector, 50 per cent were Conservative, with Alliance and Labour each drawing one-quarter of the vote. Overall, the relationship between source of income and vote was very limited; the Index of Determination was 42 per cent, and the Standardized Index was 9 per cent. There was a better fit than the virtually nil relationship with production workers, but it is nonetheless low by comparison with conventional measures of occupational class.

Subjective class

Theories of class determining voting normally assume that an individual's class is given by occupation rather than being a matter of subjective choice. However, the social psychological approach to politics assumes that perceptions can be as important as material conditions in society. It implies that people who do not identify with a class will not vote for the party of the class to which sociologists say they belong.

When British voters are asked whether or not they think of themselves as belonging to a class, only half reply that they do, and this proportion has remained virtually constant for two decades (Butler and Stokes, 1969: 66ff). The electorate can be divided into three groups: consciously middle class voters, who can be expected to vote Conservative; consciously working class voters, who can be expected to vote Labour; and those who do not identify with a class, who can favour the Alliance.

TABLE 3.8
Vote by subjective class identification

Total %		Con.	All'ce (% all votes)	Lab.
21	Middle class	**12** *	5	4
47	None/Don't know	25	**12** *	10
32	Working class	9	8	**15** *

Index of Determination, 39 percent; Standardized, 13 percent.

Source: British Election Study, 1983.

The indeterminateness of class structure is further emphasized by the fact that most people do not vote in accord with their subjective class identification (Table 3.8). In 1983 less than half those thinking of themselves as working class voted Labour, and little more than half thinking of themselves as middle class voted Conservative. Among those who did not proffer a class identification, the Alliance took only one-quarter of the vote. The Standardized Index of Determination is thus low, 13 per cent. When respondents who do not offer a class identification are forced to place themselves by a follow-up question from the interviewer, this increases the proportion of the electorate with at least a latent middle class or working class identification, but it only increases the Standardized Index by two per cent.

The schema compared

Examining many different stratification schema is a very strong test of class determination of voting, for each has features of general theoretical interest, and some have been intended to correct for the presumed weaknesses of others. If the closed-class model is to be accepted as valid today, one or more of the schema reviewed here should fit the behaviour of most voters.

TABLE 3.9
Comparing the Index of Determination for class and vote

Schema	Fits Standard Index	Of which M.C. Con.	Of which Inter. All'ce	Of which W.C. Lab.	Does not fit
	(% all votes)				
Heath, Jowell, Curtice: Head of household	18	24	6	17	53
Butler-Stokes	18	25	n.a.	23	52
ABC1/C2DE	15	22	n.a.	22	56
Robertson	15	19	5	21	57
Heath, Jowell, Curtice: Respondent	15	18	9	15	57
Subjective class	13	12	12	15	60
Public/Private production	3	30	n.a.	10	60

M.C.: middle class.
W.C.: working class.
Source: British Election Study, 1983.

Whatever theory and method is used to define class, the result is the same: *most British voters do not have their vote determined by occupational class* (Table 3.9). Given differences between concepts of class in theory, it is specially noteworthy that all measures of class are limited in their ability to distinguish Conservative from Labour or Alliance voters. In every instance but one, the Standardized Index of Determination is in the range 18 to 13 per cent, small enough for the differences to reflect sampling fluctuations. For production classes, the Index drops to 3 per cent.

To reject the closed-class model of electoral competition is not to deny that there is some association between class and vote. The foregoing tables give evidence of this. But deviation from pure randomness is not proof of strength. The association between class and party can be weak rather than strong, and this is the case in Britain today.

A consistently weak relationship

The above analysis of class and voting is unambiguous in its conclusion. But before it can be regarded as robust, it must be tested by additional methods of analysis. Two are especially appropriate here: the examination of within-class differences in voting, and trends in class determination across the decades.

Within-class analysis of voting is the conventional form of examining the relation between class and party. Voters are first of all divided into classes, and the percentage voting Conservative, Alliance and Labour is then calculated. For each stratum the total sums to 100 per cent. Insofar as the percentage share of the vote within a class departs from the overall distribution in the electorate, this is considered as indicating an association within that class between class and party. But it is not evidence of the influence of class upon the electorate as a whole. The influence may not be registered in every class in the stratification schema. Moreover, the results cannot, as in a matrix, be summed to show the impact upon the total vote.

TABLE 3.10
Voting within classes

Total %		Con.	All'ce %	Lab.
	Middle class	(56)	(27)	(16)
2	Upper (A)	68	21	7
13	Middle (B)	61	25	13
24	Lower middle (C1)	52	28	18
	Working class	(36)	(26)	(37)
31	Skilled (C2)	40	27	31
18	Semi-skilled and unskilled (D)	31	25	41
12	Welfare recipients (E)	30	24	43

Source: Gallup Campaign Study, 1983.

When votes are percentaged within each of the Market Research Society classes, the middle class does differ from the national voting pattern. Whereas at the 1983 election the Conservatives won 44 per cent of the vote in Britain (excluding Northern Ireland), in the middle class their vote share was higher, ranging from 68 per cent in the upper middle class to 52 per cent among lower middle class voters (Table 3.10). In terms of electoral competition, the important point is that the relationship is weaker as the strata increase in size.

The relationship between class and party in the working class is very slight; in 1983 no party succeeded in winning a majority of the votes of skilled workmen, semi-skilled workers, or of welfare recipients. The Conservatives were the largest group in the skilled working class, but their 40 per cent share was four per cent below the national Conservative share of the vote. Labour took an above-average share of the vote among less skilled manual workers, but this was 42 per cent, less than half.

In terms of electoral competition, an important feature of the within-class division of the vote is its asymmetry. The middle class is more Conservative than the working class is Labour; this has been consistent through the years (Rose, 1980: Table 8). In social terms, manual workers are often more homogeneous (for example, lacking capital, job security, and so forth) than the middle class, whose heterogeneity is often indicated by a negative description, non-manual. Yet notwithstanding greater social homogeneity, the working class is not cohesive electorally. The asymmetry is a necessary condition of the Conservatives competing with Labour, for the Conservatives need a large minority of working class voters to win an election.

A second weakness in the relation between class and voting is that each class now divides its vote three ways rather than two. Among working class voters, no party gets as much as two-fifths of the vote. The Conservative Party appears to be the dominant party in the middle class only because of divisions among its opponents. If the Alliance and Labour votes are added together, then these two parties have 43 per cent of the middle class vote, only 13 per cent less than the Conservative share and only 6 per cent less in the lower middle class (Table 3.10).

Whereas conventional theories describe classes as favouring a particular party, in 1983 it would be as appropriate to speak of negative voting. Within the working class, upwards of two-thirds of manual workers did not vote for each of the parties. In the middle class, five-sixths rejected the Labour Party, nearly three-quarters rejected the Alliance, and the Conservatives were rejected by nearly half. In all three groups of manual workers and in the lower middle class no party had a clear preponderance of support in 1983. Since these four strata together account for 85 per cent of the British electorate, the British class structure does not inhibit open electoral competition.

So strong is the evidence of indeterminate voting in 1983 that it prompts the question: Is the idea of closed-class competition a myth of a golden age when the electorate was entrapped in what Max Weber regarded as an Iron Cage of class? Or was 1983 a deviant election occasioned by the disastrous state of the Labour Party? A third hypothesis is that social and political changes have gradually weakened the link between class and party. The three alternative theories can be tested for the seven elections since 1964, the first year in which British Election Studies were conducted.

TABLE 3.11
Changes in the Index of Class Determination, 1964–83

Schema	Fits Standard Index	Of which M.C. Con.	W.C. Lab.	Does not fit
	(as % all votes)			
1964	25	20	39	41
1966	25	19	41	39
1970	20	21	35	44
1974 Feb.	19	19	31	49
1974 Oct.	19	19	33	48
1979	17	23	28	49
1983	18	25	23	52

Source: British Election Studies.

In 1964, when the vote was divided almost evenly between the Conservative and Labour parties, there was more of a fit between class and voting than today (Table 3.11). In all, 59 per cent of the electorate consisted of either middle-class Conservatives or working-class Labour voters. Two decades later, the proportion had fallen to 48 per cent. The use of the Standardized Index of Determination controls for the effect of the gradual, albeit limited change in the size of the middle and working class. The Standardized Index also fell, from 25 per cent in 1964 to 18 per cent in 1983 (see also Kelley et al., 1985).[6]

The decline in the class determination of voting is asymmetrical. Notwithstanding the ups and downs of the Conservative Party in the period, its class-determined middle-class vote has been constant or rising; it was 20 per cent in 1964, and 25 per cent in 1983. By contrast, the Labour Party's class-determined working-class vote has fallen from a high of 41 per cent in 1966 to 31 per cent in February 1974 and 23 per cent in 1983.

By comparison with the electoral influence of religion in Northern Ireland, the influence of class in Britain has been relatively limited. It would be an oversimplification to regard the working- class, even in a period of Labour election victories, as a closed class. In the 1980s, insofar as the electorate is viewed in class terms, the crucial political division is *within* the working class. It is therefore necessary to consider alternative social structure determinants of the vote.

Notes

1. In the unusual circumstances of Single Transferable Vote Proportional Representation, there is also competition within each religious bloc. Here again it is minimal; two parties — Official Unionists and Democratic Unionists — compete for Protestant votes, and two parties — the Social Democratic & Labour Party and Sinn Fein — compete for Catholic votes (Diskin, 1984; McAllister and Rose 1984: chapter 7).

2. That is

$$\frac{89.5\%-48.1\%}{100\%-48.1\%} = \frac{41.4\%}{51.9\%} = 79.8\%.$$

The same conclusion — that religion determines voting — is shown by all correlation statistics; Kendall's tau beta, used by Butler and Stokes, is .88.

3. Of the 44 per cent of voters for class-typical parties 10 per cent is not attributable to random voting. It is divided by the 66 per cent of the total vote not attributable to randomness, to produce a Standardized Index of 15 per cent. The correlation produced by Kendall's tau beta is .12. Statistical significance tests are not used in this book because they are sensitive to sample size. The large samples used here should consistently produce high levels of significance. As would be expected with 7,709 cases, the differences are statistically significant at the level of 0.0000, with 15 degrees of freedom and a chi square value of 550. Levels of significance say nothing about the degree of association.

4. Given the absence of any positive gender effect, we have followed the normal survey analysis practice of assigning class on the basis of head of household in order to avoid inconsistencies in the treatment of employed and non-employed women, and to prevent multiplication of analytic categories leading to more and more complex tables without any gain in explanatory power.

5. Minor transfer payments insufficient to provide a full subsistence, such as children's allowance and sickness benefit, are not included here.

6. The tables presented by Heath, Jowell and Curtice (1985: chapter 3) show a similar pattern of some decline from starting point that is not polarized. Consistent with their practice of describing any variation from randomness as evidence of class voting, the authors conclude that the data therefore show that class remains important. We would interpret it as showing that a big decline has not occurred in the past two decades because class has never had the electoral importance attributed to it in theory.

4
Expanding the analysis of social structure

The closed-class model of electoral competition is too simple by half, for it reduces social structure to a single dimension, setting aside the possible electoral influence of such basic social differences as age, gender and national identity. Moreover, concentrating upon stratification by occupation ignores the potential influence of other economic influences such as trade union membership, income and housing. Given that all measures of occupational class show a consistently weak influence upon voting, further efforts to redefine class are likely to be in vain. It is more reasonable to seek a ''class plus'' explanation of voting.

The most immediately relevant influences to test are economic differences additional to occupation. Material differences in trade union membership, housing and income are each relevant to materialist theories of political behaviour, yet to a greater or lesser extent cut across occupational strata (see Rose, 1974: 531). Insofar as such influences are important, they refine and strengthen theories of the economic determination of voting, albeit not in conventional occupational class categories.

It can be argued that income, housing and trade union membership are simply different attributes of class, which can then be defined as a complex of more or less related economic characteristics. But this approach creates fresh problems. Defining a number of attributes as intrinsic to class assigns a majority of the electorate to mixed classes which are middle class in terms of some attributes and working class in others (Rose, 1974: 510; Rose, 1980: Table 14).

Social structure includes non-economic as well as economic distinctions. Societies divide for many purposes along lines of biological differences such as gender or age; potentially, these differences can have political consequences. Cultural divisions along lines of religion, nation or region can be salient too, and in many Continental European countries have been historically more important politically than class (Lipset and Rokkan, 1967).

The traditional class-equals-party model of voting is inadequate precisely because it is traditional, that is, it presupposes static rather than dynamic electoral competition. Occupational class is treated as a constant influence upon voters; the only changes that could occur would result from a gradual change in the occupational structure of the population and individual occupational mobility. When social structure is seen as multi-dimensional, then changes in voting can occur because of alterations in the relative importance of class and non-class determinants of voting (Rose, 1974b; Rose and Urwin, 1969). The best way to discriminate between economic characteristics that do and do not influence voting is to examine, one at a time, the conjoint influence of occupation plus one other social structure characteristic.[1]

The multiple dimensions of economic interest

To expand the analysis of determinants of voting to include trade union membership, housing, and income is to recognize the existence of economic interests independent of conventional occupational strata. The interests of a trade union member are not determined by whether a person is a manual worker, but by the specific concerns of that union, which may organize middle-class employees, such as teachers or professional civil servants, or manual workers, such as car workers or railwaymen. The interests of home-owners as against council tenants are affected by housing costs, and not by occupation. Income can vary independently of occupational status, as between a clergyman and a plumber or electrician. Within a class, life styles can differ as between those reading newspapers such as the *Daily Express* or the *Guardian*.

The first point to establish is whether differences in economic interests lead to differences in voting behaviour within a given occupational class: e.g. do trade union members vote differently from electors who do not belong to trade unions? This requires controlling for the effect of occupational class. Otherwise, what appears as a link between trade union membership and voting may simply reflect the fact that trade union members tend to be manual workers, and non-members to have middle-class occupations.

In testing within-class differences, it is desirable to consider divisions within the middle class and the working class, in order to see whether voters at the upper end of the manual strata differ in class-plus influences from those at the bottom. The middle class is here divided into a solid middle class (groups A and B in the Market Research Society schema), and the lower middle class (C1); the working class is divided into the skilled (C2) and non-skilled (D and E).

Because the introduction of a second non-occupational influence subdivides each of the four classes, the resulting proliferation of categories requires a survey well above average in size in order for the results to have a high degree of reliability, and not simply reflect sampling fluctuations. The Gallup Campaign Studies consistently provide such a sample; the BBC Gallup Survey and the 1983 British Election Study are often large enough to provide reliable results after subdivision.[2] When studies do not provide adequate numbers for reliable subdivision, the middle and working class are not subdivided.

Since some social structure influences could be *more* important than occupational class, the first part of each table presents a matrix of association with voting. Thus, an Index of Determination can be calculated, and compared with occupational class. The second part of the table tests for the class-plus influence. The net effect within each class can be calculated by taking the arithmetic difference in party preferences between those with and those without a given social characteristic. For example, among skilled manual workers, 44 per cent of union members voted Labour in 1983 as against 34 per cent of non-union members, an effect of 10 per cent.

Union membership

The hypothesis that trade unions influence voters independently of occupational class recognizes that even though one particular trade union usually organizes a class-specific group of workers, the Trades Union Congress (TUC) represents middle class as well as manual workers. Union membership and occupational class are in no sense synonymous. Nearly half of the electorate does not conform to a class-typical pattern of trade union membership; three fifths of the working class are not in trade unions and one third of the middle-class are. In the working class as well as in the middle class, the majority of Britons do not belong to a union.

Trade union membership can be expected to increase Labour voting for three reasons. First of all, the Labour Party is organizationally linked with trade unions, providing it with members and money, and claiming the bulk of votes in the party's Annual Conference and committees. In ideology and organization the Labour Party is not a free-standing body, but one wing of the Labour movement; trade unions are the other wing. That trade union members ought to vote Labour is the view of the TUC as well as of the Labour Party. Secondly, unions bargain for wages and benefits for their members. Trade unions see their role as encouraging (or even compelling) a Labour government to provide more public social benefits and to follow policies that promote job security for union members. Thirdly, unions give workers greater collective authority at work. By mobilizing union authority on behalf of employees, they establish a countervailing force to the authority of higher-status occupations.

Since a significant fraction of the electorate is not employed, surveys ask whether the respondent and/or spouse is a union member. It could be hypothesized that those who actually belong to a trade union would be more likely to vote Labour than those who only have another family member in a union, for the daily routine of working with fellow trade unionists affects the former but not the latter. In fact, there is virtually no difference in voting between those who are themselves in a union and those whose connection is through the family. In 1983, union members were only one per cent more likely to favour Labour than those who had a member in their family but did not themselves belong to a union. It is thus appropriate to think in terms of union families and non-union families, and not just of individual members.

TABLE 4.1
Trade union membership and voting

Total %		Con.	All'ce (% all votes)	Lab.
A)	Matrix of Determination			
62	Non-member	**32***	14	15
38	Union member	13	11	**14***
Index of Determination, 46 percent, Standardized, 14 percent.				
B)	Controlling for class		(% within row)	
	Solid middle class (AB)			
11	Member	40	37	22
17	Non-member	65	27	8
	Difference	25	10	14
	Lower middle class (C1)			
5	Member	45	29	23
13	Non-member	65	20	15
	Difference	12	9	8
	Skilled working class (C2)			
12	Member	30	25	44
13	Non-member	42	23	34
	Difference	12	2	10
	Non-skilled working class (DE)			
10	Member	26	23	50
20	Non-member	41	20	37
	Difference	15	3	13

Source: British Election Study, 1983.
Union member includes member in the family.

Notwithstanding union organization for collective action in the market place, unions cannot maintain solidarity in the privacy of voting booths. In 1983 more than three-fifths of all those in trade union families did *not* vote Labour; the Labour Party polled 37 per cent of the vote among trade unionists, only three per cent more than the Conservatives. Only 14 per cent of the electorate were Labour-voting trade unionists. *Not* belonging to a union is more important electorally; in 1983 nearly one-third of the electorate consisted of Conservative voting non-members of unions, and Labour won less than one-quarter of the vote among those not in unions. The Index of Determination was 46 per cent, and the Standardized Index 14 per cent (Table 4.1A).

Trade union membership does influence the voting of people within the same class. In the solid middle class, non-union members are 25 per cent more likely to vote Conservative, and 20 per cent more likely to do so in the lower middle class (Table 4.1B). Union members in the skilled working class are 10 per cent more likely to vote Labour, and non-skilled manual workers, 13 per cent more likely to vote Labour.

The effect of union membership is consistently in the direction predicted, but it is not symmetrical. It is stronger among middle- class voters than among working-class voters; the difference between members and non-members averages 16 per cent for the three parties among the solid middle class voters, and 8 per cent among skilled manual workers. The effect is also asymmetrical because it is greatest for Conservative voting. The difference in Conservative support between members and non-members averages 18 per cent across four classes; for Labour, 11 per cent; and for the Alliance, 10 per cent. The Conservatives thus gain more votes from non-union members than Labour does from union members. Belonging to a trade union does *not* imply acceptance of the political loyalties of the Labour movement. Not belonging to a union reflects a conscious commitment to anti-union views.

The limited association between union membership and Labour voting demonstrates the extent to which people today segregate their social values and roles. Belonging to a union that seeks higher wages is often independent of endorsing the political commitment of union leaders. Even on a host of issues concerning the role of trade unions in society, union members on average differ by only 8 per cent from non-members (Gallup Political Index No. 301: 25). The expansion of trade union membership by almost half from 1964 to 1980 has encouraged more individuals to insulate their commitments. Union membership whether voluntary or the product of closed-shop agreements has been accompanied by a *decline* in the proportion of trade unionists voting Labour (Rose, 1968: 360; 1974: 507, 1980: 25). Between 1964 and 1983, the Standardized Index has fallen from 22 per cent to 14 per cent.

The interests of members of one union often conflict with those of other trade unionists. This is demonstrated by every strike about wage differentials or demarcation disputes between unions. In the words of Fabian Society leader Brian Abel-Smith (1984), 'While socialism is about equality, trades unionism is about differentials'. Conflicts can be found within a union too. The 1984-85 coal miners' strike, held without a ballot of members because the leader feared the divisions it would reveal, spectacularly demonstrated this. A number of NUM members continued at work, notwithstanding the leadership's call for strike action. The result of the strike has been the creation of a breakaway union from the NUM.

Housing

The division of the electorate into two substantial and different groups, home-owners and council house tenants, can be important electorally, for each group is a substantial part of the electorate. In 1983, 67 per cent were in owner-occupier households, as against 26 per cent in council tenancies; only 7 per cent of voters are tenants of private landlords.

Economic interests are one reason why housing can influence votes. Home-owners are expected to vote Conservative; the party proclaims it favours a property-owning democracy, maintaining tax relief for interest payments on mortgages, and the right of council tenants to buy their houses. Labour favours more council housing and low council-house rents, with subsidies from central government or from rates paid principally by owner-occupiers and local businesses. The Conservative Party has favoured unsubsidized council-house rents, with means-tested rebates for families who cannot afford to pay an economic rent.

Home-owners anxious to keep their rates down would not be expected to favour Labour, identified as the party of high local rates, just as council tenants favouring low rents should be pro-Labour. Electors concerned with the cost of their monthly mortagage payment (three-fifths of all owner-ocupiers) favour low interest rates. Under Mrs. Thatcher the Conservative identification with home-ownership is qualified by the fact that the party supports high interest rates to combat inflation. Because interest rates also reflect world economic influences, Labour governments too have presided over increases in mortgage costs.

Secondly, the segregation of owner-occupiers and council tenants into separate neighbourhoods creates a social structure in which home-owners daily associate with other home-owners, and council tenants with other tenants. For most people a parliamentary constituency is not meaningful as a community. The local community is defined as the neighbourhood within walking distance from a house, and is normally homogeneous in housing. The line between a council house estate and owner-occupiers' residences is a recognized social boundary between neighbourhoods, and differences in architecture, shopping patterns and road and bus routes reinforce these distinctions.

Within a neighbourhood people will form friendships and close personal ties that encourage the development of group norms. Because neighbourhoods are defined by housing type, they can be occupationally cross-class. Home-owners are today divided almost equally between the middle class and the working class; home-owning is thus of major importance in assimilating half the working class to property-owning norms. By contrast, council house tenants are more than four to one working-class. Council estates are thus a device for maintaining working-class social solidarity — albeit for less than half the working class (Harrop, 1980; Rose, 1973).

TABLE 4.2
Housing and voting

Total %		Con.	All'ce (% all votes)	Lab.
A) Matrix of Determination				
67	Owner-occupiers	**36** *	18	13
7	Private tenants	3	**2** *	2
26	Council tenants	6	5	**14** *
Index of Determination, 52 percent; Standardized, 22 percent.				
B) Controlling for class			(% within row)	
	Solid middle class			
24	Owner-occupier	56	31	12
1	Private tenant	62	33	5
2	Council tenant	33	30	32
	Difference	23	1	20
	Lower middle class			
13	Owner-occupier	65	22	12
1	Private tenant	67	15	18
3	Council tenant	33	27	37
	Difference	32	8	25
	Skilled working class			
15	Owner-occupier	46	27	26
2	Private tenant	32	29	35
8	Council tenant	18	17	64
	Difference	28	10	38
	Non-skilled working class			
15	Owner-occupier	47	23	29
2	Private tenant	35	27	38
13	Council tenant	23	18	56
	Difference	24	5	27

Source: British Election Study, 1983.

The relationship between housing and voting is as predicted; the Index of Determination is 52 per cent, and the Standardized Index, 22 per cent. In 1983, 36 per cent of voters were home-owning Conservatives, 14 per cent Labour-voting council tenants, and 2 per cent private renters favouring the Alliance (Table 4.2A). Moreover, the influence of housing is symmetrical. Among council house tenants 54 per cent voted Labour, and among owner-occupiers 53 per cent voted Conservative. Private tenants divided their vote in almost exactly the same proportions as the electorate as a whole. By contrast with occupational class, the effect of housing upon voting is also increasing; the Standardized Index was 20 per cent in 1964 and 22 per cent in 1983.

The effect of housing independent of class is shown by the fact that the Conservatives receive more votes than Labour among owner-occupiers in all classes, and Labour receives more votes from council tenants everywhere but in the solid middle class (Table 4.2B). The effect of housing differences within a class averages 27 per cent for the Conservatives. Similarly, Labour support within a given class averages 28 per cent higher for council house tenants than owner-occupiers. The effect is strongest among skilled workers, where 64 per cent of council tenants favour Labour, as against 26 per cent of home-owners. The Alliance vote is little affected by housing; on average owner-occupiers are 5 per cent more likely than council tenants to vote Alliance.

Income and consumption

In the abstract the income of a voter ought to provide a good overall indicator of an individual's material circumstances, but in practice the concept of income is very difficult to apply. The first obstacle is that 62 per cent of the electorate does not have an income from fulltime employment or self-employment. According to the Gallup Poll, those not earning a fulltime income include: pensioners, 20 per cent; housewives, 17 per cent; part-time employees, 13 per cent; the unemployed, 9 per cent; and students, 3 per cent. Just as most voters derive their occupational class from the employment status of the head of household, so too they derive most of their income from transfer payments within or from outside the family.

Whereas voting is an individual concern, income is normally a family matter. The great majority of individuals live in a household with more than one weekly income, whether from two persons working fulltime, one fulltime and another part-time, or from one in employment and another drawing a cash benefit from government (Rose, 1985a). A household's income is first of all a function of the number in paid employment in the family. Moreover, the number of dependents in a family, especially children, greatly affects the use of income; a one-income family with three children in school will have to spend more money on necessities than a one-income family with no children living at home. Even when class remains constant, a family's spending needs and income vary greatly through the life-cycle.

Sample surveys do not normally ask about household income when collecting data about individual voters. One reason is that many respondents do not know their family income; they are not in work, or their earnings are only a limited part of total household income. Even when an income figure is reported, this may not be consistently accurate, because of confusion between gross earnings and weekly take-home pay, and fluctuations in earnings through the year. It is not surprising, therefore, that neither the British Election Study nor the Gallup Poll collected income data in 1983; to do so properly requires a study in itself (Pahl, 1984).

The analysis of consumption provides an alternative way to examine the influence of material living standards upon voting. The more income a household has, the more it can spend to buy consumer goods. Moreover, in an affluent society the lack of purchasing power may make an individual depend upon the public provision of goods and services. For example, the division between owner-occupiers and council house tenants reflects differences in household income: most people with the money to do so buy a house, and those with insufficient income are council tenants.

To think of electors as consumers implies a significant theoretical shift by comparison with conventional occupational class models (Rose, 1974: 531ff; 1980: 51ff). Consumption standards are changed much more easily than occupational class. Growth in the gross national product and the development of new consumer goods — cheap cars, colour television, and home video-recorders — raise consumption levels by diffusing benefits to workers while leaving unchanged their occupational status. Insofar as persons with higher consumption levels are more likely to vote Conservative and less likely to favour Labour, then increasing affluence will alter voting behaviour.

Any association of consumption patterns with voting must be qualified. In the contemporary mixed economy, electors depend upon a mix of market and state activities for their wellbeing (Rose, 1985a). Nine-tenths of the electorate has someone in the family enjoying a major state benefit, such as education, a pension, hospital care, or a council house; and virtually 100 per cent consume goods and services in the market.

Relative deprivation may cause people to feel less well off even when they consume more, because their own consumption is less than that of others with whom they compare themselves, or less than their own expectations (Runciman, 1966). Insofar as advertising creates a desire for people to buy more, then wants can exceed earnings. In a period of economic recession, growth in income could easily lag behind consumer expectations for more and more goods. Alternatively, people could expect drastic losses of income and feel reprieved when this did not occur, a form of relative gratification (Rose, 1980a).

Marxists and neo-Marxists have a particular concern with the consumption approach to political behaviour, for it is in apparent contradiction to the conventional Marxist definition of classes by an individual's relationship to the means of production (Saunders, 1984). Whereas the schemes of stratification reviewed previously are within the Marxist approach because they emphasize such things as authority and autonomy at work, the division of the electorate into home-owners and council tenants, or car-owners and non-car owners, is independent of a person's relation to the means of production. Patrick Dunleavy (1979) has argued that a new political cleavage is occurring between voters with sufficient income to purchase a high standard of living, and those who remain dependent on public services and goods. The former would vote Conservative, and the latter, Labour.

While a division of the electorate into two consumption classes — public and private — would meet the logical criterion for closed electoral competition, in practice this is a non-starter (see Franklin and Page, 1984). Two of Dunleavy's important examples of public versus private consumption cleavages — education and health — cannot sustain electoral competition, because they tend to unite the electorate. More than 90 per cent depend upon state education and upon the national health service; private health care and fee-paying education are consumed by only a minority of the middle class. Mrs. Thatcher has given implicit recognition to the cross-class importance of these welfare state services by *not* scheduling them for privatization, a step that would risk electoral suicide.

To serve as an indicator of income, consumption goods must meet several criteria. The first is that they should be affordable by many but not all households. A consumer product found everywhere, such as television sets today, cannot influence voting because it is invariant, not a variable. Secondly, the consumer good must be sufficiently expensive to require more than a minimum income. A telephone can no longer serve as a primary indicator of consumption, since the cost of having a telephone is now less than the cost of smoking. The telephone is rapidly changing from being a selective good to a universal good. Housing is a good indicator of consumer income, because house purchase represents a long-term commitment, thus implying a stable income and an income above the minimum.

Ownership of a motor-car provides the best available indicator of income additional to housing. To have a car not only requires money or credit to make an initial purchase, but also a weekly income to meet running costs. Not to have a car consigns a family to relative deprivation in a society where car-ownership is now the norm. It also creates dependence upon public transport. Transport services and fare structures are determined by how much government is prepared to subsidize bus and rail costs. In Britain today 70 per cent of the electorate is in a family with a car and 30 per cent is not.

TABLE 4.3
Car ownership and voting

Total %		Con.	All'ce (% all votes)	Lab.
A) Matrix of Determination				
72	Car in family	**37** *	19	16
28	No car	9	6	**13** *
Index of Determination, 50 percent; Standardized, 15 percent.				
B) Controlling for class			(% within row)	
	Solid middle class			
25	Car	56	31	12
3	No car	43	29	27
	Difference	13	2	15
	Lower middle class			
14	Car	63	22	14
3	No car	40	24	33
	Difference	23	2	19
	Skilled working class			
18	Car	42	24	33
7	No car	22	24	52
	Difference	20	0	19
	Non-skilled working class			
14	Car	42	23	33
16	No car	31	19	49
	Difference	11	4	16

Source: British Election Study, 1983.

Dividing the electorate into those with cars and those without produces a weak relationship between car-owning and voting; the Standardized Index of Determination is 15 per cent (Table 4.3A). As expected, the Conservatives draw a majority of votes from car owners, and Labour a plurality from non-motorists. But Labour still draws more of its vote from car owners than from non-car owners.

Within each class, there is a consistent but limited effect of car ownership upon voting; those with a car in the family are more likely to favour the Conservatives (mean effect, 17 per cent) and those without, Labour (mean effect, 17 per cent). The mean effect of car ownership for the Alliance (2 per cent) is very small. Although car ownership has had a persisting but secondary association with voting in the past (Rose, 1968a: 366; Rose, 1974: 505; Rose, 1980: 28), its future effect is likely to decline, as car ownership becomes more and more a matter of consumer choice free of any income constraint.

To a substantial extent, whether a family owns a car (and even more, two cars) is a function of family composition, place of residence and working patterns. A family with one adult will have no need for more than one car. Whether a family with two adults needs two cars depends upon employment circumstances. Living in a city as against a suburban or rural area where public transport is limited affects buying a car, or even two cars (Kelley and McAllister, 1983). Of the quarter of families having two cars in Britain, half are working class. Of those without a car, nearly one-quarter are middle-class families who have no particular need to keep a car.

If the whole electorate were car owners, then the distribution of car owners' votes would be identical with the national vote. The Labour Party leadership knows that it is electoral suicide to be identified exclusively with those dependent upon public transport, because they are a minority of the electorate. Revealingly, in the 1985 Commons budget debate Labour leader Neil Kinnock attacked the Conservative government not only for raising the national health service prescription charge to £2, but also for raising the cost of a gallon of petrol to £2.

Alternative dimensions of social structure

Social structure is intrinsically multi-dimensional. In addition to economic differences, societies can be divided according to such criteria as age, gender, or religion. Non-economic dimensions of social structure can potentially influence voting independently of class. Insofar as biologically determined social differences are politically relevant, then closed voting is strengthened, for these characteristics are fixed for life in a way that occupation is not. By controlling for class, we can test whether non-economic social differences are important in themselves, or in addition to class.

Age and generation

Age can influence voting in either of two distinctive ways. The life-cycle (or senescence) theory posits that party preferences change as people grow older. Casual journalistic writing often assumes that young people ought to be change-oriented, thus voting Labour or Alliance, and older people ought to be conservative and vote Conservative too. Generational experiences offer an alternative theory. Because young people are politically less set in their ways, they can be influenced by political trends prevailing when they first come of voting age; this generation-specific pattern of voting is then conserved through a lifetime. Butler and Stokes (1974:62) argue: 'We must ask not how old the elector is but when it was that he was young'.

The tendency for older voters to be more Conservative, observed in previous general elections (Gallup, 1976), could result from the fact that most older voters had established their party loyalty before Labour was a major party. The generation theory implies a steady growth in Labour support, as elderly voters socialized to support the Conservatives die and are replaced by a new generation more often socialized to vote Labour. At the 1983 election anyone under the age of 69 would first have voted in the 1945 landslide Labour election victory or later. Those age 30 or less would first have voted in 1974 or later, when the tide has been away from Labour.

The electoral effect of age is virtually nil. In 1983 the Conservatives were in the lead among all age groups (Table 4.4). Had voting at the 1983 election been confined solely to those aged 18 to 29, the Conservatives would have won with 39 per cent of the vote, only 5 per cent less than their overall British figure. When the electorate is divided at age 45, the Standardized Index of Determination is very low, 2 per cent.

When controls are introduced for class, a limited difference in party preferences emerges. In the middle class, the oldest group, the over 65s, is 18 per cent more Conservative than the youngest. But young middle-class Britons are not attracted to the Alliance, as might be American Yuppies (Young Urban Professionals). Within the middle class, the Alliance vote is virtually the same for all age levels. Labour did best among young, non-skilled manual workers, winning 48 per cent of their vote. But this group constitutes only seven per cent of the total electorate. The effect of age, after controlling for class, is on average 12 per cent for Conservatives, 6 per cent for Labour, and 5 per cent for the Alliance.

The passage of two decades allows a further test of generational change (cf. Butler and Stokes 1969: 62-64; 263-741). Political generations are defined by the period in which a group cast its first vote, and the particular political party favoured then (cf. Table 2.6). The generation coming of age before the Second World War, when Labour was a nascent or weak party, should therefore be more likely to favour the Conservatives. A person first voting in 1945 or in a

TABLE 4.4
Age and voting

Total %		Con.	All'ce (% all votes)	Lab.
A) Matrix of Determination				
17	65+	**8** *	4	5
15	55–64	**7** *	4	4
15	45–54	**6** *	4	4
27	30–44	12	7	**7** *
27	18–29	10	7	**9** *
Index of Determination, 37 percent; Standardized, 2 percent.				
B) Controlling for class			(% within row)	
	Middle class			
6	65+	65	23	12
6	55–64	60	26	13
5	45–54	60	24	14
12	30–44	55	29	15
10	18–29	47	28	22
	Difference	18	5	10
	Skilled working class			
4	65+	44	22	32
4	55–64	41	28	30
5	45–54	34	29	35
9	30–44	44	25	30
9	18–29	39	31	28
	Difference	5	9	4
	Non-skilled working class			
7	65+	39	22	37
5	55–64	34	25	39
4	45–54	29	28	41
6	30–44	28	25	45
7	18–29	25	24	48
	Difference	14	2	11

Source: Gallup Campaign Study, 1983.
Middle-class strata merged to maintain reliability of sample.

subsequent election involving duopolistic competition should be inclined to favour Labour, and since 1974 a person first voting in conditions of multi-party electoral competition would favour the Alliance. A transitional generation, first voting in the 1960s, can also be examined. Since the occupational class structure tends to be much the same from one generation to the next, there is no need to control for within-class differences.

In fact, the generational theory appears of little relevance today (Table 4.5). The Labour vote drops, and drops substantially in each of the political generations, including that first voting in 1945. The

Alliance vote goes up substantially in all generations, and the Conservative vote goes up very consistently. The fall in Labour support is greatest among those first voting in a period of nominal Labour dominance, 1964-70; so too is the rise in Alliance support. In contemporary Britain, influences from two, three or four decades ago appear to be of relatively little influence (see also, chapters VI, VII).

TABLE 4.5
The effect of generations upon voting

Total %		Con.	Lib./All'ce (% within row)	Lab.
	Old multi-party competition			
Born pre-1914; voting by 1935				
44	1964 vote	48	9	43
12	1983 vote	55	19	25
	Difference	7	10	18
	Closed-class competition			
Born 1914–38; voting first 1945–59				
48	1964 vote	37	13	49
38	1983 vote	44	24	31
	Difference	7	11	18
	Transition party system			
Born 1939–52; voting first 1964–70				
8	1964 vote	38	7	54
27	1983 vote	46	27	26
	Difference	8	20	28
	Open competition			
Born 1953 or later; voting first 1974 or later				
n.a.	1964 vote	n.a.	n.a.	n.a.
22	1983 vote	41	27	30

Source: British Election Studies, 1964 and 1983.

Gender

Historically, men and women have differed greatly in political rights, for extensions of the franchise beginning in 1832 only affected men. Women were first given the right to vote at the 1918 election, and women first voted on the same qualification as men in 1929. However, very few women in the electorate today came of age without the right to vote; hence, gender differences arising from past history are likely to be negligible by 1983.

A variety of hypotheses can be advanced to suggest why women should differ from men in voting. An inclination to favour the Conservatives was once thought to follow from the more "domestic" nature of women, and the Conservative Party's presumed identification with family values (cf. Reid and Goot, 1977). An apparent association between gender and voting could be spurious; for example, women are likely to live longer than men and older people are more Conservative, and older people are more likely to go to church and churchgoers are more Conservative (Butler and Stokes, 1974: 160n). Since 1979 the Conservatives have offered a very specific attraction, a woman leader. However, many of Mrs. Thatcher's views, for example, about defence and unemployment, are tough rather than the tender views alleged to characterize women.

The creation of pressure groups propagating a radical feminist ideology has challenged older assumptions about women favouring the Conservatives. From a feminist perspective, women ought to vote Labour, the party believed to be more likely to support legislation promoting equal opportunities for women. Social change, independent of ideological change, can also affect the voting patterns of women. Housewives not in paid employment are less directly subject to occupational class influences than are men. The effect of participation in the labour force could cause women in paid employment to vote differently from women who are housewives.

In fact, women divide their votes in virtually the same way as men (Table 4.6). Mrs. Thatcher demonstrates the equality of sexes by her ability to draw votes in almost equal proportions from men and women. According to the 1983 British Election Study, 45 per cent of men and 45 per cent of women voted Conservative. When women in employment (two-thirds of all women) are compared with housewives, a very similar distribution of party preferences is found. The Standardized Index of Determination is two per cent, and this is the case whether all women are assumed to vote Conservative and all men Labour, or all persons in work vote Labour and all housewives Conservative. Whatever effects may once have created a slight pro-Conservative bias among women have now virtually disappeared (cf. Gallup, 1976: 211; Sarlvik and Crewe, 1983: 91).

The absence of a gender effect is in part a function of party tactics. Since women are slightly more than half the electorate, no party wanting to win an election would consciously offend so large a bloc of voters, just as it would not offend men, who also constitute almost half the electorate. Parties can appeal to both men and women voters, for women do not share a common set of political attitudes (Rose, 1985b: Table 5.2). Most British women do not have a work-oriented feminist ideology; instead, they place a high value on home and family concerns (National Opinion Polls, 1984: 14-32). A group divided in political views will also divide its votes.

In conventional survey research, married women are assigned a class according to the occupation of their husband, and not on the basis of their own employment status. When the voting patterns of men, working women and housewives are compared, controlling for head of household's class, there is virtually no effect of gender or employment (Table 4.6B). The mean difference between men and housewives is 4.5 per cent for the Conservatives and 3.5 per cent for Labour, and under 3 per cent for the Alliance. Similarly low differences are registered as between men and working women.

TABLE 4.6
Gender and voting

Total %	Con.	All'ce (% all votes)	Lab.
A) Matrix of Determination			
18 Housewives	**9** *	4	5
35 Working women	**15** *	10	10
47 Men	21	11	**14** *
Index of Determination, 38 percent; Standardized, 2 percent.			
B) Controlling for class		(% within row)	
Solid middle class			
5 Female, housewife	55	31	12
8 Female, working	54	30	15
14 Male	55	32	13
Difference	0	1	1
Lower middle class			
3 Female, housewife	67	18	14
7 Female, working	51	26	21
8 Male	64	20	14
Difference	3	2	0
Skilled working class			
4 Female, housewife	35	26	39
8 Female, working	34	28	36
13 Male	38	21	40
Difference	3	5	1
Non-skilled working class			
6 Female, housewife	41	21	37
12 Female, working	38	24	36
12 Male	31	18	49
Difference	10	3	12

Source: British Election Study, 1983; head of household class.

Feminists criticize the convention of assigning a woman's class on the basis of her husband's occupation, arguing that status should be attributed to women by their own occupation, whether current or previous to becoming a housewife. Insofar as married couples both have the same occupational status, doing this will not make any difference in the fit between gender and voting behaviour (cf. Table 3.6). Insofar as class lines are crossed within the marital home, typically with a wife in an office job and a husband a skilled manual worker, then one of three effects could result. Feminists propose that a woman should vote her class, and the husband vote his. A second alternative is that both partners would reject class differences, and opt for the Alliance as the anti-class party. Insofar as a couple in work is much more likely to have a middle class income, both partners may tend toward middle-class voting patterns.

The extent of cross-class differences in work among married couples is very limited. For 71 per cent of the electorate, a conflict cannot occur because it is a single-person household, the couple are retired, or only one partner is employed and the other stays in the house. For an additional 20 per cent, both husband and wife work at the same class level, whether manual or non-manual. Only 10 per cent of the electorate consists of voters working at a different class level than their spouse. When the electorate is stratified to differentiate those in cross-class homes from those in a consistently middle-class or working class home, the Standardized Index of Determination is 17 per cent, one per cent lower than when the same respondents are classified according to the occupation of the head of household (cf. Table 3.3). In that tenth of the electorate with married partners working across class lines there is no evidence of class polarization in the home; support for the three parties tends to fall midway between that of unambiguously middle-class and working-class couples.

Religion

Historically, religion was an important division within society, because the Church of England, as the state church, derived privileges from its association with political authority. Until well into the nineteenth century, disabilities were placed upon the substantial fraction of the population who were not adherents of the State Church, including the disqualification of non-conformist Protestants, Roman Catholics and Jews from voting or from holding public office. The introduction of compulsory education in 1870 raised contentious issues about the role of the state religion in the schools. In Scotland, Wales and Ireland, the fact that the State Church was episcopal and Anglican created further difficulties.

Excepting Northern Ireland, religion is today of limited social importance. But divisions derived from religion can persist independent of church attendance (only one in five claim they go to church at least once a month) or doctrinal belief (heterogeneous within as well as between religions, as Anglican bishops show). People who have grown up in a non-conforming household may differ in voting from those whose religious identification is with a state church. Those identifying with the Church of England (once called the Tory Party at prayer) will be expected to vote Conservative, non-conformists to favour the Liberals or the Alliance, and three minorities — Roman Catholics, non-Christians, and the irreligious — to favour Labour. The Church of Scotland, as an Established Church, would be expected to have its adherents favour the Conservatives, though less so than Anglicans in England.

TABLE 4.7
Religion and voting

Total %		Con.	All'ce (% all votes)	Lab.
A) Matrix of Determination				
49	Anglicans	**26** *	12	11
5	Church of Scotland	**2** *	1	2
7	Protestant non-conformists	3	**2** *	2
12	Roman Catholic	4	3	**5** *
26	None	11	7	**8** *
Index of Determination, 43 percent; Standardized, 10 percent.				
B) Controlling for class			(% within row)	
	Middle class			
23	Anglican	64	26	10
2	Church of Scotland	46	32	15
3	Protestant non-conformist	53	30	15
4	Roman Catholic	51	29	20
13	None	49	30	20
	Difference	15	4	10
	Working class			
26	Anglican	42	24	34
3	Church of Scotland	22	19	53
4	Protestant non-conformist	29	34	34
8	Roman Catholic	26	17	55
13	None	36	21	41
	Difference	6	3	7

Source: British Election Study, 1983.

Secularization has advanced to the extent that when British people today are asked if they belong to any particular religion, one-quarter say they have none. Thus, the 49 per cent who are Anglicans have a positive identification, and are not assigned to that church as a residual category. Among self-reported Anglicans, the Conservatives are the favoured party, with more than half the vote. Catholics are most inclined to be Labour, and least inclined to be Alliance, an indication that the support of the Alliance for permissiveness (David

Steel sponsored an Abortion Act, and Roy Jenkins was a reforming Home Secretary) is a handicap with practising Catholics. Those who report no religion divide like a cross-section of the electorate. The Standardized Index of Religious Determination is 10 per cent (Table 4.7A).

Controlling for class differences shows two types of effects, after discounting the peculiar position of Church of Scotland adherents, who may also vote Scottish Nationalist (Table 4.7B). Among middle-class Anglicans, 64 per cent favour the Conservatives as against 49 per cent of those without any religion. The irreligious in the middle class are 10 per cent more likely to vote Labour than are Anglicans. Within the working class, the major division is between Anglicans and Roman Catholics. Catholics are 21 per cent more likely to vote Labour, and 16 per cent less likely to vote Conservative than Anglicans. The anti-Conservative orientation of working-class Catholics is not the result of left-wing theology but of a tradition of Irish nationalism, refusing votes for a party that in an Irish context has been Unionist rather than Republican.

Nationality

National differences have always existed within a multi-national Crown combining English, Scots, Welsh and Irish (Rose, 1982). But since nearly all Irish Nationalist MPs left the House of Commons in 1918 after insurrection in Ireland, parliamentary representation has been almost exclusively in the hands of parties contesting elections Britainwide, and voters have almost invariably supported these rather than nationalist parties.

National differences can be registered in two different ways. Voting for nationalist parties demanding independence from the Westminster Parliament is the most dramatic method, but it is not common. Even at its relative height in October, 1974, the Scottish National Party was rejected by 70 per cent of Scots, and in 1983 by 88 per cent. In Wales Plaid Cymru has consistently been rejected by about 90 per cent of Welsh voters; in 1983 it polled only 8 percent of the vote there. A second way in which national differences can affect voting is if Scots and Welsh tend to vote differently, e.g. opposing the more Unionist Conservative Party. To the extent that Scotland or Wales is disproportionately working class, Britainwide patterns of class voting would produce fewer Conservative and more Labour votes there.

A simple hypothesis that electoral competition is determined by national differences must be rejected, for if that were true, then the Conservatives, as the English (sic) party, would win every general election, since England contributes five-sixths of the United Kingdom electorate. In 1983 the largest proportion of the electorate consisted of English who vote Conservative (38 per cent); second and third in size were groups of English voters favouring Labour and the Alliance. Scots and Welsh voting Labour constituted only 3 and 2 per cent of the vote respectively. The Standardized Index of Determination was thus only 7 per cent.

There are two reasons why national differences do not have a major impact on voting. The first is that national identities are not fixed by the place of residence; a substantial minority of Scots and Welsh first of all identify themselves as British (Rose, 1982: Table 1.1; Miller, 1982; Balsom et al., 1983). Even among those who see themselves as Welsh or Scots, this need not exclude a British identity or a preference for Britain-wide parties. Moreover, within Scotland, there are divisions about political responses to nationalism, and in Wales about language, for Welsh is a minority language there (Madgwick and Rawkins, 1982; McAllister and Mughan, 1984).

The secondary effect of nationality is evident, even after allowing for the effect of social class (Table 4.8). Middle-class voters in Wales are 10 per cent less likely to vote Conservative and in Scotland, 11 per cent less, after controlling for the lower vote for the Britainwide parties because of Nationalist parties. In the working class, there is a complementary effect: Labour's vote in Scotland is 13 per cent higher than in England and also 13 per cent higher in Wales. The Alliance vote profile is hardly affected by national differences.

TABLE 4.8
Nation and vote, controlling for class

Total %			Con.	All'ce	Lab. (% within row)	Nat.
	Middle class					
33	England		59	25	16	n.a.
4	Scotland		44 (48)	28 (31)	20 (22)	8
2	Wales		43 (49)	23 (27)	22 (25)	12
	Difference,	England-Scotland	(+11)	(−6)	(−6)	
		England-Wales	(+10)	(−2)	(−9)	
	Working class					
50	England		35	28	37	n.a.
7	Scotland		21 (24)	23 (26)	44 (50)	12
3	Wales		26 (28)	23 (25)	45 (48)	6
	Difference,	England-Scotland	(+11)	(+2)	(−13)	
		England-Wales	(+7)	(+2)	(−13)	

( ) Percentage of votes for Britain-wide parties only.
Source: BBC Gallup Study, 1983; for Wales, McAllister and Rose, 1984: Table V1.2.

English regions

Within England, regional differences between the North and South are often discussed as if they were tantamount to differences in national identity. Maps of election results can produce a distorted appearance of regional effects. Showing seats won in a region masks very great divisions in votes within regions; the leading party may have less than half the vote. Secondly, maps cannot control for differences in occupational structure as between the industrial North, agricultural East Anglia, and London. Thirdly, maps do not display the degree of difference — small or large — that remains after controlling for differences in occupational structure. Moreover, the rationale for expecting regional voting within England — the persistence of traditional cultural differences — can be opposed by a contrary rationale, nationwide media, nationwide industries and trade unions, and nationwide party competition making regional differences negligible (McAllister and Rose, 1984).

Any attempt to divide the whole of England along a simple North-South axis faces two great difficulties. The first is: Where to draw the line between North and South? If industrialization is the test, then the North should include the Midlands, a historic industrial centre but not a historic centre of Labour strength. London presents a second problem. Geographically, London is undoubtedly in the South of England, but it is not a sleepy cathedral town full of thatched-roof cottages, like a prototypical Southern shire village. Among other things, London is full of Labour voters.

Detailed ecological analyses reported elsewhere (McAllister and Rose, 1984: chapter 5) distinguish between four English regions — the North, the Midlands, the South of England shires, and London — each varying in the strength of Conservative, Labour and Alliance vote. When the North/South line is drawn south of the Midlands the Standardized Index of Determination of the vote within England is only 2 per cent (Table 4.9A). Even if the line is drawn so that only the North of England is regarded as Labour, region does not become the determinant of Labour vote, for in 1983 the Conservatives won a larger proportion of the North of England vote than did Labour.

Within-class comparisons of voting test the influence of region additional to occupational class. If the regions are arrayed from most to least Labour, this produces the curious geographical effect of Greater London being closer to Newcastle upon Tyne than to Birmingham! After controlling for class, London voters are usually more Labour and less Conservative than those in the Midlands (Table 4.9B). The maximum regional effect can be calculated by comparing the two extreme regions — the North of England and the South — each with nearly one-third of the English electorate. There is a consistent albeit consistent albeit limited secondary effect of region upon voters. Both middle-class and working-class voters are more Labour in the North of England, and more Conservative in the South. The mean regional effect is 15 per cent for Labour, and 8 per cent for the Alliance and for the Conservatives.

TABLE 4.9
English regions and voting

Total %		Con.	All'ce (% vote in England)	Lab.
A) Matrix of Determination				
37	South	**19** *	11	6
14	London	**6** *	3	4
19	Midlands	9	5	**6** *
30	North	12	7	**11** *
Index of Determination, 42 percent; Standardized, 2 percent.				
B) Controlling for class			(% within row)	
	Solid middle class			
6	South	64	26	9
3	Greater London	65	22	12
3	Midlands	67	23	9
4	North	58	22	19
	Difference	6	4	10
	Lower middle class			
9	South	57	32	11
4	Greater London	53	26	20
5	Midlands	56	27	16
7	North	51	27	21
	Difference	6	5	10
	Skilled working class			
10	South	47	33	19
4	Greater London	43	24	32
7	Midlands	46	25	28
10	North	37	23	40
	Difference	10	10	21
	Non-skilled working class			
8	South	39	34	27
5	Greater London	34	26	38
6	Midlands	33	22	45
11	North	30	23	47
	Difference	9	11	20

Sources: Calculated from data in McAllister and Rose (1984: Appendix A); 1983 Gallup Campaign Study Aggregation of Standard Regions as follows: North (Northern Yorkshire and Humberside, North West); Midlands (East, West); Greater London (GLC boundaries); South (South East except for Greater London, South West, East Anglia).

Urban-rural

Insofar as conventional ideas about classes are derived from urban industrial settings, differences between urban and rural voters should arise, for rural voters are less likely to live in a self-consciously industrial environment, where Conservative vs. Labour competition is the norm. This tendency should be reinforced to the extent that deference, that is, a tendency of manual workers to favour the Conservatives, characterizes rural English society (Stacey, 1960; Newby, 1979). However, the dispersion of industry produces coal mining in rural areas, and the impact of conurbations, especially Greater London, can be felt throughout the whole of its rural hinterland. There are also rural areas in which religious non-conformity and tenant versus landlord differences can produce a dissenting vote.

TABLE 4.10
Urban-rural differences and voting

Total %		Con.	All'ce (% all votes)	Lab.
A) Matrix of Determination				
19	Rural areas	**9** *	6	4
21	Cities under 50,000	**10** *	6	5
61	Cities over 50,000	25	15	**20** *
Index of Determination, 39 percent; Standardized, 7 percent.				
B) Controlling for class			(% within row)	
	Solid middle class			
3	Rural areas	65	23	11
3	Cities under 50,000	61	30	8
8	Cities over 50,000	61	23	15
	Difference	4	0	4
	Lower middle class			
4	Rural areas	57	30	10
5	Cities under 50,000	58	28	13
15	Cities over 50,000	49	28	21
	Difference	8	2	11
	Skilled working class			
6	Rural areas	42	36	20
6	Cities under 50,000	46	26	27
19	Cities over 50,000	38	24	37
	Difference	4	12	17
	Non-skilled working class			
5	Rural areas	36	27	31
6	Cities under 50,000	33	29	37
19	Cities over 50,000	29	22	47
	Difference	7	5	16

Source: Gallup Campaign Study, 1983.

Urban voters may be expected to vote Labour, and rural voters Conservative. When urban-rural differences are examined in the whole electorate, the Standardized Index of Determination is 7 per cent; class divisions occurring within cities and within the countryside are greater than the small differences between them (Table 4.10 A).

When urban and rural voters are compared, controlling for occupational class, a small but consistent effect is found. In all classes urban voters are more likely to favour Labour than rural voters by an average of 12 per cent. Rural voters, and particularly working-class rural voters, are more inclined to favour the Alliance, doing so at the expense of Labour. The mean effect is 13 per cent for Labour, 6 per cent for the Conservatives, and 5 per cent for the Alliance.

Contextual influences

It has long been held that the social context or environment in which a voter lives has an influence over and above his own individual characteristics. A wide range of British studies have argued that manual workers living in predominantly non-manual areas will be more Conservative than similar workers living in manual areas, while non-manual workers living in manual areas will be disproportionately Labour (Butler and Stokes, 1974: 130-32; Garrahan, 1977; Miller, 1978).

The influence attributed to context is based on a spurious relationship, caused by a failure to control for other influences. Butler and Stokes (1974: 130ff), for example, only controlled for whether or not a voter was a manual or a non-manual worker. Kelley and McAllister (1985) have shown that being a manual or a non-manual worker is also related to differences in education, family background, housing and other socio-economic influences on voting. Unless these are also controlled for, their influence is erroneously attributed to context. Once controls are introduced for individual characteristics, the context is shown to have virtually no effect on British voting.

Something more than class

Nearly every characteristic of social structure examined here appears to have *some* influence upon voting. Just as Alice found that in a Wonderland game all had won and all should have prizes, so it appears that everything can influence voting — at least a little bit. There are theoretical as well as empirical reasons why the influences tested here — housing, trade union membership, consumption and religion — should make a difference in how people vote.

Each influence upon voting can be ranked by the Index of Determination (Table 4.11). When this is done, housing is *the* most important social characteristic influencing voting; its Standardized Index of Determination is 22 per cent, as against 14 per cent for the average Index measuring occupational class (cf. Table 3.9). Yet it would be wrong to conclude from this that housing completely determines voting. The Index is 78 per cent short of complete determination, and it is less than one-third the Index for religion and voting in Northern Ireland. Yet by British standards, the relation between housing and voting is outstanding.

TABLE 4.11
Comparing the Indexes of Determination for social structure and voting

	Fits Standard Index	Con.	Of which All'ce (% all votes)	Lab.	Does not fit
Housing	22	36	2	14	48
Car ownership	15	37	n.a.	13	50
Union membership	14	32	n.a.	14	54
Religion	10	28	2	13	57
Nation	7	38	n.a.	5	57
Urban/rural	7	19	n.a.	20	61
English regions	2	25	n.a.	17	58
Age	2	21	n.a.	16	63
Gender	2.	24	n.a.	14	62

Sources: Tables 4.1 to 4.10 above.

The shift from occupational class to alternative economic determinants of voting is underlined by the fact that motor-car ownership and union membership show a Standardized Index of 15 per cent and 14 per cent respectively, the same as the average class Index. If occupational class is regarded as a traditional influence in decline (cf. Table 3.11), it has gone into decline more rapidly than religion. This nineteenth-century influence upon party loyalties even today can produce a Standardized Index of Determination of 10 per cent. Two other cultural influences — nation, and urban-rural differences — are also of some significance. Three non-economic social differences — English regions, age and gender — have virtually no direct influence upon voting.

Given that occupational class and housing appear of principal but not exclusive importance for voting, we can also think of a class-plus approach. When social influences are ranked according to the influence they exert in addition to occupation, housing again appears most important, with a mean effect of 20 per cent (Table 4.12). There are also class-plus effects of 10 per cent or more for trade union membership, car ownership, nation, and region. While social characteristics of little direct influence can register a secondary influence, they are not necessarily significant electorally, especially when a difference involves a small substratum of the electorate, such as the Welsh middle class. For a big electoral impact, effects must involve a large bloc of voters. This impact is best measured by the Standardized Index of Determination (cf. Table 4.11).

TABLE 4.12
The effect of social structure plus class on voting

	Mean effect				
	Solid middle %	Lower middle %	Skilled working %	Non-skilled working %	All classes (avg.) %
Housing	15	21	25	19	20
Union membership	16	12	8	14	12
Car ownership	10	15	13	10	12
English regions	7	7	14	13	10
Nation[a]	– 8 –		– 12 –		10
Age	– 11 –		6	9	9
Religion	– 10 –		– 5 –		7
Urban-rural	3	7	11	9	7
Gender	1	2	3	8	3

Source: Calculated from Tables 4.1 to 4.11 above. [a]Average for Scotland and Wales.

The influence of social structure upon voting, whether modified by class or independent of class, must be qualified in three ways. First and foremost, the differences are of degree not kind. On scales that run from 0 to 100, each influence is much closer to 0. Secondly, the influence of social structure is not consistent. Most potential social determinants have a secondary influence. Moreover, the influences are not equally strong in all classes; they are sometimes more apparent in the working class and sometimes in the middle class. Nor is the influence of social structure symmetrical between parties. Social structure influences Conservative and Labour support more than the Alliance. Whatever the subdivisions of the electorate, Alliance support is normally within a few per cent of being an exact cross-section of the electorate. The distinctive feature of the Alliance vote is its social representativeness.

All in all, the electorate today is far better described as open than closed. The idea of determination by social structure, emphasizing an almost mechanical cause-and-effect relationship, is unsuitable in contemporary electoral analysis. While it is possible to identify some social characteristics that have some influence, these are fewer and their their degree of influence far less than sociological theories hypothesize. Even more important politically, the influence of social structure is *not* sufficient to determine which party wins an election.

Notes

1. Doing this avoids the problems that multi-collinearity can produce in regression analysis (cf. Weatherford, 1980).

2. For an example of ignoring the limitations of sample size, see Dunleavy and Husbands (1985 Table 5.18), which divides 760 respondents into 39 cells with an average of 19 respondents each.

5
Restructuring the electorate

In an electorate of more than 40,000,000 people, politicians and parties cannot appeal to individuals; of necessity politicians must address their appeals to masses of voters. Campaigning by appeals to individual concerns was destroyed by the introduction of mass suffrage (Rose, 1967: chapter 1; McAllister, 1985). Today, campaign walkabouts or pressing the flesh only make sense if the intimate contact between politicians and ordinary electors is televised, simulating for a mass audience the directness of person-to-person communication.

The practical problem facing political parties today is: What are the principal groups within the mass electorate? In a closed-class system, both parties and voters knew where they were. Insofar as class determined voting, parties could concentrate upon mobilizing the maximum of support from their own class. But in an open electorate, classes do not respond to traditional appeals with traditional enthusiasm.

The opening up of the electorate does not mean that social structure now lacks all influence upon the vote. Nearly every social characteristic examined in the preceding chapter registers at least a little influence upon voting. There is thus a need to restructure the electorate in order to identify the combination of social characteristics influencing British voters today.

Identifying what does not influence voting is relatively easy; identifying what does is more difficult. The simplest alternative is a mono-causal theory, replacing class by one other influence. But this risks exchanging the shortcomings of an oversimplified class model of voting with another one-dimensional oversimplification. As Chapter IV demonstrates, only one influence, housing, is stronger than occupation, and no one influence is all-important.

Multivariate statistical analysis is an appropriate method for identifying the dimensions of social structure that jointly influence voting. By examining a multiplicity of influences together, it is possible to remove spurious effects that may arise from the intercorrelation of occupation, union membership, and housing, and also to identify influences of secondary importance; social characteristics of no importance can be discarded.

The first task is to set out a precise statistical analysis of the most important social determinants of the vote. Secondly, the chapter compares influences on the 1983 vote with the pattern at every British election since 1964. Has the influence of social structure been declining, or is consistently low? It is then possible to restructure the electorate to identify those groups that *do* give a high level of support to the Conservative or Labour parties today, and those that are especially open to move between parties.

The combined effect of social structure: a multivariate analysis

Given that many social characteristics appear to exert some influence upon voting, which are most important statistically? Equally, which are most meaningful politically? A good statistical analysis should identify groups that a party can consider its own; it should also identify swing groups, evenly divided in voting and therefore deserving a high degree of competitive attention from all parties.

The multivariate statistical technique used here is AID (Automatic Interaction Detector algorithm), familiarly known as tree analysis (Sonquist, et al., 1973). AID is appropriate, because it is constructed according to the same logic as the preceding matrix tables. It reviews the influence upon voting of a variety of social characteristics, and initially divides the electorate into two groups according to the social characteristic that creates the greatest party difference among voters. After the first split, each group is examined separately, to see which social characteristic can best discriminate further between partisans. For example, if occupational class proves the strongest initial influence, then middle-class voters might be further subdivided into upper-middle versus lower-middle class groups, and working-class voters into trade union versus non-trade union members. The process of reviewing all social characteristics in order to select the one with the most effect upon voting continues until no further subdivision can explain one-half of one per cent of the total variance among voters. Social characteristics are omitted from the tree if they add nothing to the explanation of this variance.

The branching logic of AID accounts for its description as tree analysis; the diagrammatic representation of the results resembles an inverted tree with the trunk (that is, all voters) at the top. At each branch, increasingly homogeneous social groups are created, consisting of individuals who have one or more social characteristics in common *and who are relatively homogeneous in voting*. The identification of groups of voters with common social characteristics follows Weatherford's (1980: 461) comment that notwithstanding the repertoire of new statistical techniques 'old-fashioned physical controls, i.e. by cross-tabulation' are best to display the reality of voting by social groups.

The information generated by tree analysis readily lends itself to political interpretation. First of all, at each branch the vote of a given social group is calculated, showing the extent to which voters with one or more social characteristics in common also have the same party preference. At each branch of the tree, groups tend to become more and more politically homogeneous. The tree can recognize that manual workers who are also council house tenants will be more Labour than workers considered without regard to housing. However, the purer a group is in terms of voting as a bloc, the smaller its proportion of the electorate, for subdivision necessarily diminishes size. Furthermore, at each stage from the second branch onwards, one group will tend to regress toward the mean voting pattern, for it is defined by lacking a characteristic of the more partisan group (for example, being working class yet not council tenants). In a single process tree analysis identifies both open and closed groups within the electorate.

The nine social structure influences tested here have been selected because of their theoretical potential as determinants of the vote: occupation, housing, trade union membership, education, age, gender, nation of residence, car ownership, and telephone ownership. This also permits direct comparison with previous AID analyses of British general elections since 1959, employing the same social structure influences (Rose, 1980).[1] Chapter VI and VII consider social psychological influences, such as parents' party preference and political principles. To examine the subjective perceptions and attitudes of voters first is a mistake, for this implies that the voter makes his or her own world. In fact, social structure is *prior* to an individual's experience. What is there to be perceived affects what an individual thinks about politics.

Because AID divides voters into two groups, it is particularly suitable for testing the closed-class model at the 1983 election, concentrating initially upon social differences between Conservative versus Labour voters. Insofar as the proportion of the variance explained statistically is high, then the party system is closed, but insofar as the variance explained is low, the party system can be regarded as open.

At the 1983 election housing not occupational class was most important in distinguishing Conservative from Labour voters (Figure 5.1). Among owner-occupiers, 73 per cent voted Conservative; among tenants in council houses or in the private sector, 58 per cent voted Labour. In the initial branch of the tree, housing accounted for 9.6 per cent of the variance explained in the Conservative-Labour division of the vote.[2] Among owner-occupiers trade union membership came

FIGURE 5.1
Multiplicity of influences upon the Conservative vs. Labour vote

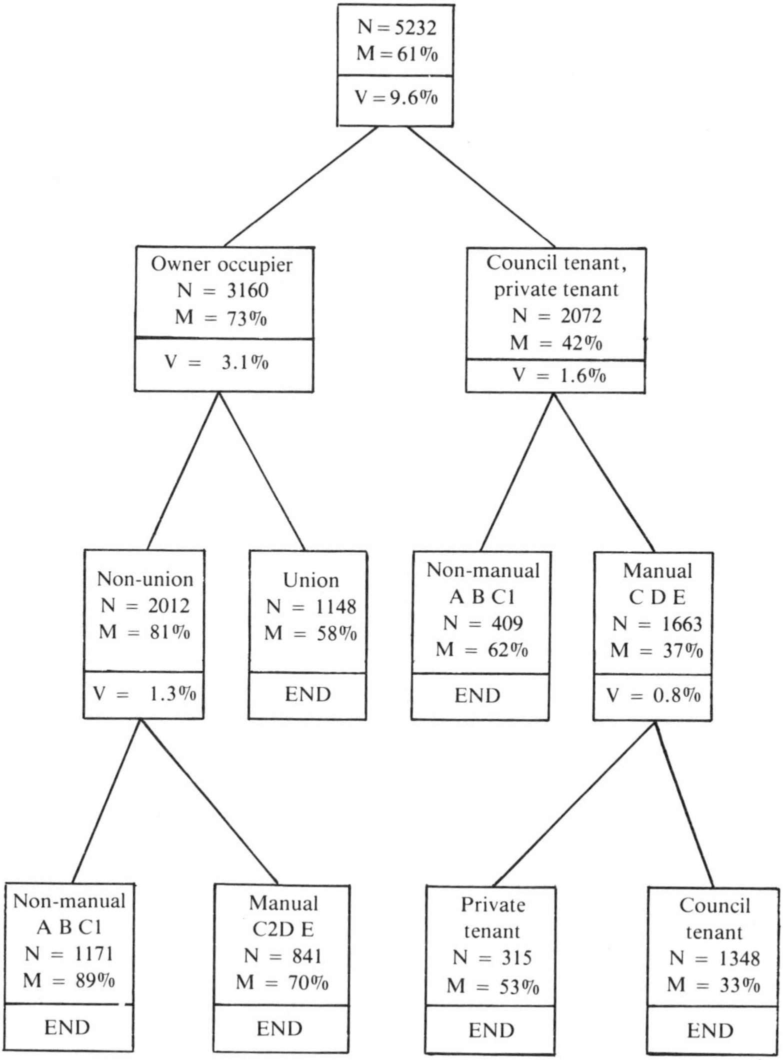

M = % Conservative
N = Number of respondents
V = Variance explained

Total variance explained: 16.4%
Source: 1983 Gallup Campaign Study.

next as an influence, explaining an additional 3.1 per cent of the variance in voting. Of those who do not belong to a trade union 81 per cent voted Conservative, and among home-owners who belong to a union, 58 per cent. Occupational class is third in significance for Conservative support which increases to 89 per cent among non-union voters who are owner-occupiers and also middle class. The limited influence of occupational class is shown by the fact that 70 per cent of manual workers who are non-union home-owners also voted Conservative. In the pro-Labour tenant sector, additional social differences are of little electoral importance. At the second branch, Labour voting rises four per cent among tenants who are working class, removing the private tenants at the third branch raises Labour suppport to 67 per cent among working-class council tenants.

Tree analysis confirms asymmetry in the social determination of voting. Whereas the most homogeneous Conservative end group in the branching process of Figure 5.1 is 89 per cent Conservative (owner-occupiers who are non-union and middle class), the most Labour end group (council house tenants who are working class) is 67 per cent Labour. The political significance of asymmetry is heightened by the fact that owner-occupiers outnumber tenants by a margin of six to four. The tree analysis also identifies a fifth of the electorate who are fairly evenly divided between the parties; among home-owners who also belong to trade unions, 58 per cent voted Conservative and 42 per cent Labour in 1983.

Of the Conservative-Labour division of the vote, 16.4 per cent of the variance is explained by the combination of three social characteristics: housing, union membership, and occupational class. It is also important to note that education, age, gender, nation and two indicators of income, car and telephone ownership, add nothing to the discrimination of Conservative from Labour voters. However, the three social structure influences are not of equal significance. Housing accounts for nearly two-thirds of the influence of social structure, and trade union membership and occupational class for about one-sixth each.

When minimal party competition was the norm the need to dichotomize the dependent variable, party vote, created no problem, for the Conservative and Labour shares were complementary, summing to 100 per cent of the total vote. But the rise of multi-party competition makes this condition restrictive. To explain 16.4 per cent in the variance of the Conservative and Labour vote in 1983 is to explain 70 per cent of the total United Kingdom vote (that is, 11.5 per cent). Yet to include all three parties in an AID analysis would require setting the Conservative vote against the Labour plus Alliance vote, or Labour against Conservative plus Alliance vote. Combining voters for two different parties reduces the amount of variance explained; it does not alter our understanding of the relationship between social structure and voting.[3] The same three influences — housing, trade union membership, and occupational class — show up with the same relative significance. They also remain important when the data is analysed by multiple regression methods (see Appendix C).

If the Alliance has a socially determined vote, then tree analysis should show support by distinctive groups, whether the same or different from influences upon Conservative and Labour voters. Alternatively, if the Alliance appeals to a cross-section of the electorate, thus having very weak links with social structure, a tree analysis of its vote should explain less variance.

When Alliance voters are contrasted with those who vote Conservative or Labour, social structure accounts for 0.0 per cent (less than one-half of one per cent) of variation in the vote. There is not a single branch, for Alliance voters so closely resemble British society as a whole that they cannot be separated from the rest of the electorate.

The social distinctiveness of the Alliance vote can also be tested separately against support for the Conservative and Labour parties.

FIGURE 5.2

Multiplicity of influences upon the Alliance vs. Conservative vote

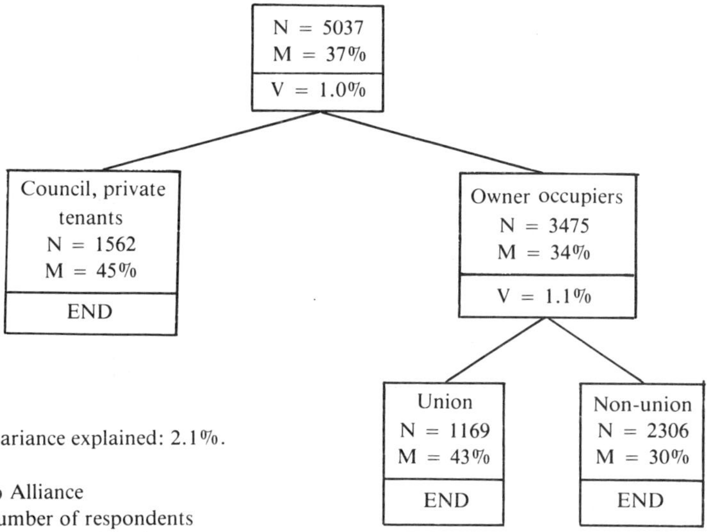

Total variance explained: 2.1%.

M = % Alliance
N = Number of respondents
V = Variance explained

Source: 1983 Gallup Campaign Study.

FIGURE 5.3
Multiplicity of influences upon the Alliance vs. Labour vote

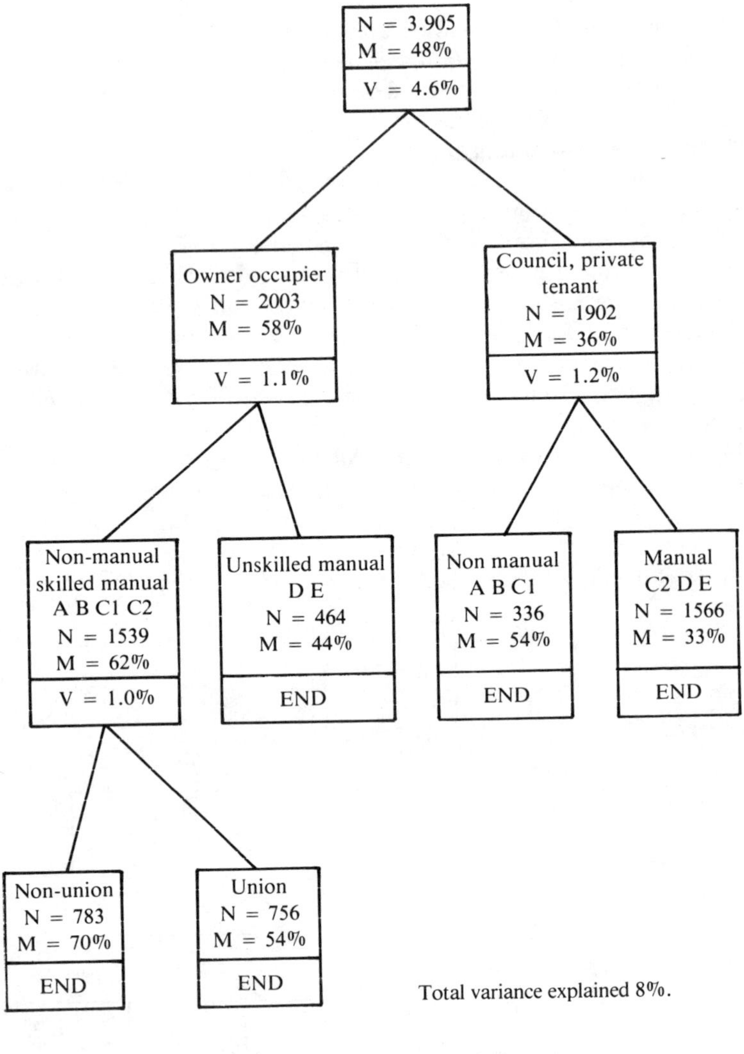

M = % Alliance
N = Number of respondents
V = Variance explained

Source: 1983 Gallup Campaign Study.

When the Alliance is compared with the Conservative vote, no social difference is of any substantial importance; only 2.1 per cent of the total variance is explained (Figure 5.2). The initial division is between owner-occupiers and tenants; both groups remain predominantly Conservative. The secondary influence, union membership, divides home-owners. The most pro-Alliance group consists of tenants (45 per cent Alliance as against 55 per cent Conservative) and the least of non-union owner-occupiers (30 per cent Alliance), a difference of only 15 per cent between them.

A comparison of Alliance and Labour voters shows somewhat more differentiation of supporters, albeit the 8.0 per cent of variance explained is less than half that between Labour and Conservative voters (Figure 5.3). The most important difference in this half of the electorate is between owner-occupiers (58 per cent Alliance) and tenants (36 per cent Alliance). Subsequent branches in the tree reflect occupational and trade union influences. The two most distinctive voting groups are non-union home-owners in middle-class occupations (70 per cent Alliance as against 30 per cent Labour), and working class tenants (33 per cent Alliance).

Within a segment of the electorate — working-class council house tenants — Labour can win two-thirds of the vote in competition with the Conservatives and the Alliance. But this is not an electoral advantage, for this group constitutes only one-fifth of the electorate. Labour's opponents are satisfied to draw most of their votes by appealing to social groups that constitute a substantial majority of the electorate today.

Comparing social influences

Comparison is a powerful means of evaluating the extent to which an electorate is open, closed, or changing. If the electorate is changing, then comparing the influence of social structure upon voting in elections since 1959 should show the direction of a trend. Comparing changes in the relative importance of different social influences, such as occupation and housing, can show to what extent the determinants of the vote today differ from a generation ago. Comparing the electoral influence of social structure in Britain with other Western nations can demonstrate whether, by international standards, British voters are closed or open.

If social structure is a constant influence upon voting, then the proportion of the Conservative and Labour vote explained by tree analysis should remain virtually the same at each election since measurement commenced in 1959. If social changes encouraged the creation of a new anti-class or extra-class bloc, a rise in voting for third-force parties would cause the proportion of the total vote explained to fall. But the variance explained in votes for the two class parties could remain the same or even increase, as each became purer with class-typical voters remaining within a closed world of highly determined Conservative and Labour supporters.

A second possibility is that the relationship between social structure and party preference is changing. Attempts to re-define class in terms of exercising authority at work or consumption cleavages suggest that occupation, accepted in Britain (but not in the United States) as the primary social influence, is not the sole determinant of political behaviour. Even if the total variation explained remained constant, the determinants could alter from more or less fixed occupational classes to groups defined by union membership, housing or motor cars.

A third alternative is that the influence of social structure upon voting for the traditional closed-class parties is declining in the electorate. This theory, not inconsistent with electoral competition being closed in the past, emphasizes that today the electorate is increasingly open.

Since 1959 voting has been less and less determined by social structure (Table 5.1). In 1959, 21.0 per cent of the Conservative and Labour vote could be explained by the influences examined here; this was nearly one-fifth of the total vote. A quarter of a century ago the chief influence on voting was occupation: middle class voters were 84 per cent Conservative, and working-class voters were 60 per cent Labour (Rose, 1980: 59). The strength of class determination is particularly striking, for the 1950s was meant to be an era of Butskellite consensus in which centrist politicians such as R.A. Butler and Hugh Gaitskell avoided stressing class appeals. Moreover, interpretations of British politics often allege that class conflict is increasing in the 1980s (e.g. Middlemas, 1979; Dunleavy and Husbands, 1985).

The influence of social structure upon the vote continued in the 1960s, even though Harold Wilson's rhetoric emphasized the national (that is, open) appeal of the Labour Party. In 1966, the year of a Labour landslide victory, nearly one-fifth of the variance was explained by social structure, and occupational class remained of greatest importance. Two-thirds of manual workers voted Labour, and two-thirds of the middle-class voted Conservative. Variations between home-owners and council tenants replaced trade union membership in the working-class electorate as of secondary importance, reflecting the cumulative effect of postwar changes in housing. In the 1960s, a big Labour vote was consistent with a substantial amount of structural determination of the vote.

The break in the social determination of the vote was first registered in 1970, and confirmed subsequently at later elections in the decade. The proportion of the Conservative-Labour variance explained fell to 13.8 per cent, and the proportion of the total vote explained fell to 12.3 per cent, one-third less than in 1959. Moreover, housing now became of principal importance; 61 per cent of tenants voted Labour, and 65 per cent of owner-occupiers Conservative. Occupation was relegated to second place in importance. The two elections of 1974 led to an increase in the social determination of Conservative and Labour vote, reflecting a purification of their support by the rise in votes for the third-force Liberals. But by October 1974, Conservative and Labour support was no longer on a traditional occupational basis; housing was of much greater importance. In 1979 the decline in determination by social structure continued, accounting for only 12.1 per cent of the established parties' vote, and less than one-tenth of the total vote. The importance of housing was confirmed, and occupational class was of virtually no account (Rose, 1980: 62-65).

TABLE 5.1
The declining influence of social structure upon voting 1959–83

Election	Variance explained as % of	
	Con./Lab. vote	Total[a] vote
1959	21.0	19.6
1964	19.6	17.2
1966	19.2	17.3
1970	13.8	12.3
1974 Feb.	17.6	13.2
1974 Oct.	18.9	14.2
1979	12.1	9.8
1983	16.4	11.5

Source: Rose, 1980: Table 17 and Figure VI.1; analysis of Gallup Campaign Studies.
[a]Variance explained multiplied by the Conservative plus Labour share of the total United Kingdom vote.

Comparing the influence of social structure in 1983 with past elections shows a definite decline in the social determination of the vote. The proportion of the vote explained was at its height in 1959. By 1983 the variance explained in the Conservative-Labour vote dropped by more than one-fifth, and in voting for all parties by more than two-fifths. The evidence is particularly strong, since it is based upon elections in which the Conservatives did well. Labour did well, and in which the two parties were evenly matched.

Comparing voting in 1983 with the 1970s emphasizes a second major development, the effect of support for a party whose vote is not determined by social structure, the Liberals and Alliance. Whereas in

1970 the Conservative-Labour share of the vote was less influenced by social structure than in 1983, the overall level of determination was higher, since the third-force parties took only one-third of the vote that they won in 1983. In the two 1974 elections, when the Liberal vote was high, the determination of the two-party vote rose as it became smaller; this also occurred with the surge in votes for the third-force Alliance in 1983.

Since non-economic influences are consistently unimportant in Britain, economic dimensions of social structure appear important by default. The tree analyses in the past eight elections of the influence upon voting of age, gender, religion, education and nation find each of nil or very slight importance (Table 5.2). Economic differences, strong or weak, are the only aspects of social structure that have a noteworthy influence upon British voters. Of all the variance explained by tree analyses, occupation accounts for two-fifths, housing for one-third, and trade union membership for a fifth. Together, these three influences explain more than nine-tenths of the variation in voting attributable to social structure, and in 1983 explain all the variance.

TABLE 5.2
The influence of social structure upon party choice: an AID trend analysis, 1959–83

Election	Occup. class	Housing	Union	Tele-phone	Educ.	Reli-gion	Gender	Age	Total
		(% variance explained, Con. and Lab. vote)							
1959	15.0	–	3.7	1.2	0.6	–	0.5	–	21.0
1964	13.5	–	3.8	1.1	0.5	0.6	–	–	19.6
1966	9.7	5.8	3.1	–	0.5	–	–	–	19.2
1970	4.1	7.1	2.1	–	–	–	–	0.5	13.8
1974 Feb.	9.6	3.1	4.1	0.8	–	–	–	–	17.6
1974 Oct.	3.1	11.9	3.9	–	–	–	–	–	18.9
1979	0.7	8.4	2.5	–	–	0.5	–	–	12.1
1983	2.9	10.4	3.1	–	–	–	–	–	16.4

Source: Rose, 1980: Table 17 and Figure VI.1; analysis of Gallup Campaign Studies.

The decline in the electoral influence of social structure has been accompanied by a major shift in the importance of particular influences. Between 1959 and 1983 the influence of occupational class has dropped from explaining 15.0 per cent to 2.9 per cent of the variance in the vote. The influence of union membership has remained virtually constant, explaining from two to four per cent of the variance. Concurrently, housing has moved from being of no importance in 1959 to being of similar importance with occupation and union membership from 1966 to February 1974, and of primary importance since October 1974 (Table 5.2).

Generalizations about the influence of class upon voting should not be confused with statements about the influence of all dimensions of social structure. The same period that has seen occupational class decline as a major determinant of voting has seen the importance of housing increase. In 1983 housing was a more important influence upon voting than occupational class had been at any British general election since 1966.

Since class is meant to be of pervasive importance in Western industrial nations, international comparison is appropriate to measure the relative importance of social structure in Britain, for class is not a uniquely English phenomenon like public schools. Studies confined to comparisons within the English-speaking world — the United States, Canada, Australia, and Ireland, (see Alford, 1963; Robertson, 1984) — conclude that British voting is relatively determined by class. However, since class is not a characteristic confined to English-speaking countries, comparison should be made with the majority of advanced industrial societies.

When social structure influences are examined in Scandinavia and Continental Europe, the British electorate appears open rather than closed. In a comparative analysis of the social structure of the vote in 15 different Western nations, Britain ranked thirteenth in the proportion of total variance explained by social structure (Rose, 1974b: 15). First came the Netherlands, where more than half the total variation could be explained, and religion has been the chief influence. Religion explained a larger share of the vote in Austria, Belgium, France and Italy than all social structure characteristics could do in Britain. Occupation explained as much as 32 per cent of the vote in Sweden, as against 4.1 per cent of the vote in Britain in 1970, placing Britain ninth in the importance (or relative unimportance) of occupation as a determinant of voting.

The weakness of occupational class in Britain is particularly significant, inasmuch as the evidence comes from voting patterns in the late 1960s, when class was still assumed to be a strong influence upon British voting. In most Western nations the influence of social structure upon voting has tended to decline since (see for example, Dalton, Flanagan and Beck, 1984). Britain has had a head start, for the influence of class was already low.

The socio-economic interests that count

In the 1980s the British electorate is not so much unstructured as it is differently structured than before. The challenge to parties and to psephologists is to identify the groups that count most in determining the outcome of elections.

The political significance of social groups is not measured in the same way as statistical significance. In electoral competition two kinds of groups are important, each very different in character. Groups that are absolutely strong in support for one party give it a core base of support. However, since this support is not enough to win an election, a party must also win votes from social groups that are more or less evenly divided electorally. An even division of votes within a group indicates opposing pressures, for example, trade union membership encouraging a Labour vote, home-ownership encouraging a Conservative vote, and the joint effect encouraging an Alliance vote. Electoral victory is won by a combination of three strategies: mobilizing a maximum of support among core groups; doing better than breaking even among evenly divided groups; and/or increasing support within an opponent's core group.

The size of a group is as important as its partisan cohesiveness. For example, a party is competitively better off mobilizing the votes of home-owners, more than half the electorate, than council tenants, a quarter of the electorate. The stability of a group's voting pattern is also important. A core group should favour the same party at election after election, whereas a group subject to conflicting pressures has more voters ready to float between parties.

Tree analysis effectively restructures the contemporary British electorate because it identifies, from among dozens of potentially salient categories of voters, the groups whose votes are most and least determined. It produces more than a simple division by a single social characteristic, while avoiding the proliferation of small groups lacking in electoral significance. For example, subdividing the electorate by all nine of the social structure characteristics initially examined in the AID analysis would fragment the electorate into 512 categories.

TABLE 5.3
Party preferences of the socio-economic interests that count

Total %		Con.	All'ce (% of group)	Lab.
40	Owner-occupiers, non-union	62	24	13
27	Owner-occupiers, union	40	32	28
16	Transitional tenants	39	24	34
17	Council tenants, working class	19	18	61

Source: British Election Study, 1983.

The social structure of the British electorate today can, for purposes of electoral competition, be divided into four groups according to their socio-economic interests. The first distinction of importance is between owner-occupiers and tenants. Housing has been the primary electoral determinant since October 1974, and a significant influence even longer. Further divisions are not symmetrical. Owner-occupiers can be divided by whether or not they are members of a trade union, but tenants by whether they are working class or middle class. The four groups are distinctive electorally, and in the mix of socio-economic interests that each represents (Table 5.3).

Owner-occupiers, non-union (40 per cent of the electorate)
The most politically homogeneous group consists of a mixture of middle-class (57 per cent) and working-class electors (43 per cent). The two social characteristics they share in common, being home-owners and not belonging to a trade union, operate instead of occupational class; among manual workers, they operate against class. Within this group, 62 per cent voted Conservative in 1983, and only 13 per cent Labour. The Alliance took its average share of the vote.

Council tenants in the working class (17 per cent)
This group is as strongly Labour (61 per cent) as the preceding group is pro-Conservative. The big difference is that the core social group supporting Labour is less than half the size of the core group supporting the Conservatives. The votes of working-class council tenants are not particularly influenced by union membership: those who belong to trade unions are 67 per cent Labour, only 10 per cent more than those who are not members.

Owner-occupiers in trade unions (27 per cent)
This group receives conflicting cues about voting, for home-owning has favoured the Conservatives and union membership has favoured Labour. Conflicting cues can lead a voter to resolve the pressures by voting Alliance as a compromise; the Alliance share of this group's vote, 32 per cent, is higher than its national total. The Conservative share is lower at 40 per cent, and Labour is at its national figure, 28 per cent. Occupational class does nothing to resolve conflicts. The crucial characteristic of this group is a tendency to divide like the electorate as a whole.

Transitional tenants (16 per cent)
In contemporary Britain voters can be described as in transition if they have not achieved home-ownership or, in the working-class, the secure tenure of a council-house. The transitional status of this group is

indicated by its relative youth; one in five is under the age of 25. There is always a small fraction of the electorate — students, geographically mobile workers and so forth — who are temporarily renting accommodation. Middle-class private tenants usually want to own their own home in future, and middle-class council tenants may buy their council tenancy or move to an owner-occupier estate. Working-class tenants of private landlords can aspire to a council tenancy, or to buying a house. The sixth of the electorate in transition are heterogeneous in social terms, and their votes are distributed between parties as in the electorate as a whole.

The influence of socio-economic interests is stable; it is not a unique product of the 1983 election (Table 5.4). Whatever the Conservative, Labour or Liberal/Alliance level of the vote, since 1964 more than three-fifths of owner-occupiers who are not in trade unions vote Conservative, and more than three-fifths of working-class council tenants vote Labour. Equally important, the two groups with conflicting cues — owner-occupiers in trade unions, and tenants in transition — have not given as much as half their vote to any one party since 1970, when a majority of home-owning union members voted Labour.

The dynamics of change in social structure have been helpful to the Conservatives, increasing the size of their core group, non-union members who are owner-occupiers, from 34 per cent in 1964 to 40 per cent in 1983. The core Labour group, manual workers in council houses, has declined in size since 1964 from 22 per cent of the electorate to 17 per cent. House-building in the 1950s and 1960s greatly reduced the demand for council housing from private tenants, and the return of a Conservative government in 1979 has further dampened new housing construction by local councils as well as promoting the sale of council houses (McAllister, 1984; Rollett, 1972). In social terms, the electorate is much more polarized between owner-occupiers and council tenants than was the case twenty years ago — and Labour has the shorter end of the pole. The other group to increase in size since 1964, home-owning trade unionists, is subject to conflicting electoral pressures. Hence, its doubling in size has not been an advantage to Labour.

Whereas the influence of class has been declining in the past two decades, socio-economic interests have become more associated with party loyalties. The Standardized Index of Determination for the Butler-Stokes class schema was 25 per cent in 1964; by 1983 it had fallen to 18 per cent (cf. Table 3.11). By contrast, the Standardized Index for socio-economic interests increased from 19 per cent in 1964 to 22 per cent in 1983 (Table 5.5).

A very high Index of Determination would imply no electoral

TABLE 5.4
Party preferences of end groups, 1964–83

Total %		Con.	Lib. (% of group)	Lab.
	1964			
34	Owner-occupier, non-union	64	14	22
13	Owner-occupier, union	35	14	51
31	Transitional tenant	38	9	52
22	Council tenant, manual	19	6	75
	1966			
23	Owner-occupier, non-union	59	11	29
9	Owner-occupier, union	33	11	56
51	Transitional tenant	38	8	55
16	Council tenant, manual	17	5	77
	1970			
37	Owner-occupier, non-union	61	8	28
15	Owner-occupier, union	34	7	57
27	Transitional tenant	45	7	47
21	Council tenant, manual	27	7	62
	1974 Feb.			
34	Owner-occupier, non-union	60	19	20
19	Owner-occupier, union	31	25	43
25	Transitional tenant	33	20	45
22	Council tenant, manual	15	14	67
	1974 Oct.			
34	Owner-occupier, non-union	60	21	18
21	Owner-occupier, union	29	24	45
24	Transitional tenant	35	20	42
22	Council tenant, manual	14	13	69
	1979			
31	Owner-occupier, non-union	69	13	16
27	Owner-occupier, union	42	18	38
19	Transitional tenant	43	12	44
23	Council tenant, manual	26	12	60
	1983			
40	Owner-occupier, non-union	62	24	13
27	Owner-occupier, union	40	32	28
16	Transitional tenant	39	24	34
17	Council tenant, manual	19	18	61

Sources: British Election Studies, 1964–83.

competition, that voting was entirely pre-determined, which is clearly not the case in Britain in the 1980s. But a trivial Index of Determination would imply that the whole of the electorate was open to vote for any party that seized the fancy of individuals for the moment, which is inconsistent with a core of stable support for established parties.

TABLE 5.5

Stability of influence of the socio-economic interests that count, 1964–83

Election	Fits Standard Index	Of which Own.-occup. non-un.	Own.-occup. union	Trans. ten.	Coun. w.c.	Does not fit
1964	19	21	2	3	16	57
1970	13	23	1	2	13	62
1974 Feb.	21	21	5	5	15	55
1974 Oct.	21	20	5	5	15	55
1979	18	21	5	2	14	58
1983	22	25	8	4	11	52

Source: British Election Studies, 1964–83, omitting 1966, for which appropriate housing and union membership data are not available. Classification as in Table 5.3.

The restructured view of socio-economic interests simultaneously identifies groups that are relatively closed, having their vote determined by their place in a multi-dimensional social structure, and groups that are open, because their social location subjects them to conflicting electoral pressures(Table 5.5). The two closed groups — owner-occupiers who are not union members and working class council tenants — constitute 57 per cent of the total electorate. This is enough to assure the Conservative and Labour parties a core of support. Electoral victory depends upon a party doing relatively well among the two competitive groups — owner-occupiers who belong to trade unions, and tenants in transition — constituting 43 per cent of the electorate.[4]

TABLE 5.6

Socio-economic interests and the vote

Total %		Con.	All'ce (% all votes)	Lab.
40	Owner-occupiers, non-union	**25** *	9	5
27	Owner-occupiers, union	11	**8** *	7
16	Transitional tenants	6	**4** *	5
17	Council tenants, working-class	3	3	**11** *

Index of Determination, 48 percent; Standardized 22 percent.

Source: British Election Study, 1983.

The restructured electorate is understandable in both economic and political terms. In political terms, the British electorate is divided into two housing groups, owner-occupiers and council tenants. The Conservative and Labour parties have each become identified with one housing bloc, owner-occupiers or council house tenants. Trade union involvement in politics has been emphasized by the Labour Party, whereas the Conservatives have argued for the separation of union activities from party politics. Because two dimensions of social structure are each important as electoral influences, it necessarily follows that there will be a bloc of voters who are caught in the middle by conflicting pressures.

The restructured electorate is understandable in social terms, for it captures important post-war changes in the structure of British society. The ideal-type manual worker, who left school at the minimum age, thought of himself or herself as working class, belonged to a trade union, and was a tenant, is a small minority of the working class today (Rose, 1980: Table 14). The ideal-type middle-class person, who has some further education, owns a home, thinks of himself or herself as middle class, and would not belong to a trade union, is also very much in a minority. More than five-sixths of the British electorate today is "mixed" in social position, having some stereotype working-class and stereotype middle-class characteristics.

What kind of theory explains the structure of the contemporary British electorate? The short answer is: a theory of socio-economic interests. The term interests emphasizes that the influences most important in the British electorate today are material, concerning housing, trade union membership and occupation. The interests are social as well as economic, for occupational strata, housing, and to some extent trade union membership have social as well as economic significance. The role of socio-economic interests in Britain contrasts with the importance of cultural interests in Northern Ireland, where religion and national identity are primary.

Ironically, as the British electorate has had its vote less determined by occupational class, voters have become more concerned with socio-economic interests. Whereas a generation or more ago, matters of peace and war and national defence could divide the electorate independently of socio-economic concerns, today these issues are of little importance compared with such economic concerns as the standard of living, unemployment, and inflation.

Home-owners see the effects of economic changes in rising or falling interest rates, and rate increases. A slowing down in economic growth limits increases in real wages, which can also be eroded by inflation. The prospect of unemployment concerns workers who may find that conventional union action does not stop redundancies.

Council house tenants may be squeezed by increases in rents prompted by government legislation, and those out of work are sensitive to a reduction in income-maintenance grants from the welfare state. The British electorate today can be just as materialist as a generation ago. But material interests are not aligned strictly according to occupational class — nor are they necessarily aligned with traditional distinctions of Conservatives versus Labour.

The political implications of socio-economic interests are open to change, whereas classic Marxist class distinctions are relatively stable. Voters who are sensitive to interest rates, unemployment rates or inflation rates have an incentive to be mobile as the economy changes. In fluctuating economic conditions, a Conservative government can push the cost of housing up by high interest rates, and Labour can become unpopular by siding with the interests of trade union elites against the inclinations of many ordinary members. When the performance of the British economy is unstable and often unsatisfactory, voters are encouraged to make the most of open electoral competition between a multiplicity of parties.

Notes

1. Given that tree analysis works by repeatedly subdividing the electorate, it is desirable to conduct analysis with a large number of respondents. Hence, the very large 1983 Gallup Campaign Study is here employed. The Gallup Poll is unusually consistent in phrasing and classifying responses to questions. Exceptionally, in 1983 religion was not included in the questionnaire; its omission is of no consequence given its very slight influence at previous elections (cf. Table 5.2).

2. Multi-collinearity is not a serious problem here, since correlations between the nine socio-economic variables are always well below the figure of 0.6 or 0.7 which Hanushek and Jackson (1977: 86-96) regard as evidence of multi-collinearity. The very low level normally registered emphasizes the independence of different socio-economic characteristics from each other. For example, the zero-order correlation between occupation and housing is .24 (see Appendix C).

3. The variance explained for Conservative vs. all other parties is 8.9 per cent, and for Labour vs. all other parties, 11.0 per cent.

4. The structural significance of these groups has altered through time. In 1964 most tenants were not transitional in the sense that they are today; manual workers had usually been private tenants for all their lives, and a majority were Labour voters. By 1983 the significance of being a tenant had changed, and the size of the group had fallen from 31 per cent to 16 per cent.

6
Discontinuity in political socialization

Theories of political socialization explain voting as the result of learning from childhood on. On election day a voter is at the exit point of a 'funnel of causality' (Campbell et al., 1960: 24), which concentrates a variety of experiences from childhood onwards upon the momentary act of voting. From this perspective, an individual does not decide how to vote, but rather learns a party identification long before becoming old enough to vote. What is learned in youth then provides a cue about how to vote as an adult (Jennings and Niemi, 1968, 1978).

Socialization theories can incorporate the influence of class as well as a host of other social structure characteristics affecting social learning. The primary influence is parental class rather than an individual's current occupation. This is consistent with the emphasis of British sociologists upon the influence of class persisting from generation to generation, usually in default of social mobility (for example, Glass, 1954; Goldthorpe, 1980). The crucial influence of class is expected to be exercised before a person is old enough to cast a ballot. Within the home a child learns a particular party identification from parents as an incidental feature of growing up in a particular class milieu. Party identification is only an intervening variable, representing the means by which political instruction is transmitted from parents to children.

The political socialization model suits the closed-class model of electoral competition. Attention is focused upon whether or not a voter grew up in a working-class or a middle-class home, and was socialized into a Conservative or Labour Party identity. The model postulates continuity in voting, as successive generations are socialized to vote like their parents. At the aggregate level, the replacement of individuals in the electorate through the inevitable processes of birth and death allows for very gradual changes in the division of the vote. Using this theory, Butler and Stokes (1969: 269) calculated class-specific birth and death rates for voters from Conservative and Labour homes in order to project swings to Labour up to the year 2015.

Since 1974 electoral competition has shown discontinuity. The problems of the Labour Party have more than offset the minor advantages that Labour might enjoy from generational changes within the electorate. The ability of the Alliance, with no claim to votes through intergenerational socialization, to poll almost as many votes as Labour in 1983 raises fundamental questions about the applicability of political socialization theories. One possibility is that the influence of intergenerational socialization was over-emphasized in previous research. A second possibility is that socialization patterns of two decades ago have been disrupted; voters today no longer act as they learned (or were taught) to think in the past, instead being far more open to current influences. This chapter first examines the influence of intergenerational socialization through parental class and party, and then looks at its cumulative effect — or lack of effect.

A little learning in the home

The irony of political socialization theories is that while in principle they are about how people learn, in practice they emphasize how little learning goes on within the adult electorate. Political socialization studies emphasize the primacy of early learning within the family. What is learned at home is regarded as primary in impact as well as first in point of time. This is considered true not only of emotional attachments within the family, but also of political attachments to the family's class and party.

What is learned within the family is deemed to last through a lifetime. Durability is particularly important insofar as early learning provides inoculation against political influences in adult life. An individual who has grown up in a working-class Labour home is not expected to vote Conservative because of taking on a middle-class job, just as a middle class person from a Conservative home will not vote Labour after becoming a member of a trade union. Primary loyalties, summed up by the term party identification, provide a mechanism for selectively perceiving political messages that reinforce the party loyalty learned within the family. What is learned in early life is expected to be reinforced rather than undermined by adult learning.

Parental class

Traditional theories of class are consistent with intergenerational political socialization theories, for parental class can be the primary determinant of what a child learns in the home. Moreover, parental class influences the occupational class that people achieve as adults. Even though a market is in continuous flux, implying the potential for changes in occupational status within a working lifetime, theorists of class such as Marx and Weber presumed the fixity of class. Weber defined class as an expression of life chances, and referred to those without the advantage of being born high in the class hierarchy as 'outcasts', a phrase redolent of intergenerational determinism (Weber,

1947: 425; Gerth and Mills, 1948: 181). An individual's position on one or the other side of the manual/non-manual divide is assumed to remain the same from generation to generation.

In examining the importance of parental class as an influence upon party preference, it is important to look at evidence from the 1964 general election, the focus of the Butler and Stokes analysis of socialization, and the 1983 election. Applying the same methods to both elections can test the extent to which there has been a substantial shift in the extent of intergenerational determination of voting.

Parental class did influence adult voting in 1964, but this closed-class influence has greatly declined by 1983. In 1964, three-fifths of those who had middle-class fathers voted Conservative, and almost three-fifths with working-class fathers voted Labour. This produced a Standardized Index of Determination of 22 per cent, similar to that for the determination of the vote by the respondent's own occupational class (cf. Table 6.1 and 3.11).

TABLE 6.1
Parental class and voting, 1964 and 1983

Total %		Con.	Lib./All'ce (% votes)	Lab.
	1964			
29	Father non-manual	**17***	6	7
5	Not known, unclassifiable	3	**0.5***	2
66	Father manual	22	6	**38***
	Index of Determination, 56 percent; Standardized, 22 percent.			
	1983			
28	Father non-manual	**15***	7	4
14	Not known, unclassifiable	6	**3***	5
58	Father manual	23	14	**20***
	Index of Determination, 38 percent; Standardized, 9 percent.			

Source: British Election Studies, 1964 and 1983.

By 1983 the link between parental class and adult voting was much looser. More persons with a working-class father voted Conservative than Labour, and among those with a middle-class father the proportion of Conservative voters fell too. The Standardized Index of Determination dropped to 9 per cent, half that for the respondent's own occupational class. The decline in the intergenerational influence of class shows the limits of a deterministic father's-class-equals-party model. One reason for this is that older as well as younger adults are shifting party preferences (Table 4.4).

Party identification

In theories of political socialization, party identification is the intervening mechanism that accounts for the persistence of parental influence throughout an adult's life. While children cannot be prepared for political events that will happen in future decades, by identifying with their parent's political party children acquire a means of evaluating future events: follow the party line. Just as national identity gives people a means of making judgements about foreigners in many different settings, so party identification is expected to lead to consistent judgements about parties in election after election. Insofar as parents transmit their party identification to their offspring, then party loyalties are, as it were, "delivered by the stork".

The extent to which the intergenerational transmission of party identification can be important depends upon two crucial assumptions. The first is that everyone learns what their parent's party is. Politics must be discussed often enough in the home to convey this information, and enough significance must be given to the subject for an impression to be left on a youth's memory. Furthermore, the cues from mother and father should be the same: to learn conflicting identifications from parents creates conflict. In 1964, however, 46 per cent did not receive an indication of partisanship from both their parents, or received conflicting cues from their father and mother (Table 6.2).

A second important assumption is that the competing parties remain the same from election to election. When Butler and Stokes wrote, the collapse of the Liberal Party meant that voters socialized in an era when the Liberals were one of the two major parties often had no Liberal candidate for whom to vote. Hence, in 1964 only one-quarter of voters from Liberal homes voted Liberal.

In 1964, 49 per cent of the electorate voted in accord with the party of their parents (Table 6.2). The Standardized Index of Determination was 28 per cent, higher than that for parental class. However, this figure exaggerates the relationship, since there is a tendency for people to align recalled party preferences with their current vote (Himmelweit et al., 1978; Katz et al., 1980). Given that party identification ought to be closely related to party preference, even to the point of being simply another name for a single phenomenon (see Budge et al., 1976), it is striking that parental party identification is *not* more strongly associated with voting. Half the electorate did not or could not vote as their parents did.

By 1983 the proportion of voters who reported knowing the party of both their parents had risen from 54 to 70 per cent; only 11 per cent said they didn't know the party of either parent. This is consistent with the full electoral mobilization of the adult population after 1918. The proportion of voters socialized with Liberal support had declined, as fewer voters had been raised in an era when the Liberal Party of Asquith and Lloyd George was a major party. The conditions for closed-class voting from generation to generation were thus more favourable than two decades earlier.

TABLE 6.2
Parents' party identification and voting, 1964 and 1983

Total %		Con.	Lib./All'ce (% votes)	Lab.
	1964			
(54)	Both parents			
24	Conservative	**18***	2	4
8	Liberal	3	**2***	3
23	Labour	3	2	**19***
(20)	One parent unknown, other			
8	Conservative	**5***	0.4	2
4	Liberal	2	**1***	1
8	Labour	2	1	**6***
(9)	Parents disagree	4	1	4
(17)	Neither parent's choice known	7	2	8
	Index of Determination, 49 percent; Standardized, 28 percent.			
	1983			
(70)	Both parents			
23	Conservative	**17***	4	2
6	Liberal	3	**2***	1
41	Labour	12	10	**19***
(10)	One parent unknown, other			
4	Conservative	**3***	1	0.5
2	Liberal	1	**0.3***	0.2
4	Labour	1	1	**2***
(9)	Parents disagree	4	3	2
(11)	Neither parent's choice known	5	3	2
	Index of Determination, 42 percent; Standardized, 19 percent.			

Sources: British Election Studies, 1964 and 1983, based on recalled parental party.

However, only 42 per cent of the electorate voted for the party of their parents in 1983. As Butler and Stokes had foreseen, the proportion of the electorate coming from homes where both parents were Labour had nearly doubled in the two decades. But the effect of this was offset by the fact that in 1983 *most voters who came from the homes of Labour parents did not vote Labour.* In 1964, four-fifths from homes where both parents were Labour voted Labour; in 1983 only 45 per cent did so. The proportion of voters from homes in which parents voted Conservative remained virtually the same; the proportion who themselves voted Conservative fell by three per cent, showing that the weakening of parental party is not just a function of the Labour Party's difficulties. The Standardized Index of Determination fell to 19 per cent, less than that for the electoral influence of housing.

A majority of the electorate does not vote as their parents. In 1964, 51 per cent of the electorate did not follow their parents' lead, and in 1983, 58 per cent did not do so. Among voters who do not know their parents' party preference or whose parents disagreed, the tendency is to divide like the electorate as a whole. Among those who have the same partisan cue from both parents, 30 per cent voted differently than their parents in 1964, and 47 per cent in 1983.

Examining the influence of parental party identification in 1964 and 1983 emphasizes the consistent *weakness* of theories of intergenerational party loyalties. While properly calling attention to the fact that political behaviour is influenced by factors long antedating a particular general election, the initial studies of political socialization tended to ignore the proportion of the electorate without any parental party identification. Moreover, attention was limited to those socialized into an unambiguously partisan family. Finally, not enough consideration was given to the fact that the earliest influences are also most remote in time from contemporary concerns.

Education

Given the very limited parental influence, the next hypothesis to test is whether the education that a voter receives in youth is, as it were, a 'ballot for life', to paraphrase the words of T.H. Marshall (1950: 65): 'The ticket obtained on leaving school is for a life journey'. Education is a crucial determinant of adult occupational status. The 1944 Education Act sought to make it easier for children from working-class families to attend grammar school and university, but retained a stratified system of education. The Labour government's promotion of comprehensive schools in 1965 was intended to provide education in a common secondary school, but not to make educational achievement uniform. Since education is a bridge between the home and the adult world, it could influence voting more than parental class. Insofar as education provides a qualification for adult employment, it anticipates a person's adult class.[1] Insofar as youthful education reflects the influence of the home, then academically successful young people may be from homes more oriented toward middle-class than working-class values. Education also reflects an individual's own aspirations.

Three levels of education have been of continuing importance, notwithstanding changes in education during the lifetime of the present electorate. A minimum education is that required by law; until 1944 this was education up to age 14, and until 1972 up to age 15; school-leaving age since then has been raised to age 16. The majority of the electorate receives only a minimum education. Their votes would be expected to favour the Labour Party, as a minimum education is likely to lead to a manual job and a below-average income. An intermediate level of education is achieved by staying at secondary school past the minimum school-leaving age, providing qualifications for entry to a more or less routine middle-class job. Hence, this group might be expected to favour the Alliance, as the party for those in the middle. Further education, achieved by about one-tenth of the electorate, involves study at university, a polytechnic, a teacher training college, or other institution providing professional qualifications or education to degree level. Recipients of an education providing entry to the highest status occupations would be expected to favour the Conservatives.

TABLE 6.3
Education and voting, 1964 and 1983

Total %		Con.	Lib./All'ce (% votes)	Lab.
	1964			
5	Further	**3***	1	1
15	Intermediate	9	**2***	4
80	Minimum	29	8	**42***
Index of Determination, 47 percent; Standardized, 12 percent.				
	1983			
11	Further	**5***	4	2
31	Intermediate	17	**8***	6
59	Minimum	24	13	**21***
Index of Determination, 34 percent; Standardized, 6 percent.				

Source: British Election Studies, 1964 and 1983.
1964: Minimum: left school at 14 or before, or if born 1931 or later, at 15. Further: beyond age 18. 1983: Minimum: left school at 16 if born 1956, or after; otherwise as for 1964. Further: beyond age 18.

The extent to which education determines the vote, as the 'ticket for life' theory suggests, is limited and declining. In 1964, when four-fifths of the electorate had only a minimum of education, nearly the whole of the Labour vote came from those with a minimum education — but so too did two-thirds of the Conservative vote. The Standardized Index of Determination was 12 per cent (Table 6.3). By 1983, the proportion receiving only a minimum education had decreased to 59 per cent. But all three parties continued to receive most of their votes from those who left school at the earliest possible opportunity. The Standardized Index of Determination was 6 per cent.

TABLE 6.4
Education and voting by class

Total %		Con.	Lib./All'ce (% within row)	Lab.
	Solid middle			
7	Further	48	39	14
13	Intermediate	57	30	13
8	Minimum	57	26	14
	Difference	9	13	0
	Lower middle			
1	Further	56	28	14
6	Intermediate	65	20	14
10	Minimum	56	23	19
	Difference	0	5	5
	Skilled manual			
1	Further	18	39	43
5	Intermediate	45	28	27
19	Minimum	35	22	42
	Difference	17	17	1
	Unskilled manual			
1	Further	39	37	21
6	Intermediate	49	22	28
22	Minimum	32	20	47
	Difference	7	17	26

Source: British Election Study, 1983.

Given that educational qualifications are an approximate rather than a certain determinant of adult occupational status, it is therefore appropriate to make a second test, comparing differently educated groups within the same occupational class. This shows that within a class the effect of education is non-linear (Table 6.4). Within a given class Conservative support is higher among those with an intermediate level of education; further education usually reduces Conservative support. Only among unskilled manual workers does Labour support decline with the rise in education. Support for the Alliance shows the only consistent relationship between education and voting. Within each class, those with further education are more likely to vote Alliance that those with a minimum of education; the average effect is 13 per cent.

Educational qualifications involving an external examination independent of school attendance can be regarded as an alternative influence upon social position and voting. When the electorate is divided into those with and those without any type of educational qualification, a majority of Conservative and Alliance voters have some qualification, and a majority of Labour voters do not. The relationship is stronger than for years of school attendance, but less than for occupation or housing (Index of Determination, 45 per cent; Standardized, 14 per cent). Among those with no qualification, the Alliance took 21 per cent of the vote; with CSE grade passes, 26 per cent; with Ordinary level, 30 per cent; Advanced level, 33 per cent; and a university degree, 38 per cent. But this does not demonstrate that more education makes people vote Alliance, for in each category the Alliance received fewer votes than the Conservative Party, the Labour Party or than both parties. The median Alliance voter, like the median Conservative had passed an Ordinary level exam; the median Labour voter had no qualification.

Social mobility

Social mobility provides an additional test of the influence of parental class upon voting. Insofar as political socialization is durable, then voters who have grown up in a working-class home should retain their parental class outlook in adulthood, even if in a middle-class job. But if adult learning is dominant, then socially mobile persons should more nearly resemble others in their present class. Social mobility has been increasing across the manual/non-manual dividing line. In 1964, 67 per cent of the electorate were in the same class as their parents; by 1983 this figure had fallen to 56 per cent. The upwardly mobile consistently outnumber the downwardly mobile by almost two to one.

Social mobility does affect an individual adult's party choices. In 1964, 70 per cent of those born in working class homes and remaining there voted Labour; among those upwardly mobile into the middle class 31 per cent voted Labour. Among those born in middle-class homes, 45 per cent favoured the Conservatives among the downwardly mobile, whereas of those remaining in the middle class 67 per cent favoured the Conservatives. The Standardized Index of Determination was 23 per cent, one per cent higher than that for parental class without controlling for the possibility of intergenerational mobility (Tables 6.1, 6.5). Social mobility showed much less an effect in 1983 than in 1964. Among those raised in working-class homes, the proportion favouring Labour fell from 42 to 18 per cent with upward mobility, and among those raised in middle-class homes the proportion favouring the Conservatives fell from 58 to 52 per cent with downward mobility. The Standardized Index for socially mobile voters fell to 8 per cent, one per cent less than that for parental class without allowance for mobility.

TABLE 6.5
Social mobility and voting, 1964 and 1983

Total %		Con.	Lib./All'ce (% votes)	Lab.
	1964			
18	Father non-manual, self non-manual	**12***	3	3
10	Father non-manual, self manual	4.5	**1***	4.5
5	Father not known	3	**0.5***	1
18	Father manual, self non-manual	10	**2***	6
49	Father manual, self manual	12	3	**33***
	Index of Determination, 50 percent; Standardized, 23 percent.			
	1983			
17	Father non-manual, self non-manual	**10***	5	2
11	Father non-manual, self manual	6	**2***	3
14	Father not known	6	**3***	5
20	Father manual, self non-manual	10	**6***	3
39	Father manual, self manual	14	8	**16***
	Index of Determinaton, 38 percent; Standardized, 8 percent.			

Source: British Election Studies, 1964 and 1983.

In aggregate, controlling for social mobility does not alter the Standardized Index of Determination for any one election. But from decade to decade social mobility can slowly alter the aggregate electorate, since upward mobility is more likely to incline a voter to support the Conservatives and reduce the size of the working class vote. The electoral effect operates at the margin of a marginal influence.

The independence of voters from parental socialization is an important pre-condition of open electoral competition. If most electors had their vote determined in childhood, this would lead to closed competition. But when most voters are open to react to adult experiences, then parties cannot rely on votes being delivered by the stork.

Even in what has been considered an era of closed electoral

competition, no party could count on as much as half its vote being delivered in the home. In 1964 half the Conservative and Labour vote and three-quarters of the Liberal vote was won by attracting electors without any parental party or a parental attachment to another party (Table 6.6). A party relying solely on the intergenerational transmission of party identification would have its vote halved. In 1983 the proportion of voters with a clear recollection of parental party was higher, but the Conservatives and Alliance won more votes in open competition than due to parental influence. Of Conservative support 56 per cent came from voters who were *not* raised in a Conservative home, as did 92 per cent of the Alliance vote.

TABLE 6.6
Intergenerational profile of party support, 1964 and 1983

	Con.		Lib./All'ce		Lab.	
	1964	1983	1964	1983	1964	1983
	(as % all voting for party)					
Both parents for party	42	37	15	7	40	66
One parent for party	11	7	7	1	12	7
Following parents	53	44	22	8	52	73
Parents disagree	8	8	13	12	8	7
Parents favour other party	23	37	42	67	23	12
Parental preferences unknown	15	11	23	12	17	8
Not following parents	47	56	78	91	48	27

Source: British Election Studies, 1964 and 1983, based on recalled parental party.

The career of the Labour Party demonstrates the importance of *not* relying upon intergenerational party loyalties. When Labour won the 1964 general election, it drew nearly half its support from voters who had not come from Labour homes. However, in 1983 the Labour Party relied much more heavily upon its cradle-to-grave supporters; 73 per cent of its vote came from those raised in Labour homes. This occurred because Labour was failing to win votes in open competition. By relying so heavily upon lifelong Labour supporters, Labour condemned itself to defeat. In contemporary Britain winning support from open voters is a necessary condition of winning a general election.

The cumulative effect

The emphasis upon youthful learning from parents is not the only model of voting that can be derived from theories of socialization. The idea that what is important is most remote in time can be rejected, and emphasis placed upon contemporary learning experiences instead. From this perspective, what is important would be the last rather than the first influences entering the funnel of causality. Adult experiences, and particularly current economic conditions, are stimuli of an immediacy and salience that can override experiences of the past. Current socialization experiences include being a council tenant or an owner-occupier, a member of a trade union, and other socio-economic interests.

Primary learning and contemporary learning can be complementary rather than mutually exclusive. What a person learns today can be in addition to what has been learned in the past or, for those with no family history of party loyalties, it can fill a void. The cumulative effect of past *and* present political socialization experiences should be much more important than either taken alone.

Tree analysis can be adapted to test the importance of both primary and contemporary social influences upon the electorate. By the use of AID-III it is possible to divide the electorate at each stage in the socialization process and calculate how much or how little influence it exerts on voting, entering influences in the sequence that they occur in a voter's life-history.[2] This version of tree analysis tests first the impact of influences that come first in time, considering the impact of generation, gender, father's class and party *before* testing the impact of contemporary influences such as occupation and housing. Since voters acquire political experiences sequentially, this model fairly matches the life histories of the electorate. The relative importance of primary and contemporary influences is shown by the amount of variance that each explains.

Insofar as political socialization cumulatively determines voting, then well over half the variance in the vote should be explained. Insofar as the electorate is moving from being closed to open, then the proportion of variance explained in 1964 should be higher than in decades since. Insofar as more than half the variance is not explained by cumulative socialization experiences, then the electorate can be described as open.

In 1964 primary pre-adult socialization explained 28.6 per cent of the variance in Conservative and Labour voting (Table 6.7). Parental class and party were the chief influences. Other potentially important conditions, such as generation, gender, religion and education were of little or no consequence. Contemporary influences explained an additional 9.6 per cent of the variance. After allowing for father's party and father's class, the one contemporary influence of substantial electoral significance was current class. Housing, nation and union membership were of little or no importance. Altogether, the cumulative socialization influences explained 38.2 per cent of total variance in the Labour and Conservative share of the vote, very high by British standards, though not by comparison with many Continental nations. Since the two parties still had a near duopoly of the vote, cumulative socialization experiences accounted for one-third of the total United Kingdom vote.

TABLE 6.7
The cumulative effect of socialization experiences, 1964, 1974 and 1983

Stage in process[a]	1964	Oct. 1974	1983
	(% variance explained)		
Primary influences			
1. Generation	0.9	0.4	0.0
2. Gender (male, female)	0.1	0.2	0.0
3. Father's class (manual, non-manual)	8.8	9.2	4.6
4. Father's party, ID (Con., Lab., other, none)	13.8	9.9	12.9
5. Religion (C of E, other, none)	1.3	2.1	1.3
6. Education (minimum, above minimum)	3.7	1.2	1.9
	(28.6)	(23.0)	(20.7)
Contemporary socio-economic interests			
7. Current class (manual, non-manual)	7.7	2.4	3.6
8. { Housing (owners, tenants)	1.2	5.5	5.2
8. { Nation (England, non-England)	0.7	0.0	1.0
8. { Union membership (yes, no)	0.0	0.8	1.7
	(9.6)	(9.7)	(11.5)
Conservative/Labour variance explained	38.2	31.7	32.2
(as % all votes)	(33.4)	(23.8)	(22.5)

Sources: AID-III analysis of 1964, 1974 and 1983 British Election Studies.
[a]The sequence in which variables were constrained to enter in the calculation of variance, except for housing, nation, and union membership, which were entered together.

By October 1974, the cumulative effect of socialization experiences had declined, explaining 31.7 per cent of the two-party vote; due to the rise of the Liberal Party, less than one-quarter of the total British vote was explained. Primary pre-adult influences remained of greater importance, but there was a decline in the influence of parental party. Among contemporary influences, current occupational class fell, and there was a substantial increase in the electoral importance of housing.

In 1983 the overall level of variance explained, 32.2 per cent, was much like that in 1974, albeit there were changes in the relative importance of specific influences.[3] Primary pre-adult influences have declined by one-quarter since 1964. Adult experiences explain a larger portion of the vote in both absolute and relative terms than in 1964. Of the current influences, housing is of greatest importance; of pre-adult influences, parent's party. Whereas father's class and current class in 1964 accounted for 16.5 per cent of variance, by 1983 they together accounted for 9.2 per cent.

Comparing the cumulative effect of socialization experiences across two decades confirms that electoral competition today is open not closed. Upwards of four-fifths of the Conservative versus Labour vote can not be explained by pre-adult primary influences (Table 6.7). While some political learning does occur in childhood, its relevance has diminished substantially not only because of social changes, but also because of political changes brought about by upheavals within the Labour Party. In 1983 those socialized to support Labour were divided into two substantial groups, lifelong Labour voters and defectors from a Labour tradition; the Labour defectors were more numerous.

The weakness of the traditional closed-class model of political socialization is just that it is traditional. It assumes that people do not think for themselves, or that learning stops as soon as a person is old enough to be independent of parents. Moreover, the model is static in its assumptions about political parties. It is assumed that the parties salient in the parents' lifetime will always be salient. This is not an assumption that any German or French person could make; throughout the Western world parties often alter their name or their appeals (Rose and Mackie, 1984), and duopolistic competition is not an accurate description of the past century of elections in Britain. The recurrence of multi-party competition in Britain demonstrates the limits of political socialization in determining the vote. The success of the Liberals and Alliance in boosting their vote, and Labour in repelling supporters, has introduced a discontinuity in the life histories of voters. In place of the dead hand of the past, contemporary circumstances gain influence.

Note

1. Status attainment models consistently emphasize the importance of education in determining occupational status (Blau and Duncan, 1967), and have conceptualized education as human capital, to be transformed into status and income (Becker, 1975).

2. The unconstrained version of AID was used in chapter 5, because of the absence of good theoretical reasons for sequencing potential influences. Given the rationale of socialization theory, AID-III is appropriate for use here.

3. Analysis of the same 1983 data by OLS regression yields a similar result, explaining 26.4 per cent of the variance, as against 32.2 per cent with AID-III. In the regression analysis father's party is substantially less important, and housing is more important. Primary influences (14.1 per cent variance explained): generation, 0; gender, 0; father's class, 4.6; father's party, 7.6; religion, 1.0; education, 0.9. Contemporary socio-economic interests (12.3 per cent): current class, 2.8; housing, 6.0; nation, 1.4; union membership, 2.1. See also Appendix C.

7
Learning through a lifetime

The influences that affect voters are multiple not singular; they cumulate through a lifetime of learning. The choice that a voter makes at a particular election does not occur in a timeless vacuum free of the influence of the family or of current socio-economic interests. Political principles developed through the years influence voting, and so too does the current performance of parties in Parliament. Just because the electoral system forces British voters to choose only one party, there is no necessity for students of voting to plump for a single influence as all-important. In a lifetime of learning, each of a sequence of influences can register a substantial impact.

To the extent that political principles and the current performance of parties are important, voting can be considered determined — but not by class. It is thus important to examine whether voters have political principles in addition to the judgements implicit in social structure and pre-adult socialization.

The good government assumption is that most voters are relatively thoughtful, actively seeking political information in order to determine how the country should be governed. The century since the introduction of mass suffrage has given politicians ample time, in the old Victorian phrase, to 'educate our masters'. If education encourages people to think independently of socio-economic interests, then an increasing proportion of the electorate should be voting on the basis of its own political principles, rather than passively reflecting views of parents or social structure. Political parties devote much effort to developing and propounding principles, in the hope that voters will cast their ballot for the party whose image is most closely associated with their own principles.

The neo-realist view of elections is that the minds of the voters are a blank. Media commentators discuss elections as if large numbers of votes were decided by a single speech or television programme, implying that voters remembered nothing from the day before, or from a lifetime of experience. Academic surveys are sometimes interpreted as supporting this view. Terms such as left and right may be said to have no meaning to most electors (cf. Butler and Stokes, 1969: 200-14), a claim challenged by other academic reasearchers (Marsh, 1977; Barnes and Kaase, 1979; Laponce, 1981; Rose, 1985b: Table 9.5). A theory of unprincipled electoral competition implies that parties will alter policies and personalities in a continuing effort to catch the votes of an electorate open to the most ephemeral and transitory of campaign influences. An electorate without an anchor in social structure and political principles would be an electorate likely to float aimlessly, responding to each passing gust of wind.

It is possible that voters do have principles, but they contradict those that parties articulate. For example, in closed-class competition, voters favouring both welfare measures and the market would be subject to conflicting pressures, since the Conservative and Labour parties each favour one principle but not both. Voters can also be under conflicting pressures if an important principle, such as traditional moral standards, is not endorsed by any party.

As well as reflecting personal judgements, political principles reflect pre-adult learning in the home and current socio-economic interests. Even if voters explain their actions by statements invoking political principles, voting can be determined by socio-economic interests or by family background. Conservative or Labour parents can inculcate partisan values in their offspring, and a voter's current socio-economic interests can lead to the endorsement of general principles. From this perspective, political principles can be considered intervening variables, which reflect in summary form more distant experiences.

Parties appeal to both interests and principles. One view of the Labour Party sees it as appealing to class interests, with manual workers voting Labour even if they think like Conservatives (see Crewe, 1982; McAllister and Mughan, 1985). Another view sees Labour as appealing to ideological principles, which creates middle-class socialists as well as manual workers voting Labour. The election of a Labour government could be interpreted as a victory for working-class interests, as a victory for socialist principles, or even as both. Similarly, the 1983 Conservative victory could be interpreted as a victory for the ideological principles of Thatcherism; for the economic interests of employed persons who expected to benefit from a Conservative government, or as the effect of a transitory event, the Falklands war, upon voters whose minds were blank. Voters who reject the socio-economic interests associated with the Conservative and Labour parties could vote Alliance as a positive way of resolving conflicts.

The first object of this chapter is to examine the extent to which the British electorate does have political principles, and to identify their salient characteristics and relevance to parties, including potential conflict between popular principles and party positions. Secondly, the chapter sets out a lifetime-learning model of voting, which systematically incorporates the influence of pre-adult socialization, socio-economic interests, political principles and current party performance.

The principles of voters

In analysing the minds of voters we should avoid setting standards too high or too low. To expect every voter to have a coherent set of values and beliefs from which political choices can be logically deduced is to ask more of the electorate than many politicians are capable of. Yet to regard the electorate as a mass audience with no political views independent of what they are told through the media is to assume that voters have no capacity to evaluate politics in the light of their own socio-economic interests and experience of parties in government.

The term political *principle* is here used to describe underlying judgements and preferences about the activities of government. Principles are general enough to be durable (for example, favouring the poor, or a strong national defence) and thus applicable in many different contexts (to public spending and taxation, or to the Falkland Islands or Russia). Just as the elements of a party image (good for the working class, stands up for the national interest) reflect durable features of parties, so political principles are lasting because they concern persisting problems of public policy. It is reasonable to think of voters using their principles to guide decisions about voting at a particular election, for principles come first in time (McAllister and Mughan, 1985).

Political principles are plural not singular; a voter holding one principle need not endorse another. Because of this, an analysis of the electorate in terms of principles differs from an analysis of ideology. An ideology consists of a number of logically consistent principles that can be related to nearly every issue facing a government. An ideology represents the ultimate in closed political thinking, for conclusions are deduced rather than tested against experience and evidence (Sartori, 1969a). In a pure model of closed electoral competition, voters would not only have their votes determined by their class, but also their political principles determined by the ideology of their class.

Political principles must be distinguished from topical issues of the moment, which are transitory by definition. The question — What should be done about the Argentine invasion of the Falkland Islands? — did not arise in 1979. A few months after Britain had successfully recaptured the Falklands, the question had become different: What should be the future role of Britain in the Falkland Islands? The problems posed by a particular strike, a particular sterling crisis or a furore about a crime or scandal are important at the moment, but lack the durability of political principles.

Political attitudes differ from principles and issues since attitudes are relatively non-specific in their relevance to government actions. For example, a list of voters' likes and dislikes about a party will catalogue many attitudes that are not on the agenda of public policy. The response of voters to questions asking for a series of adjectives to be applied to parties (for example, extreme/moderate; united/divided) or to party leaders (for example, determined, likeable or caring) may reflect something about the feelings of voters towards political objects. But the expression of such attitudes and feelings is not the same as the choice of party. Only if the electorate is moved by appeals to emotions rather than actions will such attitudes influence voting.

Concentrating attention upon political principles is a public policy approach, albeit not as that term is applied in government. A government must have detailed programmes to deal with hundreds of different policy matters: a listing of public expenditure identifies 200 separate programmes. A voter does not need detailed knowledge of public programmes; it is sufficient to have some principles general enough to be relevant to dozens of programmes or issues arising in the course of a Parliament. A few principles about economic priorities, social programmes, dealings with foreign countries, and morality can enable a voter to decide what a government *ought* to do, and to evaluate whether its actions or what it promises to do is worth voting for.

Because political principles are durable, they can properly be considered prior influences upon the choice of the vote at a particular election. By contrast, many questions about topical issues reflect judgements made after a person decides which party to support. Demonstrating a correlation between what people think about topical issues and party choice leaves open the direction of causation. Post-election analyses of issues may show a correlation between how people voted and answers to issue questions, but post hoc explanation is not a satisfactory basis for understanding future voting.

The raw materials for identifying major political principles in the minds of the electorate are readily available — a battery of British Election Studies' questions about political phenomena. Once it is clear what one is looking for — underlying, durable political judgements held by the mass electorate — the task of excluding as well as including questions is greatly simplified. In analysing principles, questions concerning political personalities and generalized party images should be excluded, as well as questions concerning topical events. Principles are meant to have a persisting quality; so too should the questions used to measure them. Analysis here is concentrated upon those questions that could be asked at each election over a decade or more. The phrasing of policy questions is one of the more variable elements in a British Election Study questionnaire; major changes occurred when responsibility for the direction of the studies changed hands between the 1970 and 1974 elections. Hence, analysis concentrates on surveys in October 1974, 1979 and 1983, covering three consecutive elections in which the influence of social structure on voting was indeterminate, and there was multi-party competition.

Factor analysis provides an appropriate statistical method for deriving political principles from the responses of voters to a host of questions about public policies (Kim and Mueller, 1978). Factor analysis can identify what is common in a number of questions: this commonality is the underlying principle causing people to give similar responses to questions about different topics. For example, if a voter favours nationalization, trade unions, and a more equal distribution of wealth, we would consider these answers as reflecting a single underlying socialist principle, not a random association. Similarly, if a person endorses repatriating immigrants and believes that anti-discrimination laws have gone too far, this too would reflect an underlying racialist principle.

Insofar as voters make principled judgements about public policy, then a factor analysis should explain most of the variance in answers given to a variety of survey questions. Insofar as thinking is ideological, only one factor will be prominent, reducing views about many different questions to a single dimension. Insofar as thinking is principled but non-ideological, then several unrelated factors would be identified, including some inconsistent with conventional political ideologies and party images. Insofar as voters' minds are blank, then no underlying principle should appear and the proportion of variance explained would be low.

The first step in a factor analysis is to identify a variety of public policy questions suitable for testing whether and in what ways responses reflect underlying political principles. Initially, a pool of 14 different questions asked across a decade was factor analysed in order to identify opinions having a significant loading on a particular factor. In 1983 the median loading for the opinions related to a factor is .74; questions that did not correlate with others to form a common factor were excluded from analysis.[1] Moreover, the questions employed here are significant to voters; the proportion of don't knows averaged 8 per cent in 1983, and 5 per cent in 1979 and 1974.

The factor analysis consistently identifies eleven views reflecting four political principles, which together account for 58 per cent of the variance in 1974, 59 per cent in 1979, and 54 per cent in 1983. The four factors are readily related to political principles: socialism, welfare, traditional morality, and racialism.[2] Since there is a very high degree of stability in the principles elucidated, only the results of the 1983 study are discussed here. (Table 7.1; for 1974 and 1979 see Appendix D.)

TABLE 7.1
Factor loadings for political principles, 1983

	Factor loadings			
	I	II	III	IV
I Socialism				
1. Should be more nationalization	**0.71**	−0.14	−0.01	−0.01
2. Trade unions do not have too much power	**0.63**	0.02	0.15	−0.10
3. Government should redistribute wealth	**0.62**	−0.28	0.05	−0.06
4. Government should establish comprehensive schools	**0.61**	−0.12	0.12	0.01
5. Reduction of military strength not gone far enough	**0.55**	−0.04	−0.08	−0.26
II Welfare				
1. Important to reduce poverty	0.18	**0.77**	−0.02	0.06
2. Government should spend more money on the health service	0.19	**0.75**	0.02	0.02
III Traditional morality				
1. Availability of abortion on NHS gone far enough	0.04	−0.06	**0.78**	0.04
2. Nudity and sex in media gone far enough	0.07	0.05	**0.75**	−0.06
IV Racialism				
1. Racial equality gone too far	0.02	0.25	0.21	**0.75**
2. Important to repatriate immigrants	−0.17	−0.13	0.14	**0.74**
Variance explained	22.6	11.6	10.3	9.4
(Eigenvalues)	(2.5)	(1.3)	(1.1)	(1.0)

Total variance explained, 53.9 percent.

Source: British Election Study, 1983.
Varimax rotated factor loadings from a principal components factor analysis with unities in the main diagonal. No other factor had an eigenvalue greater than one. For 1974 and 1979 results see Appendix D.

Voters are not strictly materialist in their views of public affairs, nor are they detached from material interests. The principles in their minds refer to two socio-economic concerns, socialism and welfare, and two cultural concerns, traditional morality and race relations. Moreover, interests that one person may regard as materialist, such as welfare or socialism, may reflect cultural values to another. Outlooks toward race or morality may be interpreted as reflecting socio-economic interests as well as culturai views.

Socialism (Factor 1: 23 per cent of variance)
The word socialism is often invoked as a symbol rather than as a precise guide to action. A speaker at a Labour Party Conference who refers to a resolution about nationalization or redistributing wealth as consistent with socialist principles knows the term is positively valued there. Similarly, a Conservative who denounces a measure as socialist is using the word pejoratively.

In fact, there is empirical evidence of an underlying principle linking views about the nationalization of industry, comprehensive schools, trade union power, the reduction of military strength, and the redistribution of wealth. Positive answers to these questions can properly be called socialist, since the views describe a principle that is both economic and extra-economic, and which is closely identified with the Labour Party. Reciprocally, rejecting these policies expresses anti-socialism. While it is consistent with the closed-class model that socialism is the most important principle, the minds of voters remain relatively open, since socialism accounts for less than one-quarter of the variance.

Welfare (Factor II: 12 per cent)
Public provision of welfare can be regarded as a matter of both principle and socio-economic interest. The reasons given for government provision of education, health and pensions may sound altruistic, but massive popular support for these programmes also reflects the fact that nearly every family benefits substantially from state welfare (Rose, 1985b: Table 11.5). British voters view the public provision of welfare as a principle too. Views about spending on the health service, from which everyone benefits, are strongly correlated with views about the reduction of poverty, from which only a minority benefit. Equally, people who are against public action to reduce poverty, from which they do not benefit, also oppose spending more money on a health service that benefits everyone. This questions conventional theories of elections simply as a means of voters gaining material benefits for themselves. Popular principles about social welfare account for no more variance in political outlooks than do such non-economic principles as racialism and morality.

Traditional morality (Factor III: 10 per cent)
Moral principles antedate political principles in the minds of most voters; long before gaining the right to vote people are expected to

adhere to moral standards, whether laid down by law, by religion, or group norms inculcated by socialization. Today, moral standards establish how individuals expect to treat others and to be treated by others in social relations (cf. Marshall's definition of class, 1950: 92). Public policies impinge upon such moral questions as abortion on the national health service, and media depiction of nudity and sex.

Traditional moral principles are independent of such party principles as socialism and welfare. This is hardly surprising, given that parties consciously try to avoid becoming entangled in debates about moral issues, regarding them as outside their competence. Parties prefer free votes on such issues in the House of Commons (Richards, 1970). Age, not party, is of crucial importance for views about morality (Rose, 1985b: Table 12.3). The efforts of parties to keep a subject off the political agenda does not mean that it is outside the popular mind. Morality account for as much variance in popular attitudes as do questions of welfare.

Racialism (Factor IV: 9 per cent)

A generation ago questions about race relations were not asked in Britain, because Britain was virtually an all-white country. The appearance of coloured immigrants from the New Commonwealth has changed all that. It has made it politically relevant to determine whether or not British people hold racialist views, and whether these views relate to other political principles. Replies to questions about coloured immigrants and the promotion of racial equality identify a factor important in the minds of voters and independent of the principle of socialism. People who evaluate government actions according to socialist principles are as likely to hold racialist as anti-racialist principles, and racialists are as likely as anti-racialists to endorse socialist views.

The extent to which underlying principles account for voters' views rejects the proposition that the mind of the electorate is blank. If that were the case, then there would be no coherence in views, and no meaningful factors could be identified. As it is, more than half the variation in views can be accounted for by four principles. Each is clear enough to be widely understood by voters, and general enough to provide the basis for the electorate to judge a host of problems facing government.

The variety of principles rejects the assumption that voters' minds are committed to a closed partisan ideology. If that were the case, views about socialism would be integrally related to views about welfare, morality and racialism, forming a single factor statistically. But there is very little correlation between a voter's views on one principle and another.[3] There is virtually nil association between anti-racialist views and socialism, or permissiveness and socialism. The dissociation between popular principles and party principles is also apparent in a comparison of views about socialism and welfare. The Labour Party would claim it stands for both, and Thatcherite Conservatives sometimes claim that they oppose both — except in a general election campaign, when to attack welfare programmes would be electoral suicide (Rose, 1984: Prologue and Epilogue). At the mass level views about welfare are independent of views about socialism (Table 7.1).

It is sometimes argued that political principles are not so much the reflection of the minds of voters as they are of socio-economic interests. Of the four principles, socialism and welfare are conventionally regarded as relevant to socio-economic interests; racialism may be so regarded too (whether considered a working-class or a lower middle class phenomenon), and traditional morality may reflect age if not class differences. It can be hypothesized that socio-economic interests determine principles rather than principles reflecting a more or less autonomous judgement of individual voters (Scarbrough, 1984: 24ff; 39ff).

If principles are simply derivative of socio-economic interests, then middle-class voters should differ substantially from working-class voters. In order to test this hypothesis, it is necessary to create a standardized score summarizing the views of voters about the multiplicity of questions that constitute each principle.[4] If a group of voters completely endorses a principle, its score will be 100, and if a group completely rejects it, the score will be 0. For political principles to be distinctive between social groups, one group's views should approach 100, and the other, 0.

Middle-class and working-class voters structure their political thinking in much the same way. There is only a three-point difference in the mean scores of the two classes about traditional morality (69 and 72 respectively) and about racialism (52 and 55 respectively). Very positive endorsements of welfare are given by both the middle class and working-class (85 and 91). The mean scores for socialism are relatively close, 33 for the middle class, and 45 for the working class; the distance between the two classes is small by comparison with divisions about socialism within the working-class. For the four principles, the average class difference is only six points, thus rejecting the theory that political principles are derived from location in the class structure.

Reviewing all the dimensions of social structure examined in previous chapters shows virtually no link with any of the political principles identified here (Scarbrough, 1984). Principles differ little between social groups. With regard to socialism, the greatest difference is between owner-occupiers who do not belong to unions (31) and working-class council tenants (52); this emphasizes divisions about socialist principles among council tenants. The only other difference of this size is about traditional morality, between the old (80) and the young (59). Even here, a majority of young as well as elderly people endorse traditional morality.

For principles to produce closed competition between parties, Conservative, Alliance and Labour voters should have very different positions on each principle. Insofar as those voting for different parties have much the same principles, then the electorate is open. Voters find movement between parties easier when there is not the inhibition of differences of political principles. *Inter*-party similarity is greater the closer mean scores are to each other, whether high, low or in the middle. *Intra*-party consensus is greater the closer the score approaches either 100 or 0.

TABLE 7.2
Similarities between partisans in political principles, 1974–83

	Con.	Lib./All'ce	Lab.	Difference Con.-Lab.
	(Mean score for party's voters)			
Socialism				
1974 Oct.	27	38	56	29
1979	23	34	50	27
1983	24	43	61	37
Welfare				
1974 Oct.	77	80	86	9
1979	57	61	61	4
1983	80	92	97	17
Traditional morality				
1974 Oct.	71	66	67	4
1979	71	66	72	1
1983	72	69	70	2
Racialism				
1974 Oct.	53	47	48	5
1979	50	43	44	6
1983	57	52	50	7

Source: Calculated from factor analyses reported in Table 7.1 and Appendix D.
All answers standardized on a scale from completely negative (0) to completely positive (100). See footnote 4 for details.

For three of the four principles, there is inter-party consensus among voters (Table 7.2). There is intra-party consensus on the welfare principle; the mean score is 97 for Labour, 92 for the Alliance and 80 for the Conservatives; and about traditional morality too for the factor scores are Alliance, 69; Labour, 70; and Conservatives, 72. The principle of racialism divides the electorate and creates intra-party disagreement; the mean racialism score is 50 for Labour, 48 for the Alliance, and 43 for the Conservatives. The closeness of the scores shows inter-party similarity in divisions about race.

Only one of the four issues — socialism — shows much difference between supporters of the different parties; the distance between Labour and Conservative voters is 37 points, with Alliance voters halfway between. Socialism divides Labour voters. There is less unity in the Labour Party in support of socialism (mean, 61) than there is among Labour voters in supporting traditional morality (mean, 70). Moreover, Conservatives are closer to rejecting socialism completely than Labour voters are to endorsing socialism completely.

Inter-party consensus has been consistent amongst voters for the past decade. At all three elections since October, 1974, the views of Conservative and Labour voters on traditional morality and racialism have been within a few per cent of each other, and attitudes toward welfare have also been close (Table 7.2). In 1983 they appeared to move apart only because of the extremely high degree of endorsement of welfare principles in all three parties. Only socialism has shown a tendency toward increasing disagreement. As Labour's vote declined drastically in 1983, Labour voters became a little more socialist. From the evidence of the 1970s, an increase in the Labour vote would attract more voters who do not subscribe to socialist principles, increasing inter-party agreement and dissensus within Labour's ranks.

The electorate's principles are a constraint upon party competition. Electoral competition is not wide open, as would be the case if catchall parties without any principles appealed to voters whose blank minds were so suggestible that they would respond to transitory stimuli from the media, current events, or political personalities. Voters tend to have some political principles that persist from election to election. But party competition cannot be described as closed, because there is a very high degree of overlap in the principles of Conservative, Alliance, and Labour voters. Moreover, there are conflicts between party leaders and voters about racialism and traditional morality, and about welfare between Conservative voters and Mrs. Thatcher's rhetoric.

The best way to describe the relationship between the principles of the electorate and the parties is to say that no party represents the constellation of principles widespread in the electorate. A voter who favours welfare and traditional morality and rejects socialism may feel out of tune with all parties, and the same is true of a voter who gives priority to socialism, traditional morality and racialism. Voters have minds of their own, and blocs of voters can readily be identified who have distinctive political principles. But the bundles of principles common in the electorate are not consistently linked with the choices that the parties offer voters.

The reasonable electorate

The division of academic labour normally concentrates attention upon a single set of influences upon voting behaviour, whether pre-adult socialization, social structure, political principles, or the relatively transitory events of a Parliament or election campaign. However, the distinctive feature of an election is that voters are subject to all these influences *simultaneously*.

To view voters as accumulating a lifetime of influences from childhood onwards is not to suggest that a voter consciously makes a rational calculation about the relative importance of each influence before casting his or her vote. A generation of empirical research into the minds of voters has emphasized that the association between political attitudes, social structure and party is not exactly what rational theories assume (Campbell et al. 1960). It would be extraordinary if the median British voter, a working-class person leaving school at 15, thought about voting the same way as a middle-class PhD in public choice economics.

Since explanations can be offered for the behaviour of most voters, we emphasize the *reasonable* nature of voters. One way in which actions can be described as reasonable is if a person can offer an explanation for voting that is empirically consistent with his or her choice of party. The reason may be long-standing (I vote as my parents) or transitory (I like Mrs. Thatcher). The point is that a person can give an explanation for a vote, even if the statement is not a complex and detailed cost-benefit analysis.

Secondly, voting can be reasonable if a justification can be offered on behalf of a voter's choice. As John Plamenatz (1958: 9) has noted:

> A choice is reasonable, not because the chooser, when challenged, can give a satisfactory explanation of why he made it, but because if he could give an explanation, it would be satisfactory.

The reasons that could be offered on a voter's behalf may be the same as those articulated by an individual in response to a battery of survey questions. Or an explanation may be offered in lieu of any statement by an individual elector. For example, a person may have no political interest and be a don't know in response to a series of questions, but we would consider it reasonable if a person votes like others in the same class or like neighbours in a housing estate, or the same as parents.

The reasons that electors offer for their vote need not be taken at their face value. For example, a voter may express a belief that the party supported is best for the country, a vague statement about present competence. But if an interview discloses that the individual has always voted for the party of his or her parents, then the prior cause, parental party choice, is the underlying reason. Similarly, a voter may explain a vote by reference to political principles. But if these principles can also be linked with interests, as is the case for socialism and class, then class can be regarded as the prior cause of the voter deciding that socialist or anti-socialist principles are best.

While in theory many reasons could be relevant to voting behaviour, the preceding chapters have emphasized that in practice they are not equally relevant. For example, socio-economic interests are more important than such ascribed differences as age and gender. Moreover, no single reason can claim a monopoly of significance. For example, housing is most important, but not all-important. Pre-adult socialization, political principles and current party performance must also be taken into account.

FIGURE 7.1
A cumulative lifetime learning model of voting

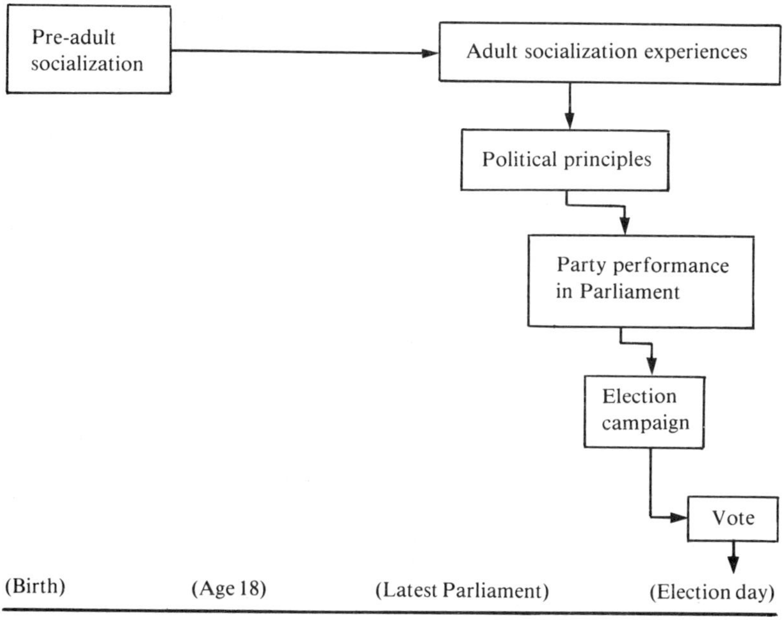

Landmark dates in the life-history of a voter

In thinking about socialization experiences, content is more important than process. Concentrating exclusively upon how people acquire political outlooks can distract attention from what is experienced. Theories of lifelong socialization are not an alternative but a complement to theories explaining how socio-economic interests influence political behaviour.

Lifetime learning

In order to understand voting, we need to think in terms of the accumulation of influences through a lifetime of learning (Figure 7.1). The analysis should be sequential, reflecting the order in which the influences occur in a voter's life history. The lifetime learning model differs from the tables in chapters III and IV, which could only test one or two influences. It differs from a conventional multiple regression analysis that considers a host of potential influences as if all occurred simultaneously. It is an empirical question whether recent influences or those that come first in point of time are more important electorally. Given that each voter is exposed to a number of varied influences — pre-adult socialization, adult socio-economic interests, political principles, the current performance of parties, and has a residual party identification — more than one influence is likely to be of some importance.

In testing the lifetime learning model, it is important to order the analysis of influences in the sequence in which they occur in the life of the voter, starting with pre-adult socialization. In chapter VI this was done with the statistical technique known as AID-III, which dichotomized the independent variables. Since political principles are continuous variable scales, hierarchical stepwise multiple regression, a technique analogous to AID-III, is here used to discriminate between those experiences in a life history that affect electoral behaviour, and those that do not.[5] Insofar as voting is reasonable, then cumulatively the influences examined (see Appendix E) should explain more than half the variance in how people vote.

I Pre-adult socialization (15 per cent of variance explained on average)

Influences that come first in time remain of some importance throughout a lifetime; pre-adult determinants of contemporary voting explain about the same proportion of variance as tree analyses of the contemporary influence of socio-economic structure (cf. Table 7.3 and Table 5.1). Consistently, father's party is the single most important early influence upon adult party choice. But its effect is limited, and in decline. It explained 10 per cent of the variance in Conservative versus Labour voting in 1974, and 7 per cent in 1983. Father's class, religion and education each have a little effect; none can be regarded as by itself of substantial importance.

TABLE 7.3
The cumulative effect of determinants of Conservative vs. Labour voting, 1974–83

	Influences	Conservative vs. Labour 1974 Oct.	1979	1983	Change 1974–83
		(% variance explained)			
I	Pre-adult socialization	(20)	(12)	(14)	(−6)
	Father's party	10	7	7	−3
	Father's class	6	3	3	−3
	Education	2	2	2	0
	Religion	2	0	2	0
II	Socio-economic interests	(10)	(12)	(13)	(+3)
	Housing	4	4	5	+1
	Union membership	4	4	3	−1
	Nation	0	3	3	+3
	Current class	2	1	2	0
III	Political principles	(22)	(22)	(29)	(+7)
	Socialism	22	19	27	+5
	Welfare	0	0	2	+2
	Racialism	0	2	0	0
	Traditional morality	0	1	0	0
IV	Current performance of parties	(18)	(17)	(21)	(+3)
	Leaders	14	16	6	−8
	Evaluation of governing party	4	1	7	+3
	Event evaluation[a]	0	n.a.	1	+1
	Campaign	0	0	0	0
	Future expectations	0	0	7	+7
V	Current party identification	(9)	(20)	(3)	(−6)
	Total variance explained	79	83	80	+1

Source: British Election Studies, 1974, 1979 and 1983.
Ordinary least squares hierarchical stepwise regression analysis; for details see Appendix E.
[a]Common Market in 1974; Falklands in 1983.

Whatever the weight accorded pre-adult influences, their significance has been declining. In 1974 pre-adult influences accounted for 20 per cent of the variance; in 1979 for 12 per cent; and in 1983, for 14 per cent. Nor is this surprising. Whereas the choice offered voters between the Conservative and Labour parties used to be relatively stable, today the names and numbers of parties are in flux, thus disrupting links with the past.

II Socio-economic interests (12 per cent)

Current occupation, housing, nation and union membership can exercise an independent influence upon a voter's current party choice. Housing is the most important, but it is not the only socio-economic interest that affects the vote. Altogether, these four interests accounted for 13 per cent of the variance in Conservative versus Labour voting in 1983, after allowing for the full impact of pre-adult influences.

Pre-adult socialization and current socio-economic interests together consistently account for about one-quarter of the variance of the vote. The relative importance of the two sets of influences is changing; in 1964 and 1974 pre-adult influences were more important. Today, current socio-economic influences have increased in importance by comparison with pre-adult socialization (Table 7.3). Voters today are no longer so inclined to vote as their parents did or in accord with parental class, because to do so is less likely to match their current socio-economic interests.

III Political principles (24 per cent)

When socialization and socio-economic interests leave three-quarters of the variance in voting open, there is great scope for political views to influence voting. Political principles explain nearly as much of the vote as do pre-adult socialization and current socio-economic interests combined, and the influence of principles has been increasing. In 1974 principles accounted for 22 per cent of the vote, as against 30 per cent for social structure influences and in 1983 for 29 per cent, against 27 per cent for social structure influences.

The importance of political principles is particularly striking, since their effect is calculated by stepwise multiple regression analysis only *after* allowing for the full impact of social structure. One principle, socialism, accounts for nearly all the impact, explaining 27 per cent of variance in 1983. Support for welfare principles cannot discriminate between parties, since virtually the whole electorate is united in favouring the welfare state. Nor can voters favouring traditional morality or opposing immigrants be much influenced, since the Conservative and Labour parties do not explicitly and consistently endorse these principles.

The electoral force of socialism benefits the Conservatives much more than Labour, because the majority of voters are *anti*-socialist. The British electorate does not divide evenly in its attitude towards socialism. The mean voter is likely to reject three-fifths of the propositions that would be endorsed by adherents of socialist principles, and this has consistently been the case.[6] Electors who are consistently anti-socialist vote Conservative. The average Labour voter agrees with little more than half the statements defining the socialist principle. Even then, Labour cannot be sure of securing the votes of all who are partly disposed toward socialism, for to some extent the Alliance also appeals to those who endorse socialist principles (Studlar and McAllister, 1985: Table 1). The importance of anti-socialism is illustrated by the fact that the socialist principle accounted for more variance in voting in 1983, when Labour had a disastrous result, than in 1974, when Labour won.

IV Current performance of parties (19 per cent)

At the start of each Parliament, most voters have a lifetime-to-date set of experiences affecting how they will evaluate the current performance of the government and opposition parties. But the period of a Parliament involves popular and unpopular changes in economic and social in party leaders; and unexpected events. During a Parliament all parties will compete to put a favourable gloss on unexpected as well as expected events. Hence, a voter will be given reason to think again about voting. In an election campaign, past performance influences judgements about which party will do best in future; the stimuli of the campaign may also lead some electors to change their vote.

The voter's evaluation of parties during the life of a Parliament accounts for up to one-fifth of the variance in Conservative versus Labour voting (Table 7.3). In 1983 the evaluation of party leaders — Michael Foot, David Steel and David Owen, as well as Mrs. Thatcher — collectively accounted for six per cent of the variance of the vote between Conservatives and Labour, a noteworthy amount but not large by comparison with the media publicity given the leaders. An index of voters' evaluation of the record of the Conservative government, based on judgements about its handling of unemployment, taxation, the cost of living and strikes, directly accounted for seven per cent of voting. Expectations of the ability of a party to improve the standard of living in the next four years accounted for another seven per cent of variance; these are linked to retrospective evaluation of the governing party's performance and that of party leaders in the past four years.[7]

Transitory events and issues appear of little direct importance on election day. The Falklands War was an important event in 1982, when it had positive consequences for the Conservative Party's morale and mid-term standing in the Gallup Poll, thus enabling the party to retain support lost during its mid-term slump. But by the time of the June, 1983 general election, it could directly add only an additional one per cent to the variance explained by what voters had earlier learned about parties. Similarly, views about the Common

Market had no independent influence on voting in 1974. After taking into account a lifetime of previous learning, the campaign appears as a transitory event of limited influence upon voters.

V Party identification (11 per cent)

If explaining variance in the statistical sense were the only object, then the ideal determinant (*sic*) would be a tautological measure, highly correlated with voting because it was simply another way of measuring current party preference. To a substantial extent, party identification is tautological. Demonstrating a high correlation between party identification and party vote supports the hypothesis that these are but two names for one thing (see Budge et al., 1976; LeDuc, 1980; Mughan, 1981).

The test of party identification as an independent influence upon voting is to calculate its impact after accounting for the effect of all other factors. When this is done, party identification is largely redundant, adding little to the influence of pre-adult socialization, socio-economic interests, political principles, and the performance of parties in the last Parliament.

Party identification is the only influence examined that is *not* consistently important. In 1983 it added only three per cent to the explanation of the variance in the Conservative versus Labour share of the vote. The apparently high level of influence of party identification in 1979 appears to reflect the fact that all other social structure and political influences were less strong at this election, thus allowing more scope for the purely residual effect of party identification.

When tested across a decade of elections, the lifetime learning model gives a clear, coherent and parsimonious account of the division between Conservative and Labour voters. At each election since October, 1974, it can account for four-fifths of the variance, an extraordinarily high proportion by comparison with conventional models of voting relying upon a single set of influences. Moreover, the two-party vote examined in Table 7.3 is now less than three-quarters of the total vote, the lifetime learning model still explains well over half the United Kingdom vote.

Political influences are more important than social structure in determining the vote. Five different types of influence affect voting behaviour. In order of their average importance they are: political principles (24 per cent); the current performance of parties (19 per cent); pre-adult socialization (15 per cent); socio-economic interests (12 per cent); and residual party identification (11 per cent). The greater importance of political principles and the current performance of parties is striking, inasmuch as the stepwise regression model measures their influence only *after* calculating the impact of pre-adult socialization and socio-economic interests.

Moreover, voters are increasingly open to political influence. In 1974, 40 per cent of the variance was explained by political principles and the current performance of parties, 10 per cent more than by social structure. By 1983, 50 per cent of the variance was explained by political principles and the current performance of parties, 23 per cent more than that explained by social structure.

Alliance support

Voting for the Alliance is best considered separately from voting for the established parties, for the Alliance rejects the idea of class parties, and preceding chapters have substantially supported this claim. The Alliance vote can be contrasted with all votes supporting the established parties, or separately against Conservative and against Labour voters. For 1979 and October 1974, the Liberal vote can provides a basis for comparison with the Alliance pattern in 1983.

When the Alliance vote is compared with the rest of the electorate, pre-adult socialization and socio-economic interests explain virtually nothing. Together, social structure explained only four per cent of the vote in 1974 — and less since then. While it is not surprising that pre-adult influences would be of no consequence, for the Alliance is a new party, it is striking that contemporary socio-economic interests are also of no importance. Differences of principle explain none of the variation in the Liberal versus established party vote in 1974 and 1979, and only four per cent in 1983. The two influences accounting for voting Alliance are the current performance of the parties in Parliament, averaging 17 per cent of the variance in three elections, and party identification, averaging 24 per cent. The influence of the performance of parties is understandable, for the Alliance and the Liberals have always depended for votes upon dissatisfaction with the party in office. The out-of-place term is party identification. It is normally considered a long-term influence, yet the Liberals and Alliance appeal to volatile elements in the electorate.

Why should party identification appear to influence voting for the most transitory of parties? The reason is that other influences collectively explain only 18 per cent of the 1974 Liberal vote, 17 per cent in 1979, and 26 per cent in 1983. Party identification becomes statistically prominent by default, notionally explaining (*sic*) an additional 20 per cent of variance in 1974, 26 per cent in 1979, and 26 per cent in 1983. But it would be false to history to interpret this as evidence of a deep lifelong party identification, for in 1983 the Alliance party was very much a novelty. Even when giving the

Alliance their vote, electors have been less inclined to identify with it. The statistical association is best interpreted as a tautology. When there is nothing else that can explain voting, then any variable such as party identification, which tends to be synonymous with the dependent variable, will by default appear important. But appearance should not be confused with reality.

The spurious association of party identification with Alliance voting is also a function of contrasting Alliance voters with both Conservative and Labour voters. As was shown by the tree analyses in chapter V, this reduces the variance explained to virtually nil. Since the Alliance is a centre party, juxtaposing it against two parties on opposite sides tends to cancel out the effect of conventional determinants, leaving scope for the residual influence of party identification.

When the Alliance vote is compared separately with Conservative and Labour votes, a different picture emerges. Pre-adult socialization was of some significance (Table 7.4). In 1983 parent's party and parent's class were as important in discriminating Alliance versus Conservative voters as for Conservative versus Labour voters (cf. Tables 7.3-7.4). Moreover, socio-economic interests accounted for 13 per cent of the variance in Conservative versus Alliance voting, the same as for Conservative versus Labour voting.

The influence of the socialist principle also differentiates Alliance voters from Conservatives in 1983, accounting for 27 per cent of the variance. Attitudes toward socialism are half as important in distinguishing Labour from Alliance voters, since both groups tend to be similarly divided about socialism. On average, political principles account for 13 per cent of the Alliance or Liberal vote in competition with one or the other class parties.

Current campaign influences have tended to be more important for the Liberal than for the Alliance vote. In October 1974 they accounted for an average of 18 per cent of the vote, and in 1979 for 22 per cent. In 1983 the proportion was down to 18 per cent for the Conservatives, since the more durable influences of socialization and party principles had registered a substantial impact; they were slightly higher for Labour.

The role of party identification is now reduced to a small residual effect. Since the first four influences explain 74 per cent of the Conservative versus Alliance vote in 1983, party identification accounts for only four per cent additional variance, virtually the same as in voting for the established class parties. Party identification appears important only when other influences are cancelled out. When each established party is contrasted with the Alliance, then party identification on average accounts for only seven per cent of the vote (Table 7.4).

TABLE 7.4
The cumulative effect of determinants of Liberal/Alliance voting, 1974–83

		1974		1979		1983	
		Con.	Lab.	Con.	Lab.	Con.	Lab.
Alliance versus		(% variance explained)					
I	Pre-adult socialization	(4)	(11)	(2)	(6)	(14)	(7)
	Father's party	2	3	2	2	7	2
	Father's class	0	3	0	1	3	1
	Education	1	5	0	2	2	2
	Religion	1	0	0	1	2	2
II	Socio-economic interests	(4)	(4)	(4)	(3)	(13)	(7)
	Housing	1	1	1	2	5	3
	Union membership	2	1	2	0	3	1
	Nation	1	1	1	0	3	1
	Current class	0	1	0	1	2	2
III	Political principles	(8)	(14)	(7)	(9)	(29)	(13)
	Socialism	8	14	6	8	27	13
	Welfare	0	0	0	0	2	0
	Racialism	0	0	1	0	0	0
	Traditional morality	0	0	0	1	0	0
IV	Current performance of parties	(22)	(15)	(26)	(19)	(18)	(22)
	Leaders	20	14	24	18	5	9
	Evaluation of governing party	2	1	2	1	6	1
	Event evaluation[a]	0	0	n.a.	n.a.	0	0
	Campaign	0	0	0	0	0	6
	Future expectations	0	0	0	0	7	6
V	Party identification	(13)	(11)	(2)	(0)	(4)	(14)
	Total variance explained	51	55	41	37	78	63

Source: British Election Studies, October 1974, 1979 and 1983. As in Table 7.3; see Appendix E for details.
[a]Common Market in 1974; Falklands in 1983.

Since the Alliance is fighting on two fronts against both the Conservatives and the Labour Party, it is to be expected that its vote would be less determined. What is striking here is that the lifetime learning model can account for more than half of the variance in the Alliance vote as against either the Conservative or Labour parties. The much higher level of determination of the Alliance vote by comparison with the Liberal showing in 1979 and 1974 indicates that Alliance support is not as shallow as Liberal support was in the past.

From either/or to both/and models

Many analyses of voting behaviour may appear convincing when examined singly, but contradictory when taken together. Any study that seeks to emphasize one influence, whether pre-adult socialization, contemporary socio-economic interests, political principles, or the current performance of parties in Parliament is bound to be partly correct, yet also incomplete. When studies concentrating upon a single influence are compared, the collective result is confusion.

To understand voting we should abandon the either/or approach, which asserts that either class or the current performance of parties determines voting, or else either socio-economic interests or political principles. We should think in terms of both/and; voting reflects the influence of *both* pre-adult socialization *and* contemporary socio-economic interests, of political principles *and* the current performance of parties.

The lifetime learning model emphasizes that the British electorate is open rather than closed. Even though given statistical priority, pre-adult socialization could on average determine only 15 per cent of the Conservative versus Labour vote, and adult socio-economic interests an average of 12 per cent. More important are political principles, which can be altered by voters of their own accord or in reaction to the current performance of parties.

The actions of voters are perfectly reasonable, since an explanation can be given for the behaviour of the great majority of voters. The reasons offered are not just speculative theories of social scientists; *all the evidence comes from statements of voters in survey interviews.* Voters can consciously articulate views relevant to an understanding of their votes.

Social science analysis should seek to understand both 'the point of view of the actor' (Campbell et al., 1960: 27) — and the political social and economic structures influencing each voter's actions (Lipset and Rokkan, 1967). This requires the inclusion of the subjective perceptions and values of voters and their family histories, an understanding of the material conditions of social structure, and observable changes in parties and their performance. Multivariate statistical analysis can reveal the latent structure of political judgements that individual voters themselves cannot articulate as a coherent whole.

The reasons given here are not the only reasons that could be advanced about why people should vote for different parties. Any social science seminar, like any TV discussion or pub conversation, can quickly generate dozens of reasons why people ought to vote one way or the other. Statements of what ought to happen sometimes blur the distinction between a moral obligation (manual workers should vote Labour) and a naturalistic hypothesis (manual workers can be expected to vote Labour). Social science research makes it possible to test whether and to what extent any of these theories are supported by the evidence. The results are tragic, in Huxley's phrase, only to individuals who want to believe what is contrary to empirical evidence. They are illuminating to those who want to understand the reasoning of voters today, and the conditions in which large numbers of voters are open to change.

Notes

1. Questions asked at only one election, reflecting changing interests of voters and the authors of questionnaires, were excluded, because durability could not be tested. The four questions developed by Ronald Inglehart(1977) for 'postmaterialist' values were not included here for three reasons. They have not been salient in electoral competition in Britain; their status as indicators of coherent principles in the minds of voters is debatable (cf. Marsh, 1975), and when included in an additional analysis, they did not alter the basic structure of outlooks identified.

2. An exploratory factor analysis utilizing virtually all 48 different attitude questions in the 1983 British Election Study produced a lower proportion of total variance explained, 46 per cent, distributed among 11 weakly defined factors. Extending the range of topics considered confirms the basic conclusions: the multiplicity of political principles, their poor fit with conventional party ideologies, and their inability to provide a complete and coherent account of the outlook of voters.

3. Correlations between factors are as follows:

Factors		II	III	IV
I	Socialism	.34	−.10	−.20
II	Welfare		−.07	−.14
III	Traditional Morality			.08

4. The scores were calculated by summing the items in each factor shown in Table 7.1 and Appendix D, and respecting signs. Missing values were coded to the mean of the item, and each was divided by its respective standard deviation in order to standardise the scores. Since the resulting variables had no natural metric, they were transformed into a 0 to 100 scale using a simple linear transformation.

5. In order to avoid an excessive proliferation of categories, only those influences already identified in previous chapters as of some importance on their own or in conjunction with class are analysed here. Those of no consequence, such as urban-rural residence, age and gender, are omitted.

6. With 100 reflecting complete endorsement of socialism by the whole electorate and 0 reflecting complete rejection, the mean score was 39 in 1983, 35 in 1979 and 42 in October 1974.

7. The interdependence of future expectations and past performance (cf. Fiorina, 1981) creates difficulties in entering the current performance variables as a bloc, the practice with other entries in Table 7.3. Future expectations are constrained to enter last, as logically they follow from judgements of prior actions. In 1983 future expectations correlated .42 with views of Thatcher; −.48 with views of Foot; .69 with evaluation of the governing party; .47 with evaluation of the Falklands War; and .04 with deciding how to vote during the campaign.

8
Are we all Alliance nowadays?

'We are all Socialists now' — a phrase used in the 1889 *Fabian Essays* and repeated by the future King Edward VII — exemplifies the adeptness of politicians in seeking consensus across party lines. When Clement Attlee and Harold Wilson spoke approvingly of patriotism and the monarchy, they too sought to associate the Labour Party with consensual values. In the 1980s the fundamental question is: Are we all Alliance nowadays?

To ask if we are all Alliance nowadays is not to imply that the Alliance has converted the great mass of the electorate to its cause. It means that in open electoral competition the old class parties are under pressure to conform to the Alliance model. Because of the size and novelty of its vote the Alliance can influence the whole electorate by the pressure it exerts upon its Conservative and Labour competitors in every constituency.

The Alliance vote is *not* determined by socio-economic interests. In this it follows the pattern of the post-war Liberal Party (Curtice, 1983). The Alliance vote is not a demand for a novel programme of government, for the principles of Alliance voters are not distinctive. Above all, the Alliance vote is a fluid vote, for a party on the rise must draw votes from other parties. In the past the Liberal Party has found that quickly won voters can quickly depart.

To suggest that all British parties are "Alliance-like" nowadays assumes that the pressures that have produced the Alliance affect the Conservative and Labour parties as well. Specifically, it implies that the Conservative and Labour vote is no longer determined by socio-economic interests, especially class; that those who vote for these parties are not distinctive in their principles; and that the vote for established parties is becoming increasingly fluid. Insofar as this is the case, then electoral competition is truly open. Rather than having two class parties and one open party, *all* the parties in the system are open.

Electoral competition can exist in the absence of pervasive differences between the parties. The alternation between Labour and Conservative governments since the 1950s has shown that there is far less difference between the parties in office than outbursts of partisan rhetoric imply (Rose, 1984). Some theories argue that the absence of difference is a predictable consequence of competitive elections; in efforts to win the median voter all parties may adopt much the same policies (Downs, 1957). Parties can differentiate themselves not by offering contrasting policies on the left or right, but by inspiring popular confidence that they are most likely to achieve consensual ends, such as peace and prosperity (see Stokes, 1963). At a minimum, every election offers voters a choice between different candidates. Even if there is little disagreement about how the country should be governed, politicians disagree about who should govern.

A fluid electorate can make competition more intense by increasing electoral uncertainty and volatility. Insofar as there is very little to differentiate Conservative, Labour and Alliance voters, then politicians cannot compete by mobilizing their traditional support, as in a closed-class system. In a multi-party system with a fluid electorate, each party is vulnerable to losses on two sides, while concurrently attempting to gain support by attracting mobile voters from both its opponents. Voters are more easily persuaded to move between parties when the barriers between them are few, and this is the case in open electoral competition.

This chapter will test whether or not each party's voters are nowadays like the prototypical Alliance voter, that is, relatively free from the influence of socio-economic interests; without a distinct set of views about political issues; and wobbling or already floating voters. While the electorate is open to change, this is not a sign of instability in the political system; open voters are oriented toward the centre, and not to the extremes.

Indeterminate support for all parties

Voters may be differently motivated from party to party: Labour voters could be class-determined, Conservatives could vote according to family tradition, and Alliance supporters might be floating voters. Only if all three parties have a similar degree of indeterminateness can we say that all voters are like the Alliance nowadays.

When the class profile of each party's vote is examined, Alliance support is almost exactly a cross-section of the national electorate. Two-fifths of the electorate is middle class, and two-fifths of the Alliance vote comes from the middle class; three-fifths is working class and three-fifths of the Alliance vote comes from the working class (Table 8.1). Even when the two principal classes are subdivided into six strata, the difference between the Alliance vote and each strata remains within the range of sampling fluctuations. The Conservative profile of the vote is also cross-class, for half the Conservative vote in 1983 came from manual workers, and half from middle-class voters. The Conservative vote differs from a stratum's share of the electorate by an average of three per cent.

In 1983 Labour's vote was less a cross-section of the electorate. It drew 79 per cent of its support from manual workers, 18 per cent more than their share in the electorate overall, and there was a reciprocal shortfall in its middle-class vote. Having most of its vote come from the working class does not make Labour the party of the working class, for this is also true of the Alliance and of the Conservatives. The average difference between Labour's support from a stratum and its proportion of the total electorate was six per cent. The Labour Party's class profile was higher than at previous elections. In 1979 the Labour vote was 13 per cent more working class than the electorate as a whole, and in 1970 10 per cent (cf. Rose, 1984: Table 3.2; Rose, 1974: Table 24). In other words, an electorally competitive Labour Party tends to draw its vote from a cross-section of the electorate.

TABLE 8.1
The class profile of support for parties

Total %		Con.	All'ce	Lab.
		(% voting for party)		
2	Upper middle	3	2	0.5
13	Middle	18	12	6
24	Lower middle	29	26	15
39	Total middle class	50	40	21
31	Skilled manual	29	32	34
18	Unskilled manual	13	17	26
12	Poor	9	11	19
61	Total working class	50	60	79

Source: Gallup Campaign Study, 1983.

Electoral pressures to appeal for votes across class lines affect all parties today. A cross-class appeal is inherent in the Alliance, which has a self-image as a party that departs from the old mould of class politics. In the case of the Conservative Party, it follows from the fact that its 'natural' class, the middle class, is a minority of the electorate.[1] In order to win a general election, the Conservatives must appeal to a substantial fraction of working-class voters too. In theory, the Labour Party could ignore the middle class and win an absolute majority of the popular vote. In practice, it cannot. For Labour to win half the vote solely by increasing its appeal to working-class voters, it would need to win five-sixths of the working-class vote, or win almost three-quarters of that vote and not lose any of its present middle-class support. Labour has not achieved this level of class hegemony at any previous election. Since the size of the working class is gradually contracting, appealing to a single class would be a recipe for electoral suicide (Kelley et al., 1985).

TABLE 8.2
The evenness of support for parties in the social structure

(% British vote)	Con. (43.5)	All'ce (26.0)	Lab. (28.3)
	(% vote by group)		
Occupation (ABC1)			
Working class	38	26	36
Middle class	56	27	16
Union			
Non-member	52	23	24
Member	34	29	37
Housing			
Owner-occupier	52	27	20
Council tenant	27	24	48
Car			
Yes	50	27	22
No	33	25	40
Age			
65 plus	49	22	28
18–29	39	27	32
Gender			
Men	45	23	30
Women	45	26	28
Religion			
Anglican	52	25	23
None	42	25	30
Region[a]			
North of England	38	24	37
South of England	53	30	16
Nation[a]			
England	46	26	27
Wales	31	23	37
Scotland	28	25	35
Urban-rural			
Cities	41	24	33
Rural	47	29	22
Average deviation	7	1.6	7

Source: As for Tables in chapter 4.
[a]Calculated from election results.

Another way to demonstrate the evenness of support for all three parties today is to compare their share of the vote among different social groups with their share of the vote in the electorate as a whole. As long as a party draws its vote evenly from all parts of society, then its share of the vote ought to be much the same among men and women, union members and non-members, or city dwellers and rural residents. But if each party draws its vote from distinctive social groups, then it should poll well above-average in some groups, and well below in others.

When the distribution of the vote is analyzed for the ten dimensions of social structure examined in Chapters III and IV, the result is clear and consistent (Table 8.2). The Alliance vote on average deviates less than 2 per cent from its national figure, which can easily be accounted for by sampling fluctuations. The average deviation for the Conservative and Labour parties is the same, a low 7 per cent. In 17 of the 21 cases examined, the Conservative vote varied by less than 10 per cent from its national total; the same is true of Labour in 18 instances. For example, to say that Labour did well in Scotland simply means that it won a 7 per cent larger share of the vote there than in Britain overall; to do badly, as among rural dwellers, means that its vote was 6 per cent lower. A good result for the Conservatives among non-union members was only 8.5 per cent better than its overall total, and a bad result in the North of England only 5.5 per cent below its nationwide total.

The Alliance is setting the pace by winning support from voters throughout British society. Since 1964 the Conservative and Labour parties have been less and less able to rely upon socialization and socio-economic influences to determine their support. To remain electorally competitive, the Conservative and Labour parties must contest with the Alliance for the favour of electors whose votes are not simply a reflection of their position in the social structure.

The openness of the electorate

Since Edmund Burke's day in the eighteenth century, political commentators have been accustomed to think of parties as organized to express political principles and interests. In a closed-class system, the Conservatives represented the principle of capitalism, and Labour represented socialist principles. The Liberals were often dismissed as representing nothing in particular because of their lack of ties with social structure and class interests (cf. Beer, 1982). Conservatives attacked Liberals as potential allies of Socialists, Socialists attacked Liberals as crypto-Tories, and Liberals often attacked each other. But a less selective reading of the English political tradition could see liberalism as a set of beliefs that was no longer distinctive to one party because it had penetrated all of them. Political values need not be confined to a sub-culture; they can be pervasive throughout society (Rose, 1965: Table 2.2; see also Scarbrough, 1984).

Alliance politicians have difficulty in trying to define a distinctive third position in a parliamentary system that is traditionally oriented toward two parties. In the House of Commons the Liberals have been either a small opposition party or, from 1977 to 1979, a very junior partner in a pact with the government. Alliance leaders have sometimes appeared to echo positions of the Labour Party (for example, endorsing the welfare state) and sometimes the Conservative Party (for example, criticizing trade unions). The Alliance can be distinctive in its mix of policies without differing from both its competitors on any particular issue.

In a system of closed-class competition, each party's supporters would view political issues differently from other parties. Agreement within the ranks of one party would be complemented by conflict with the views of other parties. By contrast, in open competition those voting for one party would not have political views marking them off from other parties. There would tend to be agreement across party lines; the overall national position would also be the dominant position in each party. This would be true whether there was consensus (for example, support for the national health service) or disagreement cutting across party lines (for example, about race relations). Cross-party consensus is *not* a pre-condition for similarities in outlooks. Parties can be similar because each is internally divided as, for example, the Conservative and Labour parties were in the 1975 European Community referendum.

The proposition — We're all Alliance nowadays — implies that the views of Alliance voters are not unique to that party. This can happen if a large majority of voters in all parties agree about an issue, or if Alliance voters divide along lines parallel with divisions in the other parties.

At the level of political principle, factor analysis showed few differences between Conservative, Labour and Alliance voters (Table 7.2). Three of the principles — welfare, traditional morality and racialism — reflected much the same distribution of attitudes within each party. On these three principles, Alliance and Liberal voters have differed by an average of 6 percentage points from Conservatives since October, 1974, and 3 points from Labour voters. Only one principle, socialism, discriminates to some extent between partisans, dividing Liberal and Labour voters, while uniting anti-socialist Conservatives.

But agreement about major political principles need not imply agreement about specific issues. It is possible for partisans to differ about the specifics of public policies, such as how much money should be spent on a particular welfare programme at a particular time. Furthermore, many issues of political concern, ranging from troops in Northern Ireland to membership in the European Community, are independent of the previously identified principles.

In a closed system of competition, party leaders know what their supporters want, and there is no pressure to alter positions in search of votes. But in an open system, each party's leaders are doubly under pressure. There is pressure within the party from those who favour contrasting positions on issues of the day. There is also competition from other parties, which can adopt positions to attract voters. The characterization (Curtice, 1983: 114) of the Liberals and the Alliance Party as having 'failed to carve out a distinctive issue space for itself' may be applicable to the Conservative and Labour parties as well.

The 1983 British Election Study provides a wealth of data about voters' attitudes toward issues, for 45 different questions were asked about actions that government could take (for example, spending more on the health service) or policy assumptions immediately relevant to public policies (for example, whether business or unions have too much power). The questions were of concern to voters; only eight per cent on average answered don't know. Since factor analysis found that three-quarters of these questions were not integrated in a set of political principles, there is much potential scope for disagreement between supporters of different parties.

The closed-class model of electoral competition implies that voters for different parties will endorse different positions on an issue. In a two-party system, this is easy to do, for there are at least two sides to every political issue. In a multi-party system, this is only possible if three or more alternatives are readily available. Otherwise, one party's supporters would disagree with two parties. Doing so is consistent with Mrs. Thatcher's view that those who are not for her are against her, whether Alliance or Labour. It is also consistent with the socialist view of the Alliance as a crypto-Conservative party forming part of an anti-Socialist front. However, in open electoral competition most voters would agree, for opinions about issues would be unrelated to party choice.

Popular views about issues of the day are open, not closed (Table 8.3). On most issues an individual who held the dominant view of the electorate could be a Conservative, Alliance or Labour voter; there is no difference in the dominant preference of supporters of all three parties on 30 of the 45 issues examined. For example, more than four-fifths of Conservative, Alliance and Labour voters agree that unemployment is not the fault of the unemployed. When there is a division within the electorate, such as about the death penalty, the

TABLE 8.3
The extent of agreement between Alliance, Conservative and Labour voters

Issues	Total	Con.	All'ce	Lab.
		(% agree)		
A) All three parties agree (30)				
If unemployed, not own fault	87	82	91	91
Spend more on NHS	87	77	92	98
Spend more to end poverty	86	77	90	96
Stay in EEC	85	95	88	66
Increase standard of living of pensioners	83	76	86	93
Help local economies	79	69	79	95
Give stiffer sentences to criminals	77	81	74	73
Create jobs	73	53	83	95
High tax makes people work less hard	71	72	71	69
Not allow revolutionaries to teach in schools	70	75	70	61
Not abolish private education	69	87	66	43
Too many rely on government handouts	69	80	62	56
Give workers more say	68	58	74	80
To cut crime, cut unemployment	68	60	75	74
Spending on education not gone far enough	67	54	77	79
Sale of council houses about right	66	69	67	60
Nudity and sex in media gone too far	66	67	62	67
Be firm on wages and salaries	64	68	65	59
Right to demonstrate and protest in armies about right	63	59	69	64
Negotiate with Argentina	62	52	70	70
Allow revolutionaries to hold public meetings	62	62	67	58
Big business has too much power	61	51	65	74
Equal opportunity for women about right	58	62	57	53
Prison should reform, not punish	57	53	58	61
Bring back death penalty	56	61	50	51
Abortion on NHS about right	56	58	59	49
Equal opportunity for blacks about right	53	56	52	48
Comprehensive schools about right	54	50	55	59
Allow racists to hold public meetings	53	54	58	48
Cutting immigration from Commonwealth	50	49	51	49
B) Alliance and Conservative agree (8)				
Trade unions have too much power	71	89	71	43
Allow private industry to keep more profits	63	78	60	42
Britain safer with own nuclear weapons	63	79	58	42
Introduce stricter laws to regulate unions	58	80	52	27
Building nuclear power stations about right	57	70	55	38
Inflation more threat to voter's family than unemployment	53	64	50	40
Welfare benefits about right	52	57	56	39
Not remove troops from N. Ireland immediately	51	61	52	35
C) Alliance and Labour agree (7)				
Not promote private medicine	51	33	61	72
Britain less safe with US nuclear missiles	48	27	59	70
Income and wealth should be redistributed	47	26	53	75
Support for more public transport	44	31	54	57
Government's fault unemployment high	41	14	50	76
Union leaders do not cause unemployment	39	23	46	50
Spend less on defence	37	16	49	61
D) Conservative and Labour agree		none		
E) All three parties disagree		none		

Source: British Election Study 1983.
All issue questions with less than 20 percent don't knows. Parties grouped according to the response endorsed by a plurality of supporters.

majority in each party is on the same side, and close to the national total. The practice of parliamentary legislation shows a similarly high level of agreement between parties. Notwithstanding the rhetoric of adversary politics in Parliament, about three-quarters of government bills presented to the House of Commons are not opposed by the Opposition on the 2nd Reading debate (Rose, 1984: Table 5.1).

All three parties have most of their voters in agreement with one or both of their competitors on the great majority of issues. Notwithstanding the Labour Party's relatively leftwing appeal in 1983, on 37 of the 45 issues most Labour voters agreed with other voters: for 30 issues, agreement was with both Conservative and Alliance voters, and for 7 with Alliance voters. On only one-sixth of issues, such as abandoning nuclear weapons and removing troops from Northern Ireland, did most Labour voters take a different position from supporters of the two other parties. Instead of showing 100 per cent disagreement with the Conservatives, Labour voters differed by 22 per cent from Conservative voters on average across all 45 issues.

Conservative voters were in the mainstream of public opinion on 38 of the 45 issues. Notwithstanding Mrs. Thatcher's readiness to emphasize differences between the parties, on 30 issues Conservatives were in agreement with both Labour and Alliance voters, and on another 8 with Alliance voters. There were only 7 issues on which Conservative voters were relatively isolated, such as promoting private medicine and spending on defence.

Most Alliance voters are invariably in the national majority in their views about issues. In addition to agreeing with both Conservative and Labour voters on two-thirds of issues, Alliance supporters agreed with Conservatives on another sixth, and with Labour voters on the remaining sixth. There is not a single issue among the 45 in which a majority of the Alliance supporters differ from a majority of both Conservative and Labour voters. The Alliance demonstrates its centrality in the electorate by the fact that its voters are usually between Conservative and Labour voters in their views; this occurs for 37 of the 45 issues. The exceptions almost invariably involve questions of morality, such as nudity, or civil liberties, such as allowing revolutionaries to hold public meetings. Alliance voters on average are only 10 per cent distant from the position of the average Labour voter, and 13 per cent from the average Conservative supporter.

Differences of opinion in the electorate as a whole are entirely consistent with similarities across party lines. If clearcut national agreement is defined as two-thirds of the electorate endorsing a particular position on an issue, such agreement is found on 18 of 45 issues. Voters are more likely to divide evenly than to show a substantial majority favouring a particular position. *The most common form of disagreement is within parties rather than between them.* Among Labour voters, there is an absence of agreement (that is, the same position taken by two-thirds of voters) for 26 of the 45 issues. Among Alliance voters, such agreement is absent on 25 issues, and on 19 issues among Conservatives. Divisions about issues within each party link voters across party lines. For example, just as there is a majority within each party favouring abortion on the national health service, so there is a substantial minority within each party opposing it.

The influence of issues upon the vote is limited, since there is not a cohesive bloc of the electorate favouring a set of issues *and* a particular party. Groups of people who think the same about an issue tend to be in ad hoc agreement; they can only be identified by asking questions about issues. *How a person votes is a poor guide to what a person thinks about most issues today.*

The ability of party leaders to lead public opinion about issues is usually overestimated — especially by party leaders. Notwithstanding the landslide Conservative victory in seats in the House of Commons, most of the British electorate has *not* followed Mrs. Thatcher's lead at the ballot box; the 1983 Conservative vote actually fell by comparison with 1979.

Whether the question is a matter of style or of substance, the results are the same. Mrs. Thatcher has not created a broad base of support within the electorate. In fact, the Prime Minister has actually been losing support for what she regards as the central issue: reducing the size of government by cutting taxes and state welfare services (Table 8.4). When Mrs. Thatcher was first returned to office in 1979, a third favoured such cuts, a third favoured increasing both taxes and services, and one-quarter wanted things left as they were. Mrs. Thatcher's period in office has resulted in an increase in the proportion opposed to her view of the role of government. In 1983 nearly half the electorate endorsed spending more on welfare even if this meant higher taxes; since then this view has gained the support of an absolute majority. Moreover, a plurality of Conservatives agree with Labour and Alliance voters in favouring higher taxes and more welfare benefits.

In her style of politics, Mrs. Thatcher has proudly boasted that she rejects consensus politics.

> I am a conviction politician. The Old Testament prophets did not say; Brothers, I want a consensus. They said: This is my faith. This is what I passionately believe. If you believe it too, then come with me. (Quoted in Rose, 1984: 4)

TABLE 8.4
Popular attitudes towards taxes and welfare benefits

	May 1979	Mar. 1981	Mar. 1983	Feb. 1985
	(% for each preferred option)			
Taxes being cut, even if it means some reduction in government servies, such as health, education and welfare	34	20	23	16
Things should be left as they are	25	23	22	18
Government services such as health, education and welfare should be extended, even if it means some increase in taxes	34	49	49	59
Don't know	7	8	6	6

Source: Gallup Political Index for months indicated.

But many voters still support consensus politics. When asked about handling five different types of political problems, an average of 40 per cent of the electorate agreed with Mrs. Thatcher's style of conviction politics. But equally important, an average of 47 per cent reject her conviction rhetoric in favour of negotiation and compromise (Table 8.5).

TABLE 8.5
Popular attitudes towards Thatcherite beliefs about politics

(Pro alternative first)	Pro	Mixed[a]	Anti
	(% voters)		
When dealing with political opponents, stick firmly to one's beliefs, or meet halfway?	50	11	39
Government can't do much to create prosperity: agree or not?	48	14	38
In difficult economic times, should government be tough or caring?	46	19	35
In dealings with other countries, is it better for Britain to stick to its own position, or meet other countries halfway?	29	12	59
In government economic policy, better to keep unions and business at arm's length, or involve them?	27	11	62
Average	40	13	47

Source: BBC Gallup Survey, 1983.
[a]Don't know, neither, both.

Divisions of opinion about political issues are not inconsistent with closed-class competition, if all who endorse Mrs. Thatcher's style vote Conservative and all who reject it vote for other parties. This would also be consistent with the official Labour and Alliance view, which is that their supporters are united in wanting to rid the country of Thatcherism.

In fact, the appeal of Mrs. Thatcher's conviction style of politics cuts across parties (Table 8.6). Among Conservative voters, 20 per cent usually endorse Mrs. Thatcher's style, only three per cent more than Alliance voters. The proportion of Labour voters who endorse Mrs. Thatcher's tough style, 25 per cent, is higher than among Conservatives! Labour voters are also less likely than Conservative or Alliance voters to be consistently anti-Thatcher. In all three parties, the pro- and anti-Thatcher groups are in a minority. Nearly two-thirds of Conservative, Alliance and Labour voters have mixed views about Mrs. Thatcher's style of politics, approving some but not all of its characteristics.

TABLE 8.6
Nil party difference in voters' views of Thatcher's style

Total	Con. %	All'ce %	Lab. %
20 Pro-Thatcher (+2 to +5)	20	17	25
63 Mixed (+1 to −1)	64	65	60
16 Anti-Thatcher (−2 to −5)	16	19	15

Source: Calculated from 1983 BBC Gallup Study questions reported in Table 8.4, scoring each pro-Thatcher statement as +1, anti-Thatcher statement as −1 and other statements as 0.

Popular views about the Thatcher style of politics reflect the fact that in open electoral competition a party leader can expect to find a measure of agreement with voters in other parties — but also a measure of disagreement within his or her own party. This is as true of Michael Foot or Neil Kinnock's Labour Party as it is of the Alliance under David Steel and David Owen, or of Conservatives facing differences between wets, dries and drips.

The bundle of policies that a party offers is only acceptable in part to its median supporter. As the salience of issues shifts, for example, because of a crisis in industrial relations or foreign affairs, voters can easily shift to another party offering a slightly different bundle. Just as party leaders cannot expect voters to be lifelong supporters because of their family background or their position in the social structure, so too they cannot count on people who voted for them at the last election to do so next time, since there is neither exclusive nor full agreement with party policies.

Floaters and wobblers outnumber committed partisans

The Alliance vote, and the Liberal vote before that, is a floating vote par excellence. A Liberal Party with a closed base would have been consigned to electoral oblivion, since the core support for the party has been very low. Recurring surges in Liberal and Alliance fortunes have demonstrated an ability to attract voters from Conservative and Labour ranks. Recurring slumps have shown the tendency of voters who float into the Liberal column to float out again (Alt et al., 1977; Lemieux, 1977; Curtice, 1983). To suggest that the electorate as a whole is becoming like the Alliance is not to forecast a big boost in the Alliance vote. Rather, it is to emphasize a weakening in the attachment of Labour and Conservative voters. In open electoral competition a large fraction of voters are predisposed to wobble in their commitment to a party and some will float between parties.

When voting is indeterminate, individuals do not need to change their class or socio-economic interests in order to change parties; all parties seek votes on a cross-class basis, appealing to many socio-economic interests. Nor do individuals need to change their principles, inasmuch as parties tend to accommodate many different views in order to recruit support from a cross-section of the electorate. A voter who is a skilled manual worker or a home-owning trade unionist may vote Conservative, Labour or Alliance, whatever his or her views about welfare policies, race relations, or traditional morality and, to a substantial degree, regardless of views about socialism. In an open electorate, the distance between parties is less and far more easily traversed than in a closed electorate, where there are social and ideological gulfs between parties.

The openness of the electorate is best measured in a series of steps and half-steps. *Stable* voters do not change their behaviour from one election to the next, or at least, do not report acting differently between elections).[2] *Mobile* voters are of three types: those who move *in-and-out* of the ranks of voters, whether because of coming of age or dying, or temporarily being non-voters (Crewe et al., 1977); *floating* voters who have moved between parties in the recent past; and *wobbling* voters, who are unsure of whether to vote the same or float to another party. In an open electorate, a majority of the electors will be mobile, and stable voters a minority.

Change from one election to the next is complex not simple. There is only one way for a voter to be stable, acting as before, but there are 30 possible directions in which a mobile voter can move (Table 8.7). Of those eligible to vote at either or both of the 1979 and 1983 elections, 58 per cent reported they were stable, acting the same at both elections; 42 per cent were mobile.

Of the stable electorate, three-quarters consisted of Conservative and Labour voters; the Conservatives were more numerous, since the party won both the 1979 and 1983 elections. Of the mobile voters, the bulk were in-and-outers. The 1979 electorate was diminished by the death of 7 per cent of voters, and the 1983 electorate was increased by 7 per cent by those too young to vote in 1979. The other group of in-and-outers consists of intermittent abstainers. Of those not voting in 1979, a third moved into the ranks of voters in 1983; of those not voting in 1983, nearly one-half reported having voted in 1979. Voters who actually float between the parties are a minority of the electorate; they constitute 16 per cent of the electors examined in Table 8.7. Moreover, floating voters are more inclined to take a half-step than a full step; 12 per cent were to-ing and fro-ing from the Liberal or Alliance parties, as against 4 per cent floating between the Labour and Conservative parties.

TABLE 8.7
Stability and mobility in the electorate, 1979–83

	1983 status					
1979 status	Con.	All'ce	Lab.	Other	Didn't vote	Departed
Con.	**26.7**	3.8	1.2	0.2	3.9	3.4
Lib.	1.0	**5.1**	0.6	0.0	0.8	0.8
Lab.	2.8	5.7	**17.1**	0.2	3.1	2.7
Other	0.2	0.1	0.1	**0.6**	0.1	0.1
Didn't vote	1.9	1.2	1.1	0.1	**8.8**	0.4
Too young	2.6	1.8	1.8	0.2	0.8	**0.0**

Source: BBC Gallup Study, 1983.
Departed estimated at mortality rate of 0.15 percent per month × 49 months = 7.35 percent of 1979 electorate, with vote apportioned according to 1979 result.

Of the total change in the electorate between 1979 and 1983, one-third reflected inevitable and apolitically induced changes in the demographic composition of the electorate through death and coming of age. The other major causes of change can be divided into those that reflect a positive shift between parties, and more ambiguous movements in or out of the ranks of non-voters. Politically induced shifts between parties are numerous enough to be decisive in a first-past-the-post British electoral system — but only in conjunction with partisan differentials in turnout, in coming of age, and in death rates.

A review of the movement of voters at successive elections for the past quarter-century emphasizes that stable voters are always a limited fraction of the electorate. Those who vote for the same party at two successive elections are a minority of the total electorate (Table 8.8). On average, only 46 per cent of electors eligible to vote at one or both of successive elections have actually reported voting for the same party both times. An additional 11 per cent are stable abstainers. The only time in which more than half the voters were stable was in the exceptional circumstances of elections close together, 1964 and 1966, and the two elections of 1974. In 1970 less than two in five of the electorate were stable voters.

Mobile voters are almost as numerous as stable partisans; they average 43 per cent of the electorate. Those shifting in and out of the ranks of voters were 32 per cent of the electorate, and those positively floating between parties, 11 per cent. The longer the time between elections, the greater the proportion of voters entering or leaving the electorate because of generational change. However, the proportion of floating voters is unaffected by the span of time between elections, and there is a noteworthy trend up in the proportion of voters floating between parties. From 1959 through 1970 the proportion of floating voters fell from 10 to seven per cent. In the 1970s, it averaged 12 per cent, and in 1983 rose to 16 per cent.

TABLE 8.8
Stability and mobility in the electorate, 1959–83

	Stable		Mobile	
	Same party	Non-voters	In/out	Floating
	(% all electors)			
1959–64	46	9	35	10
1964–66	56	14	22	8
1966–70	39	12	41	7
1970–Feb. 1974	40	9	40	12
Feb.–Oct. 1974	54	14	21	11
Oct. 1974–79	41	10	37	12
1979–83	49	9	27	16

Source: Calculated from tables in Butler and Stokes, 1974: 256, 261, 263; Sarlvik and Crewe, 1983: 44, 47, 51; and Table 8.7.

So much mobility in the electorate means that every party must run fast to stay in the same place. Between one election and the next, from a third to nearly one-half of a party's supporters will have left its ranks by a process of demographic attrition (death) or political attrition (moving to another party or into the ranks of non-voters). After winning the 1979 election, the Conservatives lost 32 per cent of their support by political and demographic attrition. Even though the Liberal vote went up due to its link with the SDP, 39 per cent of 1979 Liberal voters did not support the party at two successive elections, and Labour lost 46 per cent of its 1979 support (Table 8.9). Changes on this scale force parties actively to seek new supporters in an open electorate; they cannot rely upon a stable base of support.

TABLE 8.9
Changes in party support, 1979–83

	Con. %	All'ce %	Lab. %
Of 1979 electorate			
Retained	68	61	54
Lost to Alliance	10	n.a.	19
Lost to Con. or Lab.	3	19	9
Lost to non-voting	10	10	10
Died	9	10	9
Of 1983 electorate			
Retained from 1979	76	29	78
From Liberals[a]	3	n.a.	3
From Con. or Lab.	8	54	5
From non-voters[a]	7	7	5
From young voters	5	10	8

Source: Calculated from BBC Gallup Study 1983 data reported in Table 8.7.
[a]Includes a small number moving to/from other parties.

In order to hold their aggregate vote steady between 1979 and 1983, the Conservatives needed to recruit one new voter for every two supporters retained. Labour failed to hold nearly half of its 1979 voters, recruiting little more than one new voter for every four old voters. The Alliance success resulted from recruiting more than two new voters for every one old supporter that it held. Winning new support to replace departed voters makes the difference between victory and defeat.

An open electorate is open at all times. The proportion of voters who float on election day is smaller than the proportion who float during the life of a Parliament. The ranks of seemingly stable voters conceal a substantial portion of voters who only 'accidentally' vote the same at two successive elections. Many voters are wobbling, uncertain about how they will come off the fence at the next election.

Taking into account movement between parties during a Parliament increases the number of floating voters. Such movement is most dramatically shown in by-elections, which today register far greater movements than during the classic period of closed party competition. In the 1979-83 Parliament, six seats changed hands in 19 by-election contests, equivalent to more than 200 seats changing hands in a general election. The Conservative Party's average by-election vote fell one-quarter from its 1979 level of support. The fact that the Conservatives won back most of this support at the 1983 election shows that floating voters are frequently in motion, moving in more than one direction.

Changes in nationwide opinion polls are more representative than any by-election outcome, which by definition represents only one among 650 constituencies in the House of Commons. In the 1979 Parliament the swings in the monthly Gallup Poll were even greater than in by-elections; support reached nearly 50 per cent for the Labour, Alliance and Conservative parties in turn and their opponents plummeted (McAllister and Rose, 1984: Table 2.3).

The making of a floating voter is a process; it is not the result of an overnight conversion. It starts when a voter begins to drift away from a firm commitment to his or her usual party. The voter may still favour the party at successive elections, but as the degree of commitment weakens a voter begins to wobble, increasing the likelihood of coming down in support of another party.

From 1964 to 1983 party identification has altered marginally. Conservative identifiers have declined by four per cent and Labour by 12 per cent; the Liberal and Alliance identification has risen by 5 per cent; and the proportion identifying with no party has increased from 4 to 15 per cent. The proportion identifying with one of the two closed-class parties has thus fallen from four-fifths to two-thirds of the electorate (Table 8.10A). The fact that one-third of the electorate no longer identifies with either the Conservative or Labour parties emphasizes that multi-party competition now has a social psychological base in the minds of many voters.

While party identification is virtually synonymous with party choice in Britain, the strength of party identification can indicate how strongly committed a voter is to his or her current choice. The vote of an elector who does not identify very strongly with a party counts for just as much in the ballot box as the vote of a strongly committed partisan. But a party's ability to rely on the stable support of electors at election after election declines as party identification weakens (Butler and Stokes, 1974; Sarlvik and Crewe, 1983).

The strength of party identification is declining (Table 8.10B). In 1964, 44 per cent of the electorate identified very strongly with a party. In 1983 the proportion doing so fell by more than half; only 18 per cent identified as very strong Conservative or Labour supporters. More than four-fifths of the British electorate now think of themselves as not having a very strong party identification or are without any identification with the duopoly parties. Such voters are beginning to wobble, and are open to change their vote during the life of a Parliament or at the next general election.

An omnibus survey of British Social Attitudes (Young, 1984: 12, 38) has produced further evidence of the weakness of party identification, first of all asking voters whether they think of themselves as a supporter of any one party. Only 46 per cent of those interviewed shortly before the 1983 election campaign replied that they were a supporter of a party; the majority were open. Among those not considering themselves partisan supporters, 26 per cent said that they felt a little closer to one party, and an additional 15 per cent indicated a party for which they would vote at the forthcoming general election. Open voters can make a choice between parties, but for most electors an occasional choice is not the reflection of durable support.

TABLE 8.10
The decline in party identification, 1964–83

	1964 %	1983 %	Change %
A) Party identification			
Conservative	40	36	−4
Labour	43	31	−12
Duopoly parties	83	67	−16
Liberals, Alliance, other	13	17	+4
None	4	15	+11
Non-duopoly	17	32	+15
B) Very strong party identification			
Conservative	19	9	−10
Labour	21	9	−12
Duopoly parties	40	18	−22
Liberals, Alliance, other	4	2	−2
Not strong	56	80	+24

Source: British Election Studies, 1964 and 1983.

Given that more than half the electorate does not normally think of itself as supporting a party, the concept of party identification appears more a construct of survey researchers than a meaningful identification in the minds of voters. The presence of an interviewer will usually produce a party label if an identification is asked for (cf. Table 8.10). But for most voters the identification is stimulated by the interview. When voters are given a chance to describe their own state of mind by being asked the prior question — whether or not they think of themselves as a party supporter — most people say they do not. Follow-up panel interviews (Lievesley and Waterton, 1985: 188) have found that within a year of the election, one-quarter of voters changed the party toward which they were inclined, demonstrating the readiness to float of those who do not see themselves as partisan supporters.

A predisposition to float will be increased insofar as voters are motivated more by dislike of one party in a multi-party system than by a positive attachment. When the 1983 BBC Gallup Poll asked people to say which was stronger, their like of the party they were voting for or their dislike of an opposing party, 52 per cent replied that they disliked the alternatives, as against 35 per cent declaring a positive preference for the party they were voting for. Moreover, the extent of negative voting was virtually equal in Conservative, Labour and Alliance ranks. When nearly half a party's vote reflects the defects of opponents rather than its own appeal, a party cannot claim a positive long-term endorsement for its cause. Yet wobbling voters need a positive inducement to change parties; otherwise dissatisfaction with their previous choice may simply push them into the ranks of non-voters.

Voters who have good things to say about their own party often find good things to say about parties that they do not support currently. The 1983 British Election Study asked voters to characterize the images of each of the three parties according to four sets of positive and negative characteristics: moderate versus extreme; united versus divided; for all classes or for one class; and clear versus vague policies. In a closed electorate, voters would only endorse positive remarks about their own party; in an open electorate they could find something good to say about more than one party. In an alienated electorate, nothing good would be said about any of the parties.

The British electorate is not alienated, for voters endorse more positive than negative statements about parties. The electorate is open, for 75 per cent of voters make at least one favourable judgement about a party other than the one for which they vote, and 40 per cent make as many positive judgements about parties they do not vote for as about the party which they currently support. An individual's vote is not an exclusive endorsement of one party; it is cast with the recognition that other parties have good points too (see also Feldman and Zuckerman, 1982: 211f). Most voters do not see parties in black and white terms; they see a choice between shades of grey.

In a closed electorate the decision about how to vote is made many years before an election is held, or even before a youth is conscious of politics. In 1983, 61 per cent told the British Election Study that they had made up their minds a long time ago. Because Labour support was low, the proportion of long-term voters was highest in Labour's ranks. The proportion was lowest in the party most successful in attracting floating voters, the Alliance. Of those who said that they had made up their mind fairly recently, 9 per cent reported doing so a year before the election, 9 per cent during the election year, and 21 per cent during the campaign. The Alliance could reckon that it attracted nearly two-fifths of its vote during the campaign, and the Conservative and Labour parties about one-seventh. The number of electors who wait until after the campaign starts before making up their mind how to vote is increasing.[3]

Even after casting a ballot, a significant fraction of voters are prepared to admit that their election-day choice is not their only choice. Of those interviewed in the post-election British Election Study, 26 per cent said that they had thought of voting differently, including 20 per cent of Conservatives, 29 per cent of Labour voters, and 31 per cent of Alliance supporters. While this proportion is limited in a statistical sense, it is powerful politically. If any party had won the support of all those who at one time had thought of voting for it, its vote would have risen substantially. And if a party had lost the votes of all the wobblers who had considered floating elsewhere, it would have suffered electoral disaster.

TABLE 8.11
Committed, wobbling and floating voters

Total %	Partisan commitment score[a]	Con.	All'ce	Lab.
		(% party's voters)		
	Committed			
8	10	13	0	10
10	9	14	3	10
16	8	17	7	24
34		44	10	44
	Wobbling			
16	7	20	6	18
15	6	15	13	16
14	5	11	20	12
11	4	5	23	7
56		51	62	53
	Floating			
7	3	3	19	2
2	2	1	7	1
1	1	1	2	0
0	0	0	0	0
10		5	29	3

Source: BBC Gallup Study, 1983.

[a]Answers to five questions: Voting for same party, 1979 and 1983; considered voting Alliance; when decided how to vote; balance of likes and dislikes of parties; strength of party identification. Scored 2 for committed, 1 for intermediate, and 0 for uncommitted.

The distribution of the electorate as between committed partisans, wobblers, and floaters can be estimated by combining answers to the five different questions about partisanship reviewed above. Each committed partisan response is scored 2 (for example, very strong party identifier); an intermediate response is scored 1 (for example, fairly strong party identity); and each response that shows little or no commitment 0 (for example, not very strong or no party identification).

When voters are arrayed on a scale from most committed to completely floating, the great bulk of the electorate is neither very committed nor completely adrift (Table 8.11). Only eight per cent of the electorate consistently gives a fully committed reply, and less than one per cent is a floater in every respect. The median respondent is a wobbler, with a score of 6, showing a limited attachment to his or her current choice. In an electoral system in which a voter must plump for one party when casting a ballot, wobblers may often vote for the same party at successive elections. But their choice is not closed by pre-adult socialization or socio-economic interests: the median voter is always ready to consider voting differently, thus making electoral competition open.

The commitment of voters is lowest in the ranks of Alliance supporters, as would be expected with a new party. More than half who voted Alliance were floaters on one or more criteria; only one-tenth of Alliance voters could be classified among the committed.[4] By contrast, 44 per cent of Labour and of Conservative voters could be classified as committed. A majority of those who voted Conservative or Labour show greater or lesser signs of wobbling.

When electoral competition is open, as in the 1980s, the evidence demonstrates both the strength and the weakness of all parties. The Conservative, Labour and Alliance parties each has a potential for attracting voters — and each is also vulnerable to loss. When all parties resemble the Alliance, a generalization about the Liberal Party over the years is now applicable to all: 'support is widely if thinly spread' (Curtice, 1983: 103).

Centripetal instability: voters begin to choose

A variety of negative labels are used to characterize electoral competition in Britain since 1974. The electorate has been de-aligned; the Conservative and Labour parties are in decline; the first-past-the-post electoral system produces instability or its opposite, stagnation; and there is a need to break the mould. Such characterizations are doubly negative, implying an unfavourable judgement about what is described, and failing to describe what has replaced the old system.

Open electoral competition in Britain can be positively characterized as showing centripetal instability. *Instability* accounts for anxiety amongst persons accustomed to a Conservative/Labour duopoly of votes: the old system is no longer there. The cause of instability can be summed up in the epigram: voters begin to choose.[5] While there is great movement, it is that of voters moving around in a circle. Competition is *centripetal*, for there is a central focus and common points of reference for both parties and electors. Just as centrifugal competition would drive parties further away from each other, centripetal competition brings voters and parties closer.

The centripetal tendency of the electorate is clearly evident in the analysis of principles and issues. Conservative, Labour and Alliance voters are not polarized at the extremes, but gathered around a central tendency. This central tendency is not a do-nothing position but a clear endorsement of some measures (for example, the national health service, or stiffer sentences for criminals) and a clear rejection of others (for example, blaming the unemployed for their position). Occasionally, it reflects a more or less even division of opinion among supporters of all parties (for example, about immigration).

In a democratic system of government a central tendency in public opinion has an impact on all parties. It does not deny the existence of minority positions, but it does create a problem for advocates of minority views. Public opinion does not dictate what parties must say and do, but it does caution party leaders about what will not be popular. No party can consistently fly in the face of majority opinion and still hope for success in electoral competition. In 1983 the Labour Party offered voters a fullfledged leftwing alternative — but this was not what most voters wanted. Nor did it want a hard right programme — and Mrs. Thatcher has moderated actions in recognition of this fact. Public spending has risen under Conservative as well as Labour governments, and this is what most voters want (Rose, 1984).

The relation between social structure and voting also demonstrates centripetal instability. It is centripetal inasmuch as the vote for all three parties tends more toward a cross-section of British society. The Alliance is almost exactly proportional in its support, and to a far greater extent than the rhetoric of Conservative or Labour leaders suggests, their voters too resemble a cross-section of the electorate.

The rethinking of class structure has emphasized the growth in intermediate strata rather than the polarization of the population into two distant and antagonistic 'us-and-them' classes. The class structure is becoming more diamond-shaped; it bulges in the centre, where variously labelled groups of routine non-manual workers and skilled self-employed or supervisory manual workers are found. These groups are central, having some attributes of the conventional working class and some of non-manual workers. The resulting indeterminacy simultaneously produces more wobbling and floating voters and less class conflict between voting blocs.

Central tendencies in the electorate do not work to any one party's advantage. They could spell the *downfall* of the Alliance Party at the next election, if the Conservative and/or Labour parties successfully identify with positions that the Alliance also holds.

Instability is certain to characterize the electorate for the whole of the 1980s. No sooner was the 1983 election over than voters began sending warning signals to politicians not to take their support for granted. In response to a post-election survey, only 37 per cent said that they would definitely vote the same at the next general election (Table 8.12). The Labour Party, which had done worst, appears most protected against further defections; half said that they would definitely remain Labour supporters. The Alliance, which made the most gains, appears most vulnerable to defections; only 28 per cent said that they would definitely vote Alliance again. Notwithstanding the Conservative dominance in Parliament, only two in five of the party's voters were definitely committed to continue support.

By-elections in the Parliament elected in 1983 emphasize both instability *and* centripetal tendencies. If votes are totalled, the results show the centrality of the Alliance: in eight by-elections from Penrith & the Border through Brecon & Radnor in July, 1985, the Alliance is first, with 38 per cent of the total vote, the Conservatives second with 35 per cent, and Labour third, with 26 per cent. When seats are totalled, the result is four Conservative seats held, two Labour seats held, and the Alliance gaining two seats from the Conservatives.

At the next general election, instability can arise on many fronts (McAllister and Rose, 1984: chapter 11). Any movement in votes is likely to depart substantially from the simple one-dimensional model of swing that reflected an era of closed or fixed-track alternation in votes between Conservative and Labour. Electoral competition is now three-sided; movement can occur between the Alliance and Labour or between the Alliance and the Conservatives, as well as between the two duopoly parties. On past form, the greatest movement of votes would be both to *and* from the Alliance. No net change in Alliance support need result if, for example, the Alliance loss to Labour is offset by gains from the Conservatives.

Centripetal tendencies make it easy for party strategists to identify where the majority of the electorate stands. All parties sponsor surveys of electoral opinion, and any professional survey will show much the same profile of the electorate. The results indicate opportunities for a party to gain support — and its vulnerability to competition.

When open electoral competition becomes turbulent, the role of party leader offers great rewards and risks. The first problem of party leaders is to know where their party stands. All parties are coalitions of groups, (Rose and Mackie, 1984). This is most obvious in the case of the

Alliance, an electoral pact between two parties. Differences within each partner are compounded by differences about whether the Alliance should evolve into a single party, or remain two distinct organizations. There is a centripetal thrust within the Alliance. Whatever politicians in the Alliance think about their relationships with each other, they have an even greater concern with winning more seats and votes. At past elections the Liberal share of the vote has tended to rise less in seats where the party has previously been strong (Steed and Curtice, 1984).

TABLE 8.12
Likelihood of voting the same at next election

Total %		Con.	All'ce (as % voting for party in 1983)	Lab.
37	Definitely same	40	28	50
25	Probably same	29	33	23
14	Perhaps same	13	20	9
4	Will vote differently	2	7	6
19	Don't know	16	12	12

Source: Harris Research Centre, July 1983 survey.

The Labour Party under Neil Kinnock stands for two negatives: the rejection of Mrs. Thatcher's government, and the rejection of the Labour Party strategy that produced its disastrous 1983 election result. Kinnock's subsequent readiness to move from the left towards the centre, as Harold Wilson and Clement Attlee did before him, is a necessary but not sufficient step for a Labour election victory. The strategy cannot work as readily as in the past because Labour is no longer the sole alternative to the Conservatives.

The Conservatives have two fears. The first is that their opponents will not continue dividing half the vote almost evenly, a division that produced a Conservative landslide in 1983. The second worry is: What happens if Conservative support begins to fall? The distance between parties around the centre is not great, and most Conservative voters are not committed partisans, as in the closed-class model of electoral competition. The more that Labour and Alliance campaigners emphasize their centripetal tendencies, the easier it is for wobbling voters to float away from the Conservatives. Yet this also implies the possibility of the Conservatives readily regaining support after a slump mid-term in the life of a Parliament. If Mrs. Thatcher leads the party into a third successive election, the party will face a further problem arising from past success, the cry of 'Time for a change'.

Fifteen years ago politicians thought they knew what won and lost elections, the government's economic record. There was social science evidence that supported such a judgement (see Goodhart and Bhansali, 1970; Alt, 1979). But economic difficulties since 1973 have cast doubt on simple theories of economic determinism. Inflation rates have risen, unemployment has risen, and economic growth has slowed down, regardless of the party in office. During part of the first Thatcher administration, the gross national product contracted rather than grew. As taxes did not fall, the take-home pay of most workers was reduced. Unemployment, long considered a sure loser of votes, nearly trebled from 1979 to 1983 (Rose, 1984: chapter 7). According to earlier calculations, this should have lost the Conservatives much of their vote. Yet the Conservatives won the 1983 election.

The electorate's reaction to government and opposition parties reflects a lifetime of learning, not just a few ephemeral or immediate events. One reason why present economic difficulties have not had the expected electoral impact is that voters have learned from the setbacks of the 1970s not to expect a rapid rise in prosperity in the 1980s (Rose, 1980a; Alt, 1984). Neither pre-adult socialization, adult socio-economic interests, political principles nor the performance of parties in the present Parliament by itself determines voting; collectively, their influences are sufficiently diverse to maintain competition that is open to the point of uncertainty.

Open electoral competition can be considered a strength not a weakness of the British political system. What is pejoratively labelled as instability can also be interpreted as showing an increasing "choosiness" of voters. Uncertainty encourages politicians to pay more attention to the views of the electorate. The penalties for failing to strike the appropriate chords are severe, as shown by the defeats of Edward Heath in 1974, and of Michael Foot in 1983. There are opportunities for new politicians and, in the Alliance, a new party to come forward.

A quarter-century ago the British party system appeared stable because it was closed. Britain's position in the world appeared stable too. Today, things are not so certain. We should not expect electoral competition to remain the same, nor should we view elections by standards formulated generations ago. The whole point of representative government is that the mass of the electorate has a choice between parties, and that the choices made are reasonable.

Notes

1. The Heath, Jowell and Curtice definition of class by describing the electorate as preponderantly middle-class, is deviant in its political implications, for it implies that the Conservatives have done a bad job of mobilizing support from their natural class, and wasted effort securing working-class votes that the Oxford Group implies they do not need. The flaw in that analysis is shown by the fact that the Conservatives have not won half the vote since 1935, and their vote since 1974 was lower than in the two previous decades.

2. Much survey data about voting is obtained in interviews at one point in time, requiring the recall of past behaviour, which tends to produce responses biased toward consistency between past and present voting (Himmelweit et al., 1978; Katz et al., 1980; Sarlvik and Crewe, 1983: appendix).

3. The relatively large proportion of Alliance voters who made up their minds during the campaign is also reflected in the large number who were influenced by party political broadcasting. In both the 1979 and 1983 general elections, Conservative and Labour gains due to broadcasting tended to cancel one another out, while the Liberals in 1979 and the Alliance in 1983 made net gains of 1.5 and 3.3 per cent of the vote respectively (McAllister, 1985: Table 4).

4. The Alliance's relatively good showing in 1983 may make it easier to retain support at the next general election, since the reason most commonly given for not voting Alliance by those who had considered doing so but did not follow through is that the party had no chance of winning (Crewe, 1985: 194). For a more sceptical view, see Rasmussen (1985).

5. In German, this is a pun on the terms for voter and choice — Die Waehler beginnen zu waehlen — a shrewd comment by Ernst Gehmacher, director of IFES, Vienna.

Appendices

Appendix A: Principal data sources

Gallup Campaign Studies
Gallup surveys have been carried out at each general election campaign since 1945, and since 1964 there are surveys available measuring a large number of standard social structure characteristics of the electorate. In each election campaign, the Gallup Poll conducts large weekly surveys; four or five representative quota surveys can be pooled to produce up to 10,000 respondents. The large number of cases makes Gallup Poll data particularly suited to detailed analysis. Samples one-tenth this size risk unreliable results with numerous subdivisions. The 1983 Gallup Campaign Studies, excluding those without a voting preference, has 7,709 respondents. The survey is weighted to the election result in Great Britain, and the weighted number of respondents transformed to equal the actual number. For details of the 1964 to 1979 Gallup Campaign surveys, see Rose (1980: 17).

British Election Studies
The British Election Studies have been carried out after every general election since 1964. The samples are smaller than the Gallup Poll, but more complex random sampling procedures are used and questionnaires are longer. The samples are often further complicated by the introduction of a panel element. Details of the 1964, 1966 and 1970 surveys can be found in Butler and Stokes (1974: Appendix A), and the February and October 1974 and 1979 surveys in Sarlvik and Crewe (1983: xiv-xv). The 1983 British Election Study, conducted by Anthony Heath, Roger Jowell and John Curtice, was a random sample of the electorate collected between July and October 1983. With 3,955 respondents, it was more than double the size of every previous study except those in 1974. The median BES study, that of 1979, interviewed 1,893 respondents. The original sample drawn is larger, but non-responses substantially reduce the effective sample size (Heath et al., 1985: 234). The survey is weighted by standard region: the weighted number of respondents is transformed to equal the actual number of respondents.

BBC Gallup Studies
A particular advantage of this quota survey is that interviewing occurs on election day or one day before. Reports of voting are therefore particularly accurate. The 1979 survey had 2,434 respondents, and the 1983 survey 4,146. Each survey is weighted, the 1979 survey by standard region, and the 1983 survey by parliamentary constituency.

Appendix B: Measurement

Voting
Analyses in the tables are restricted to respondents who reported casting a vote in Great Britain in the general election; voting surveys exclude Northern Ireland. Those who reported not voting or refused to answer the question are excluded. Voters for a Nationalist party in Scotland or Wales or another minor party are included in all calculations, so that tables will reflect the distribution of the vote in Great Britain, but

since they constituted only 2.2 per cent of the vote in 1983, they are not shown in the tables. For this reason and because of minor rounding errors, some tables do not sum to exactly 100 per cent. All statistics are calculated before rounding off. A hyphen means less than 0.5 per cent, and n.a. means calculation not appropriate. Non-voters are not analysed here because their numbers tend to be under-reported in surveys, and the electoral register, the base for determining the official percentage of non-voters, is itself inaccurate (Todd and Butcher, 1982; Rose, 1980: 14). The category of non-voters at any one election resembles a shifting cross-section of voters rather than constituting a stable and distinctive group (Crewe, Fox and Alt, 1977).

Class

The one consistent measure of occupational class available in both Gallup and British Election Studies for virtually every election since 1964 is the ABC1/C2DE Market Research Society definition, the most widely used class schema. The detailed British Election Studies occupational data also make possible other measures of occupational class. The 1983 British Election Study presents a unique problem, for the directors did not include the ABC1 codes, as applied in previous British Election Studies by Butler and Stokes and the 1970s Essex surveys, and by the Gallup Poll. It can be derived with a reasonable degree of approximation from other occupational data in that study.

ABC1/C2DE

Coded for head of household by Gallup Poll interviewers, and by British Election Study coders from 1964 to 1979. For the 1983 British Election Study, classification is derived from the 11-fold Goldthorpe-Heath schema (Codebook variables I:23-24, 25-26):

A	= 1:	High grade professional and managerial
B	= 2:	Low grade professional and managerial
C1	= 3:	Routine office workers; 5: small petty bourgeoisie with employees; 6: small petty bourgeoisie without employees; 7: farmers.
C2	= 4:	Sales and personal service workers; 8: manual foremen and technicians; 9: skilled manual workers.
D	= 10:	Semi-skilled and unskilled manual workers; 11: agricultural employees.
E	= 0	not otherwise classified.

Given limited differences between semi-skilled and unskilled workers and the small size of the upper middle class, the original sixfold schema can be simplified by reduction to four strata:

Solid middle class = A, B
Lower middle class = C1
Skilled manual = C2
Unskilled manual = D, E

For a dichotomized non-manual/manual analysis, the two middle-class categories are grouped, and the two manual categories.

Butler and Stokes

As in the ABC1/C2DE schema, except that the C1 category is dichotomized on the basis of whether or not respondents supervised others at work, supervisors being coded C1A, and others C1B. Here, both C1A and C1B are assigned to the middle class, as Butler and Stokes and others have done since 1970. In 1983 the categories do not match previous years exactly. Since the 1983 British Election Study did not use the Butler-Stokes schema in coding, the categories have had to be derived from occupational data in the survey also used to apply the conventional ABC1 schema.

Robertson
From the guidelines in Robertson (1984: 112), the following classification was derived from the Butler and Stokes and Goldthorpe-Heath schemas:

Upper = A, B, C1A
Intermediate = C1B, plus manual foremen and technicians (Goldthorpe-Heath code 8) and petty bourgeoisie without employees (Goldthorpe-Heath code 6).
Lower = C2, D E

Heath, Jowell and Curtice
A sevenfold classification developed by John Goldthorpe and Catriona Llewellyn (Goldthorpe and Hope: 1974, 1983 British Election Study Codebook Variables I: 19, 20), and adapted by the organizers of the 1983 British Election Study, Heath, Jowell and Curtice exclude 10 per cent of respondents — students, participants in government training schemes, those who have never worked etc. (see Codebook variable VI:58-59). We have followed their practice when using their schema.

Given the primary importance of the household as an economic and social unit (cf. Rose, 1985a), class is coded from the occupation of the head of household. In the case of married couples, the occupational status of the male is conventionally used to classify all household members. Classifying individuals by their own occupation produces a weaker relationship between class and voting (see Tables 3.5, 3.6).

Appendix C: Regression analysis of social structure and voting
Tables 7.3 and 7.4 rely on ordinary least squares multiple regression analysis, which assumes that relations between the independent variables are, to a reasonable approximation, linear and additive (Hanushek and Jackson, 1977). Cross-tabular analyses show that these are reasonable assumptions with the data used in the tables. One familiar difficulty with multivariate analysis, multi-collinearity, proved not to be a serious problem and correlations between the major items are well below the figures of 0.6 or 0.7 which suggest multi-collinearity (Hanushek and Jackson, 1977: 86–96). Appendix Table C shows the correlations between the major social structural variables in 1983. Missing data are treated by the 'pair wise present' procedure, which is statistically preferable to the usual alternatives (Hertel, 1976).

Regression analysis was also used to cross-check the results reported in Table 6.7 based on AID-III. It confirmed the openness of the electorate explaining less variance than the AID analysis (R^2 of 12 per cent for Conservative-Labour vote and an R^2 of zero for Alliance versus Conservative plus Labour vote). The beta weights for the effect of particular influences almost exactly matched the relative ranking of variables in the class plus analysis (Table 4.12), placing housing, owner occupation, trade union membership and car ownership above such influences as age and gender, which came last. See note 3, page 114 for details.

APPENDIX TABLE C

Correlations between social structural variables, 1983

	1	2	3	4	5	6	7	8	9	10	11	12	13	14	15
1. Parents' partisanship (1 = both Labour, 0.5 = one Labour, 0 = both Conservative)		−0.37	−0.07	0.01	−0.22	0.11	−0.19	−0.17	0.16	0.06	0.08	−0.22	−0.39	0.07	−0.39
2. Father's class (1 = non-manual, 0 = manual)			−0.08	−0.02	0.34	−0.03	0.18	0.20	−0.08	−0.04	−0.02	0.26	0.14	0.02	0.14
3. Age (years)				−0.04	−0.47	−0.04	−0.09	−0.27	−0.20	−0.01	0.05	−0.05	0.06	−0.06	0.06
4. Sex (1 = male, 0 = female)					0.03	−0.04	0.02	0.09	0.08	−0.03	0.00	0.06	0.01	−0.03	0.01
5. Education (years)						−0.01	0.24	0.28	0.03	−0.06	0.01	0.40	0.07	0.08	0.07
6. Religion (1 = Catholic, 0 = otherwise)							−0.12	−0.08	0.06	0.08	−0.06	−0.06	−0.07	−0.03	−0.08
7. Housing (1 = owner-occupier, 0 = other)								0.38	0.05	−0.21	0.07	0.24	0.23	0.07	0.23
8. Car ownership (1 = yes, 0 = no)									0.07	−0.11	−0.02	0.22	0.23	0.04	0.23
9. Union member (1 = yes, 0 = no)										0.03	0.01	−0.08	−0.18	0.07	−0.18
10. Scottish resident (1 = yes, 0 = no)											−0.08	−0.04	−0.14	−0.02	−0.14
11. Welsh resident (1 = yes, 0 = no)												−0.02	−0.06	−0.02	−0.06
12. Current occupation (1 = non-manual, 0 = manual)													0.14	0.08	0.14
13. Conservative voter (1 = yes, 0 = no)														−0.52	−0.36
14. Alliance voter (1 = yes, 0 = no)															−0.57
15. Labour voter (1 = yes, 0 = no)															

Source: 1983 British Election Study.

Appendix D: Factor loadings for political principles, 1974 and 1979

	Factor loadings: varimax rotation							
	(1974)				(1979)			
	I	II	III	IV	I	II	III	IV
I Socialism								
1. Should be more nationalization	**0.73**	−0.05	−0.02	0.08	**0.74**	0.06	0.10	−0.09
2. Trade unions do not have too much power	**0.67**	0.03	−0.07	0.00	**0.63**	−0.11	−0.01	−0.07
3. Government should redistribute wealth	**0.61**	0.02	0.03	0.44	**0.59**	−0.01	0.48	−0.05
4. Government should establish comprehensive schools	**0.62**	−0.05	−0.03	0.20	**0.69**	−0.06	0.24	−0.02
5. Reduction of military strength not gone far enough	**0.51**	−0.21	−0.27	−0.15	**0.62**	0.02	−0.19	0.18
II Welfare								
1. Important to reduce poverty	0.16	−0.03	0.01	**0.77**	0.16	0.01	**0.77**	0.02
2. Government should spend more on health service	0.02	−0.09	−0.12	**0.71**	−0.03	0.03	**0.72**	0.00
III Traditional morality								
1. Availability of abortion on NHS gone far enough	−0.06	0.06	**0.82**	−0.08	−0.02	0.09	0.05	**0.81**
2. Nudity and sex in media gone far enough	−0.10	0.06	**0.82**	−0.05	0.09	0.05	−0.04	**0.79**
IV Racialism								
1. Racial equality gone too far	−0.05	**0.84**	0.06	−0.17	−0.15	**0.82**	0.10	0.09
2. Important to repatriate immigrants	−0.07	**0.86**	0.07	0.03	−0.04	**0.87**	−0.05	0.06
Variance explained	24	14	11	10	23	15	11	10
(Eigenvalues)	(2.6)	(1.5)	(1.2)	(1.1)	(2.5)	(1.6)	(1.2)	(1.1)
(Total variance explained)	(58 per cent)				(59 per cent)			

Source: 1983 British Election Study, including all factors with an eigenvalue greater than 1.0.

Appendix E: Codings: cumulative effect of determinants of voting

Variables were entered progressively in blocks under each of the five sub-headings using hierarchical inclusion, except for current performance of parties, for which the variables were entered individually in the sequence shown in the table. For Tables 7.3 and 7.4 codings are as follows:

I Pre-adult socialization

Father's class: father non-manual versus manual occupation. Father's party: father normally voted for Conservative, Labour, Liberal or Alliance. Religion: Catholic versus rest. Education: years of full time education.

II Socio-economic interests.

Current class: head of household non-manual versus manual worker. Housing: owner occupier versus rest. Nation: resident of Scotland or Wales versus resident of England. Union membership: head of household trade union member.

III Political principles

Socialism, welfare, traditional morality, racialism: see Table 7.1 for details of these multiple-item scales.

IV Current performance of parties in Parliament

Leaders. 1983: likely effectiveness of Thatcher, Foot, Steel and Jenkins as Prime Minister. 1979: rating of Thatcher, Callaghan, Steel. October 1974: rating of Wilson, Heath, and Thorpe.

Evaluation of governing party. 1983: a multiple-item scale combining the Conservative government's handling of inflation, unemployment, taxation, cost of living and strikes. 1979: the Labour government's handling of unemployment, law and order, prices, and strikes. 1974: Labour government's handling of strikes and prices, and best party to deal with housing, unemployment, and pensions.

Event evaluation. 1983: Conservative handling of Falklands. 1974: effect of Common Market on British economy.

Campaign: When the decision to vote for party taken.

Future expectations. 1983: which party best for improving standard of living in next four years. 1979: a multiple-item scale based on a factor analysis of the possibility in next ten years of an economic depression, breakdown in law and order, revolution, race riots, a general strike, and political terrorism. 1974: multiple-item scale combining future prediction about unemployment, economy, personal income.

V Party identification

References

Abel-Smith, Brian (1984), 'Social Welfare' in Ben Pimlott (ed.), *Fabian Essays in Socialist Thought* (Aldershot: Gower), 169-184.

Alford, Robert R. (1963), *Party and Society* (Chicago: Rand McNally).

Alt, James (1979), *The Politics of Economic Decline* (Cambridge: Cambridge University Press).

Alt, James (1984), 'Dealignment and the Dynamics of Partisanship in Britain' in Dalton et al. (eds), 298-329.

Alt, James, I. Crewe and B. Sarlvik (1977), 'Angels in Plastic: the Liberal Surge in 1974', *Political Studies* 25: 343-368.

Alt, James and J. Turner (1982), 'The Case of the Silk-Stocking Socialists and the Calculating Children of the Middle Class', *British Journal of Political Science* 12: 273-291.

Balsom, Denis and Ian McAllister (1980), 'Whose Vote Counts? Electoral Registration and the "40 Percent Rule"', *Political Quarterly* 51: 218-223.

Balsom, Denis, Peter J. Madgwick and Denis Van Mechelen (1983), 'The Red and the Green: Patterns of Partisan Choice in Wales', *British Journal of Political Science* 13: 299-325.

Barnes, Samuel H. and Max Kaase (1979), *Political Action* (Beverly Hills, Calif.: Sage Publications).

Becker, Gary (1975), *Human Capital* (Washington: National Bureau of Economic Research).

Beer, Samuel H. (1982), *Modern Social Politics* (London: Faber and Faber).

Berglund, S. and U. Lindstrom (1978), *The Scandinavian Party System(s)* (Lund: Studentlitteratur).

Blau, Peter and Otis Dudley Duncan (1967), *The American Occupational Structure* (New York: Wiley).

Bogdanor, Vernon (1983), *Multi-Party Politics and the Constitution* (Cambridge: Cambridge University Press).

Bott, Elizabeth (1957), *Family and Social Network* (London: Tavistock).

Budge, Ian, Ivor Crewe and Dennis Fairlie (eds) (1976), *Party Identification and Beyond* (London: Wiley).

Butler, David (ed.) (1978), *Coalitions in British Politics* (London: Macmillan).

Butler, David (1983), *Governing Without a Majority* (London: Collins).

Butler, David and Dennis Kavanagh (1984), *The British General Election of 1983* (London: Macmillan).

Butler, David and Anne Sloman (1980), *British Political Facts 1900-1979* (London: Macmillan, 5th edition).

Butler, David and Donald Stokes (1969, 2nd edition 1974), *Political Change in Britain* (London: Macmillan).

Campbell, Angus, Philip Converse, Donald Stokes and Warren Miller (1960), *The American Voter* (New York: Wiley).

Craig, F.W.S. (1981), *British Electoral Facts, 1882-1980* (Chichester: Parliamentary Research Services).

Craig, F.W.S. (1984), *Britain Votes 3: British Parliamentary Election Results 1983* (Chichester: Parliamentary Research Services).

Crewe, Ivor (1982), 'The Labour Party and the Electorate' in Dennis Kavanagh (ed.), *The Politics of the Labour Party* (London: Allen and Unwin), 9-49.

Crewe, Ivor (1985), 'How to Win a Landslide without Really Trying' in A. Ranney (ed.), *Britain at the Polls 1983* (Durham, NC: Duke University Press), 155-96.

Crewe, Ivor, Anthony Fox and James Alt (1977), 'Non-Voting in British General Elections, 1966-October 1974' in Colin Crouch (ed.), *British Political Sociology Yearbook*, Vol. 3 (London: Croom Helm).

Curtice, John (1983), 'Liberal Voters and the Alliance: Realignment or Protest?' in V. Bogdanor (ed.), *Liberal Party Politics* (Oxford: Clarendon Press), 99-122.

Dalton, Russell J., Scott C. Flanagan and Paul Allen Beck (eds) (1984), *Electoral Change in Advanced Industrial Democracies: Realignment or Dealignment?* (Princeton, NJ: Princeton University Press).

Diskin, Michael (1984), *The Development of Party Competition among Unionists in Ulster* (Glasgow: University of Strathclyde Studies in Public Policy No. 129)

Downs, Anthony (1957), *An Economic Theory of Democracy* (New York: Harper and Row.

Dunleavy, Patrick (1979), 'The Urban Basis of Political Alignment: Social Class, Domestic Property Ownership, and State Intervention in Consumption Processes', *British Journal of Political Science* 9: 409-44.

Dunleavy, Patrick (1980), 'The Political Implications of Sectoral Cleavages and the Growth of State Employment', *Political Studies* 18, 364-383, 527-549.

Dunleavy, Patrick and Christopher T. Husbands (1985), *British Democracy at the Crossroads* (London: Allen and Unwin).

Elliott, Sydney (1973), *Northern Ireland Parliamentary Election Results, 1921-1972* (Chichester: Political Reference Publications).

Elliott, Sydney and R. Wilford (1983), *The Northern Ireland 1982 Assembly Election* (Glasgow: University of Strathclyde Studies in Public Policy No. 119).

Feldman, Stanley and Allan S. Zuckerman (1982), 'Partisan Attitudes and the Vote: Moving beyond Party Identification', *Comparative Political Studies* 15: 197-222.

Fiorina, Morris P. (1981), *Retrospective Voting in American National Elections* (New Haven, Conn.: Yale University Press).

Flanagan, Scott C. and Russell J. Dalton (1984), 'Parties under Stress', *West European Politics* 7: 7-23.

Franklin, Mark N. (1984), 'How the Decline of Class Voting Opened the Way to Radical Change in British Politics', *British Journal of Political Science* 14: 483-508.

Franklin, Mark N. (1985), 'Assessing the Rise of Issue Voting in British Elections Since 1964', *Electoral Studies* 4: 37-56.

Franklin, Mark and Anthony Mughan (1978), 'The Decline of Class Voting in Britain: Problems of Analysis and Interpretation', *American Political Science Review* 72: 523-534.

Franklin, Mark and Edward C. Page (1984), 'A Critique of the Consumption Cleavage Approach in British Voting Studies', *Political Studies*, 32: 521-536.

Gallup Poll (1976), 'Voting Behaviour in Britain 1945-1974' in R. Rose (ed.) *Studies in British Politics* (London: Macmillan, 3rd edition), 204-15.

Garrahan, Phillip (1977), 'Housing, The Class Milieu, and Middle Class Conservatism', *British Journal of Political Science* 7: 125-6.

Garrard, John, D. Jarry, M. Goldsmith and A. Oldfield (eds) (1978), *The Middle Class in Politics* (Farnborough: Saxon House).

Glass, D.V. (ed.) (1954), *Social Mobility in Britain* (London: Routledge and Kegan Paul).

Gerth, H.H. and C.W. Mills (eds) (1948), *From Max Weber* (London: Routledge and Kegan Paul).

Goldthorpe, John H. (1980), *Social Mobility and Class Structure in Modern Britain* (Oxford: Clarendon Press).

Goldthorpe, John H. and Keith Hope (1974), *The Social Grading of Occupations* (Oxford: Clarendon Press).

Goodhart, C.A.E. and R.J. Bhansali (1970), 'Political Economy', *Political Studies* 18: 43-106.

Gray, A. and J. Gee (1967), *Electoral Registration for Parliamentary Elections* (London: Government Social Survey).

Hanham, H.J. (1959) *Elections and Party Management* (London: Longman).

Hanushek, E.A. and John A. Jackson (1977), *Statistical Methods for Social Scientists* (New York: Academic).

Harrop, Martin (1980) 'The Changing British Electorate', *Political Quarterly* 51: 385-407.

Harrop, Martin and Chris Rudd (1983), 'Can Labour Recover?' *Political Quarterly* 54: 383-87.

Heath, Anthony, Roger Jowell and John Curtice (1985), *How Britain Votes* (Oxford: Pergamon Press).

Hermet, G., A. Rouquie and Richard Rose (eds) (1978), *Elections Without Choice* (London: Macmillan).

Hertel, Bradley R. (1976), 'Minimizing Error Variance Introduced by Missing Data Routines in Survey Analysis', *Sociological Methods and Research* 4: 459-475.

Himmelweit, Hilde T., M. Jaeger and J. Stockdale (1978), 'Memory for Past Vote: Implications of a Study of Bias in Recall', *British Journal of Political Science* 8: 365-376.

Himmelweit, Hilde T., P. Humphreys, M. Jaeger and M. Katz (1981), *How Voters Decide* (London: Academic).

Hobsbawm, Eric (1981), *The Forward March of Labour Halted?* (London: Verso).

Inglehart, Ronald (1977), *The Silent Revolution* (Princeton; NJ: Princeton University Press).

Jennings, Sir Ivor (1961), *The British Constitution* (Cambridge: Cambridge University Press).

Jennings, M. Kent and Richard Niemi (1968), 'The Transmission of Political Values from Parent to Child', *American Political Science Review,* 62: 169-184.

Jennings, M. Kent and Richard Niemi (1978), 'The Persistence of Political Orientations: An Over-time Analysis of Two Generations', *British Journal of Political Science* 8: 333-364.

Judge, Ken, Jillian Smith and Peter Taylor-Gooby (1983), 'Public Opinion and the Privatization of Welfare', *Journal of Social Policy* 12: 469-89.

Kahan, Michael, David Butler and Donald Stokes (1966), 'On the Analytical Division of Social Class', *British Journal of Sociology* 17: 122-132.

Katz, Richard S., Richard G. Niemi and David Newman (1980), 'Reconstructing Past Partisanship in Britain', *British Journal of Political Science* 10: 505-514.

Kavanagh, Dennis (1971), 'The Deferential English: A Comparative Critique', *Government and Opposition* 6: 333-360.

Kelley, Jonathan and Ian McAllister (1983), 'The Methodology of Aggregate Analysis: Errors in Traditional Procedures and Suggestions for Improvement', *Quality and Quantity* 17: 461-474.

Kelley, Jonathan and Ian McAllister (1984), 'Ballot Paper Cues and the Vote in

Australia and Britain: Alphabetic Voting, Sex, and Title', *Public Opinion Quarterly* 48: 452-466.

Kelley, Jonathan, and Ian McAllister (1985a), 'Class and Party in Australia: with British and American Comparisons', *British Journal of Sociology* 36: 398-430.

Kelley, Jonathan and Ian McAllister (1985b), 'Social Context and Electoral Behaviour in Britain', *American Journal of Political Science* 29: 564-586.

Kelley, Jonathan, Ian McAllister and Anthony Mughan (1985), 'The Decline of Class Revisited: Class and Party in England, 1964-79', *American Political Science Review* 79: 3.

Kim, J.O. and Charles W. Mueller (1978), *Factor Analysis* (Beverly Hills, Calif.: Sage).

Kirchheimer, Otto (1966), 'The Transformation of the Western European Party Systems' in J. La Palombara and M. Weiner (eds), *Political Parties and Political Development* (Princeton: Princeton University Press), 177-200.

Laponce, J.A. (1981), *Left and Right: The Topography of Political Perceptions* (Toronto: University of Toronto Press).

LeDuc, Lawrence (1980), 'The Dynamic Properties of Party Identification: A Four-Nation Comparison', *European Journal of Political Research* 9: 257-268.

Lemieux, Peter (1977), 'Political Issues and Liberal Support in the February 1974 British General Election', *Political Studies*, 25: 323-342.

Lievesley, Denise and Jennifer Waterton (1985), 'Measuring Individual Attitude Change' in R. Jowell and S. Witherspoon (eds), *British Social Attitudes: the 1985 Report* (Aldershot: Gower), 177-194.

Lijphart, Arend (1974), 'The Netherlands: Continuity and Change in Voting Behaviour' in Richard Rose (ed.), *Electoral Behavior* (New York: Free Press), 227-268.

Lipset, Seymour Martin and Stein Rokkan (1967), 'Cleavage Structures, Party Systems and Voter Alignments' in S.M. Lipset and S. Rokkan (eds), *Party Systems and Voter Alignments* (New York: Free Press), 1-64.

McAllister, Ian (1982), 'United Kingdom Nationalist Parties: One Nationalism or Three?' in Peter J. Madgwick and Richard Rose (eds), *The Territorial Dimension in United Kingdom Politics* (London: Macmillan), 202-223.

McAllister, Ian (1984), 'Housing Tenure and Party Choice in Australia, Britain and the United States', *British Journal of Political Science* 14: 509-522.

McAllister, Ian (1985), 'Campaign Effects and Electoral Outcomes in Britain, 1979 and 1983', *Public Opinion Quarterly* 49.

McAllister, Ian and Jonathan Kelley (1985), 'Party Identification and Political Socialization: A Note on Australia and Britain', *European Journal of Political Research* 13: 111-118.

McAllister, Ian and Anthony Mughan (1984), 'Values, Protest, and Minority Nationalism in Wales', *British Journal of Political Science* 14: 230-44.

McAllister, Ian and Anthony Mughan (1985), 'Attitudes, Issues, and Labour Party Decline in England, 1974-79', *Comparative Political Studies* 18: 35-57.

McAllister, Ian and Richard Rose (1984), *The Nationwide Competition for Votes: the 1983 British General Election* (London: Frances Pinter).

McAllister, Ian and Brian Wilson (1978), 'Bi-Confessionalism in a Confessional Party System: the Northern Ireland Alliance Party', *Economic and Social Review* 9: 207-225.

McKenzie, Robert T. and Allan Silver (1968), *Angels in Marble* (London: Heinemann).

Madgwick, Peter J. and Phillip M. Rawkins (1982), 'The Welsh Language in the Policy Process' in Madgwick and Rose (eds), *The Territorial Dimension in United Kingdom Politics* (London: Macmillan), 67-99.

Madgwick, Peter J. and Richard Rose (eds) (1982), *The Territorial Dimension in*

United Kingdom Politics (London: Macmillan).
Market Research Society (1963), *Social Class Definition and Market Research* (London: Market Research Society).
Marsh, Alan (1975), 'The Silent Revolution, Value Priorities, and the Quality of Life in Britain', *American Political Science Review* 69: 21-30.
Marsh, Alan (1977), *Protest and Political Consciousness* (Beverly Hills, Calif.: Sage).
Marshall, T.H. (1950), *Citizenship and Social Class* (Cambridge: Cambridge University Press).
Middlemas, Keith (1979), *Politics in Industrial Society* (London: Andre Deutsch).
Miller, William L. (1977), *Electoral Dynamics* (London: Macmillan).
Miller, William (1978), 'Social Class and Party Choicc in England: A New Analysis', *British Journal of Political Science* 8: 257-84.
Miller, William L. (1982), *The End of British Politics?* (Oxford: Clarendon Press).
Monk, Donald (1968), *Social Grading in the National Readership Survey* (London: Joint Industry Committee for National Readership Surveys, 4th edition).
Moser, C.A. and G. Kalton (1972), *Survey Methods in Social Investigation* (London: Heinemann).
Mughan, Anthony (1981), 'The Cross-National Validity of Party Identification: A Four-Nation Comparison', *European Journal of Political Research* 9: 257-68.
National Opinion Polls (1984), *Review* (London: NOP Market Research No. 46).
Newby, Howard (1979), *The Deferential Worker* (Harmondsworth: Penguin).
Nordlinger, Eric (1967), *The Working Class Tories* (London: MacGibbon and Kee).
Pahl, Jan (1984), 'The Allocation of Money within the Household' in M. Freeman (ed.), *Law, State and the Family* (London: Tavistock), 36-50.
Parry, Richard (1985), 'Britain: Stable Aggregates, Changing Composition' in R. Rose et al., *Public Employment in Western Nations* (Cambridge: Cambridge University Press), 54-96.
Plamenatz, John (1958), 'Electoral Studies and Democratic Theory: a Continental View', *Political Studies* 6: 1-15.
Pulzer, Peter (1967), *Political Representation and Elections in Britain* (London: Allen and Unwin).
Rallings, Colin (1975), 'Two Types of Labour Voter?' *British Journal of Political Science* 5: 107-111.
Rasmussen, Jorgen S. (1985), 'The Alliance Campaign, Watersheds and Landslides' in A. Ranney (ed.), *Britain at the Polls 1983* (Durham: Duke University Press), 81-107.
Reid, Elizabeth and Murray Goot (1977), *Women and Voting Studies* (London: Sage Contemporary Political Sociology Series No. 06-008).
Richards, Peter G. (1970), *Parliament and Conscience* (London: Allen and Unwin).
Robertson, David (1984), *Class and the British Electorate* (Oxford: Basil Blackwell).
Robinson, Robert V. and Jonathan Kelley (1978), 'Class as Conceived by Marx and Dahrendorf: Effects on Politics and Income Inequality in the United States and Great Britain', *American Sociological Review* 44: 38-57.
Rokkan, Stein (1970), *Citizens, Elections, Parties* (Oslo: Universitetsforlaget).
Rollett, Constance (1972), 'Housing' in A.H. Halsey (ed.), *Trends in British Society Since 1900* (London: Macmillan), 284-320.
Rose, Richard (1965), *Politics in England* (London: Faber and Faber, 1st edition).
Rose, Richard (1967), *Influencing Voters* (London: Faber and Faber).
Rose, Richard (1968), 'Class and Party Divisions: Britain as a Test Case', *Sociology* 2: 129-162.
Rose, Richard (1968a), 'Party Systems, Class Structure and Voter Alignments in

Britain' in Otto Stammer (ed.), *Parteiensysteme, Parteiorganisationen und die Neuen Politischen Bewegungen* (Berlin: Institut fuer Politische Wissenschaft, Free University), 318-384.

Rose, Richard (1973), 'Who Lives in Council Houses?' *Daily Telegraph*, 18 May.

Rose, Richard (1974), 'Britain: Simple Abstractions and Complex Realities' in Richard Rose (ed.), *Electoral Behavior* (New York: Free Press).

Rose, Richard (1974a), *The Problem of Party Government* (London: Macmillan).

Rose, Richard (1974b), 'Comparability in Electoral Studies' in Richard Rose (ed.), *Electoral Behavior* (New York: Free Press).

Rose, Richard (1980), *Class Does Not Equal Party: the Decline of a Model of British Voting* (Glasgow: University of Strathclyde Studies in Public Policy No. 74).

Rose, Richard (1980a), 'Misperceiving Public Expenditure: Feelings about "Cuts"' in Charles H. Levine and I. Rubin (eds), *Fiscal Stress and Public Policy* (Beverly Hills and London: Sage Publications) 203, 230.

Rose, Richard (1982), *Understanding the United Kingdom: the Territorial Dimension in Goverment* (London: Longman).

Rose, Richard (1983), 'Elections and Electoral Systems: Choices and Alternatives' in Vernon Bogdanor and David E. Butler (eds), *Democracy and Elections* (Cambridge: Cambridge University Press), 20-45.

Rose, Richard (1984), *Do Parties Make a Difference?* (London: Macmillan 2nd edition).

Rose, Richard (1985), 'Opinion Polls as Feedback Mechanisms: From Cavalry Charge to Electronic Warfare' in A. Ranney (ed.), *Britain at the Polls, 1983* (Durham, NC: Duke University Press).

Rose, Richard (1985a), *The State's Contribution to the Welfare Mix* (Glasgow: University of Strathclyde Studies in Public Policy No. 140).

Rose, Richard (1985b), *Politics in England: Persistence and Change* (London: Faber and Faber, 4th edition).

Rose, Richard and Ian McAllister (1982), *United Kingdom Facts* (London: Macmillan).

Rose, Richard and Mackie, Thomas T. (1984), *Do Parties Persist or Disappear? The Big Tradeoff Facing Organizations* (Glasgow: University of Strathclyde Studies in Public Policy No. 134).

Rose, Richard and Derek Urwin (1969), 'Social Cohesion, Political Parties and Strains in Regimes', *Comparative Political Studies*, 2: 7-67.

Runciman, W.G. (1966), *Relative Deprivation and Social Justice* (London: Routledge and Kegan Paul).

Sarlvik, Bo and Ivor Crewe (1983), *Decade of Dealignment* (Cambridge: Cambridge University Press).

Sartori, Giovanni (1969), 'From the Sociology of Politics to Political Sociology' in S.M. Lipset (ed.), *Politics and the Social Sciences* (New York: Oxford University Press), 65-100.

Sartori, Giovanni (1969a), 'Politics, Ideology and Belief Systems', *American Political Science Review* 53: 398-411.

Sartori, Giovanni (1976), *Parties and Party Systems* (Cambridge: Cambridge University Press).

Saunders, Peter (1984), 'Beyond Social Classes: The Sociological Significance of Private Property Rights in Means of Consumption', *International Journal of Urban and Regional Research* 8: 202-27.

Scarbrough, Elinor (1984), *Political Ideology and Voting* (Oxford: Clarendon Press).

Schattschneider, E.E. (1960), *The Semi-sovereign People* (New York: Holt, Rinehart and Winston).

Scheuch, Erwin K. (1966), 'Social Context and Individual Behaviour' in Mattei Dogan and Stein Rokkan (eds), *Quantitative Ecological Analysis in the Social Sciences* (Cambridge, Mass: MIT Press), 131-168.

Sonquist, John A., Elizabeth Baker and James N. Morgan (1973), *Searching for Structure* (Ann Arbor, Mich: Survey Research Center).

Stacey, Margaret (1960), *Tradition and Change* (London: Oxford University Press).

Steed, Michael and John Curtice (1984), *One in Four: An Examination of the Alliance Performance* (Hebden Bridge, Yorks: Association of Liberal Councillors).

Stokes, Donald E. (1963), 'Spatial Models of Party Competition', *American Political Science Review* 57: 368-377.

Studlar, Donley, T. and Ian McAllister (1985), *Protest and Survive? Alliance Support in the 1983 British General Election* (Glasgow: Uuniversity of Strathclyde, Studies in Public Policy No. 143).

Studlar, Donley T. and Susan Welch (1981), 'Mass Attitudes on Political Issues in Britain', *Comparative Political Studies* 14: 327-56.

Todd, Jean and Bob Butcher (1982), *Electoral Registration in 1981* (London: OPCS Social Survey Division).

Treiman, Don (1977), *Occupational Prestige in Comparative Perspective* (New York: Academic Press).

Van Mechelen, Denis P. (1982), *The Growth of Third Party Support in Britain* (London: London School of Economics unpublished PhD thesis).

Wald, Kenneth D. (1982), 'Realignment Theory and British Party Development: A Critique', *Political Studies* 30: 207-220.

Wald, Kenneth D. (1983), *Crosses on the Ballot: Patterns of British Voter Alignment since 1885* (Princeton: Princeton University Press).

Wattenberg, Martin P. (1984), *The Decline of American Political Parties 1952-1980* (Cambridge, Mass: Harvard University Press).

Weatherford, Stephen (1980), 'Comment on Franklin and Mughan', *American Political Science Review* 74: 460-462.

Weber, Max (1947), *The Theory of Social and Economic Organisation* (New York: Free Press).

Williams, Philip (1985), 'Party Realignment in the United States and Britain', *British Journal of Political Science* 15: 95-115.

Young, Ken (1984) 'Political Attitudes' in R. Jowell and C. Airey (eds.) *British Social Attitudes: the (1984), Report* (Aldershot: Gower), 11-45.

Index

Since the whole of the book is about voting for the Conservatives, Labour and the Alliance, there are no special index references for the names of these parties, or for voting behaviour.